THE HISTORY AND GROWTH OF VOCATIONAL EDUCATION IN AMERICA

THE HISTORY AND GROWTH OF VOCATIONAL EDUCATION IN AMERICA

Howard R. D. Gordon
Marshall University

Allyn and Bacon
Boston • London • Toronto • Sydney • Tokyo • Singapore

Series Editor: Virginia Lanigan
Series editorial assistant: Bridget Keane
Marketing manager: Ellen Mann Dolberg/Brad Parkins
Composition and prepress buyer: Linda Cox
Manufacturing buyer: Suzanne Lareau
Cover designer: Brian Gogolin
Editorial-production service: Shepherd, Inc.
Electronic composition: Shepherd, Inc.
Signing representative: John Coleman

Copyright © 1999 by Allyn & Bacon
A Viacom Company
Needham Heights, Massachusetts 02194

Internet: www.abacon.com
America Online: keyword:College Online

Library of Congress Cataloging-in-Publication Data

Gordon, Howard R. D.
    The history and growth of vocational education in America / Howard
R.D. Gordon.
        p. cm.
    Includes bibliographical references and indexes.
    ISBN 0-205-27512-5 (hardcover)
    1. Vocational education—United States—History.   I. Title.
LC1045.G67   1998
370.11'3'0973—dc21   98-23667
                                                        CIP

Printed in the United States of America

10 9 8 7 6 5 4 3 2 1   02 01 00 99 98

To my parents, wife, children, and relatives

CONTENTS

PART III

PART IV

FOREWORD

THE HISTORY AND GROWTH OF VOCATIONAL EDUCATION IN AMERICA

I believe there are four basic cornerstones that one must understand to build an intellectual "foundation" for vocational and technical education, as we practice it today in the United States: philosophy, history, legislation, and structure.

- Our philosophy informs us of why we do things as we do. What could be more foundational than philosophy?
- Our history explains how we came to be as we are. One cannot understand vocational education without having at least a feeling for its history.
- Federal legislation provides only about ten percent of the funding for vocational education in this country, yet, federal legislation has fundamentally shaped and directed the development of the profession over the years. To understand vocational education in America, one must understand the effects,whether positive or negative, of the various national initiatives in our profession's development.
- Finally, when I speak of the structure of vocational education, I mean its programmatic framework—how vocational education delivery systems are organized. One cannot truly be conversant about vocational education without understanding the various federal, state, and local delivery systems.

The first time I became aware that no single text existed to deal adequately with these four foundational cornerstones was during my doctoral program at Georgia State University. It was during a course entitled History and Philosophy of Vocational Education and the "text" was a reading package assembled by the professor. The second time was when I started teaching a graduate course at Virginia Tech entitled Foundations of Vocational and Technical Education. To provide readings on the history of vocational education, I had to assemble extracts from many sources, including a seventy-year old work by Charles Bennett and a 20-year-old book by Melvin Barlow. Three books provided readings on Philosophy underlying vocational education: Charles Prosser from the 50s, Arthur Wirth from 1980, and Mel Miller's 1985 text. To address the delivery structure of vocational education I used a wide assortment of articles, state department of education manuals, and other sources. To address our "Legislation" cornerstone was even more difficult. The bottom line: no book has ever been written to adequately address the foundations of vocational and technical education from the perspectives of history, philosophy, legislation, and structure—until today.

Imagine my delight when, about a year ago, an old friend and colleague contacted me regarding this book. Now that I have had an opportunity to read the manuscript, I am doubly delighted. Not only has Dr. Gordon provided an examination of those four foundational cornerstones, but he has provided an examination of the pressing issues of the relationship of vocational education to gender, ethnic, and special needs populations. This is the foundations book for which I have been looking for over twenty years.

William G. Camp, Professor
Agricultural Education
Virginia Polytechnic Institute and State University

PREFACE

History is the cumulative record of our journeys—of people, civilizations, and nations. Whether novice or scholar, we are all participants, able to share its lessons. For five decades or more it has been difficult for people in the field to study the background of vocational education. The story of vocational education since 1917 has not been readily available to the person who desires to develop some background information on its more recent aspects.

This book has been written because there are no books that focus specifically on the history and growth of vocational education in America. Students will gain a better understanding of grassroots information, which formed the cornerstone for vocational education. Today's vocational education professionals need to keep current in the materials they use to help tomorrow's workers. However, the history has remained buried in thousands of pages of reports, magazine articles, and other unorganized literature.

Every topic in this book was selected to provide an intimate knowledge of the history and growth of vocational education in America. This book is divided into four parts. Questions for discussion and suggestions for activities appear at the end of each chapter. Part I presents an overview of the early beginnings of vocational education in America and leaders influencing vocational curriculum development. Part II describes the impact of land-grant institutions on the professional growth of vocational education, selected factors that influenced vocational education development, and the evolution of federal legislation that has shaped vocational education. Part III is concerned with the participation of women and special needs populations in vocational education. Part IV addresses an overview of vocational student organizations, which are an essential component of each of the vocational instructional programs. The preparation of vocational education teachers is also reviewed.

This book is especially designed for use in teacher education programs of vocational and technical education. This book is uniquely designed for undergraduate and graduate courses in history, philosophy, and foundations of vocational education. It will be useful as a source of information to vocational directors, teachers of vocational education, and other individuals interested in programs of vocational education.

This book is committed to the idea that vocational education does make a contribution to our educational progress. Vocational education was added to the school's curriculum to achieve a particular set of purposes. Those purposes are still valid by most vocational educators in spite of the fact that we now have a society that differs from the society of the early 1900s.

Finally, I wanted to write a book that would not be a crashing bore to read. Colleagues and students who have read the material tell me that for the most part I have succeeded. This work sets forth the historical foundations of vocational education as they have developed. Vocational educators need to understand this wealth of historical information if they are involved in planning programs for, advising students in relation to, and making judgments about vocational education. To the future of vocational education, the most important record is the story of those principles and how they evolved.

ACKNOWLEDGMENTS

An ancient saying reminds us, "When you drink the water, remember who dug the well." Many generations of academicians and practitioners provided the scholarship that gave intellectual life to this book.

Appreciation is expressed to Dr. LeVene A. Olson, Professor/Division chair of Human Development and Allied Technology at Marshall University, and the faculty and staff of the department for their interest and encouragement.

Appreciation is also expressed to Dr. William G. Camp, Professor of Agricultural education (my former advisor and mentor) at Virginia Tech, and other members of the faculty and staff.

Facts and ideas from many sources have been incorporated in the book, and I gratefully acknowledge my indebtedness to those sources. I am especially grateful to Dr. Gary Moore of North Carolina State University and Dr. Deborah Griffin and Dr. Ray Herren of the University of Georgia for granting permission to quote portions of their materials. Thanks also to the vocational student organizations for contributing illustrations and for providing membership information. Special thanks to Ms. Vickie E. Adkins, assistant principal at Cabell County Vocational-Technical Center (West Virginia) for providing some of the photographs used in the first edition of this book.

Thanks to the staff of Allyn and Bacon, beginning with Virginia C. Lanigan, senior editor, and Kris Lamarre, editorial assistant, for their excellent production work. I am grateful to the reviewers, Curtis "Paul" Scott, Altamaha Technical Institute, Jesup, Georgia, John P. Mundt, University of Idaho, Boise Center, and Ray Ryan of Ohio State University, for holding me to such high standards of precision.

In any project of this magnitude, assistance comes from many sources. I gratefully acknowledge Mrs. J. Renee Clay and Mrs. Maggie E. Fannin, graduate students in the department of Adult and Technical Education, for word processing the first edition of this book. Finally, I want to thank my wife for her support while I wrote this book.

I know there are others I have unwittingly left out; for that I am sorry. Those who have helped me are not responsible for any faults and limitations of this book. Any errors are mine only.

ABOUT THE AUTHOR

 Howard R. D. Gordon is a professor in the Department of Adult and Technical Education at Marshall University in Huntington, West Virginia. A native of Jamaica, West Indies, Dr. Gordon has made numerous contributions to the discipline through research, presentations, and publications.

Dr. Gordon has been a member of the College of Education faculty since 1991. Before joining the faculty at Marshall University he worked as a science/horticulture teacher at Prospect Heights high school, Brooklyn, New York and also as a community college instructor in floral design and management at Florida Community College, Jacksonville, Florida. Since 1994, he has served as the Historian for the American Vocational Education Research Association (AVERA), an affiliate of the American Vocational Association (AVA).

His academic preparation includes college courses at the Jamaica School of Agriculture, B.S. in Animal and Poultry Sciences, and M.S. in Vocational Education/Agricultural Education from Tuskegee Institute. His doctorate is in Vocational and Technical Education with minors in Rural Sociology and Educational Research from Virginia Polytechnic Institute and State University. His present interests are in assessment of vocational education, program evaluation, and research methodology.

1

EARLY BEGINNINGS OF VOCATIONAL EDUCATION IN AMERICA

The program of vocational education, as we know it today, had its origin in the early part of the twentieth century. The causal factors of the vocational movement in education occurred, however, during the nineteenth century, and the historical roots can be traced to ancient times with significant European connections.

During the latter part of the nineteenth century, the need for vocational training produced a number of private trade schools. Although there were many different kinds of trade schools, organized for many different purposes, the schools can be described as belonging to one of three types: (1) schools that offered only trade training, (2) schools that offered a combination of trade training and general education, and (3) schools that apprenticed their students to the boards of trustees in addition to offering trade and general education.

In addition to trade schools, a large number of private business schools were organized throughout the nation, and supplied vocational preparation for the business world. It was also possible to find a few schools offering instruction in agriculture.

A second major development, prior to the beginning of the twentieth century, was the establishment of programs—in the public schools—known as manual training, commercial training, domestic science, and agriculture.

At the turn of the century, some of the farsighted people in the manual training area observed that many of their graduates were using the skills and knowledge gained in manual training classes for vocational purposes. This was not the major intent of manual training programs: the proponents claimed educational rather than vocational purposes. However, the manual training leaders were encouraged to develop a separate system of vocational education that would achieve vocational goals on purpose, rather than by accident. Business leaders, represented by the National Association of Manufacturers, complained that the factory system had largely destroyed apprenticeship as a source of skilled labor. Finally, the start of World War I cut off a traditional source of the highest skills—highly skilled artisan immigrants from Europe.

The current structure and growth of vocational education in the United States are the product of an extended form of the evolutionary process. With the continued changing federal role in vocational education, it has become increasingly important to understand and appreciate the historical evolution of vocational education in the United States. Therefore, attempts to address current issues without an understanding of the past will prove arduous at best.

The first chapter is an introduction to the early beginnings of vocational education in America. Emphasis is placed on the following topics: European Influence, Apprenticeship in America, Industrial Revolution, the Manual Training Movement, and Evolutionary Phases of Technology Development.

EUROPEAN INFLUENCE ON VOCATIONAL EDUCATION

Traditionally, vocational education has consisted of practical and applied instruction armed at matching students with work positions in industry and commerce (Benavot, 1983). Because of this purpose, vocational education is known by various names, including industrial education, manual education, and career education (Grubb and Lazerson, 1975). Vocational education's allegiance with the workplace becomes evident when one examines its historical roots and particularly its roots in nineteenth century Europe.

During the 1800s schools were divided by social class and the purposes of educational institutions were much different for those who came from wealthy classes as compared to those from working class or indigent backgrounds. One of the most obvious differences was that manual training became a central part of the curriculum for the lower classes. In all grades of these schools, handwork was carried on in connection with the other branches of instruction (Bennett, 1937).

Germany was the center of this manual training movement for the middle and lower classes. Unlike France and England, Germany's trade guilds retained their power throughout the nineteenth century and they continued to encourage apprenticeship programs. Also, Germany's elementary schooling was both free and compulsory so there was a ready educational foundation on which to build industrial training (Bennett, 1937). Among the noted exponents of these ideas were Jean Jacques Rousseau and Johann Heinrich Pestalozzi.

Jean Jacques Rousseau (1712–1778)

Rousseau was born in Geneva Switzerland. In 1762, Rousseau published a highly controversial novel *Emile.* According to Culver (1986), Rousseau's novel was the story of an orphan boy who was removed from society and had access only to his tutor as a companion. The boy discovers cognitive information through objects or things (no books) and in this natural manner, he develops physically, intellectually, and morally until he is ready to take his place in society.

Rousseau viewed education as a means to free man from social status and permit enjoyment of senses. In essence, Rousseau advocated that manual arts could serve as a means of mental training and thus paved the way to a new era in vocational education.

Johann Heinrich Pestalozzi (1746–1827)

Pestalozzi was born in Zurich, Switzerland. Davidson (1900) cites that Pestalozzi, who admittedly borrowed from Rousseau's work, believed that formal education must be open to all children, that teaching methods should cultivate learning and the desire to learn, and that education should be based on facts and the practical circumstances of society as opposed to theoretical constructs.

Pestalozzi's ideas about vocational education can be considered under three headings: the principles of vocational training in agreement with those of other branches of education; his views on industry, its dangers and means of overcoming them; and finally his ideas on the education of the poor and his attempts to carry them out in the first decade of the nineteenth century (Silber, 1965). Pestalozzi insisted that children should learn not only to think, but also to do, and hence that education should consist largely of manual labor. Pestalozzi's ideas about the importance of a vocational component in the school curriculum for all students spread across Europe and into the United States. One of his teachers at Burgdorf, Joseph Neef, opened a school in Philadelphia in 1809, based on the Pestalozzian method (Barlow, 1967). Early instruction in manual training in normal schools is directly tied to Pestalozzi's influence. The Oswego State Normal School, organized in 1861 by Edward A. Sheldon (1823–1897), superintendent of schools in Oswego, owed its curriculum and educational philosophy to Pestalozzi (Bennett, 1937). Other schools, based on the Oswego model, sprang up in neighboring areas. By 1891, similar schools had developed in Massachusetts, New Jersey, Connecticut, Pennsylvania, Maryland, Texas, and California (Report of the Commission, 1893).

Many other nineteenth-century educational reformers contributed to the growth of the concepts of vocational education. Among them were Friedrich Wilhelm Augustus Froebel, Uno Cygnaeus, Otto Salomon, Johann Friedrich Herbart, and Tuiskan Ziller. Their contributions and views of activity, handwork, and industry all added emphasis to the necessity of vocational education. See Appendix B for more information on European-American evolution of vocational education.

APPRENTICESHIP IN AMERICA

Apprenticeship is the oldest known type of vocational education in the United States. Programs pertaining to apprenticeship have long been a basic method of obtaining occupational competence. Education for the worker took the form of apprenticeship. This type of vocational education was not regarded as part of the school curriculum. The apprenticeship process involves a formal agreement covering a definite period of time that binds the employer to provide training in return for the work of the apprentice.

Apprenticeship came to the New World in the early colonial period. This type of training in the colonies resembled that of the mother countries. There were no guilds or similar craft organizations, as such, in colonial America. The English apprenticeship system was modified to suit conditions in the New World, and apprenticeship in colonial America became the most important educational agency of the period of colonization and settlement (Roberts, 1957).

The colonists brought the custom of apprenticeship with them from European countries and it constituted the main form of training for industrial employment until well into the period of machine production. The inadequate labor supply in the colonies and the surplus population in England were the factors promoting the indentured servitude that has been so identified with apprenticeship in this period.

With the development of slavery, this form of white servitude declined. In the New England colonies, where the conditions of apprenticeship were based largely on the English Statute of Artifices of 1562, the educational aspects of apprenticeship were sufficiently stressed to keep it distinct from servitude. The indenture of children of paupers, vagrants, and large families provision was made to secure the child (1) training in the trade of the masters, (2) education in the common branches, and (3) instruction in sound ethics. For the poor, at least, the institution of apprenticeship offered almost the sole opportunity to secure an education in colonial times. It was not until well into the nineteenth century that the free public elementary school became an established American institution and gradually relieved apprenticeship of its general education functions (Hawkins, Prosser, and Wright, 1951).

Statute of Artificers and The English Poor Law of 1601

The Statute of Artificers, passed in 1562, transformed apprenticeship from a local to a national system in England. This act codified the various local laws and regulations relative to employment of servants and apprentices. This action was made necessary by the countless number of local statutes, many of which were out of date or contradictory. The need to reform had been evident for some time, and a general law seemed to offer the best possibility for meeting this need (Roberts, 1971).

Late in the sixteenth century, rising prices and growing unemployment created distress among the poor of England. A series of "poor laws" was passed to help impoverished families survive the shift from agriculture to manufacturing that was occurring throughout the country. The English Poor Law of 1601 provided that church wardens and overseers could place children of poor families with an acceptable master until the girls were twenty-one and the boys were twenty-four. The law's basic intent was to equip the children of poor families with a salable skill. This approach was considered very successful and greatly influenced vocational education in America (Thompson, 1973).

Kinds of Apprenticeship

There were two kinds of apprenticeships. One was the voluntary form, which followed European customs and traditions, but was not subject, in general, to particular provisions of law, although such agreements were entered in the town records. The second was involuntary apprenticeship, which provided a means of taking care of poor children and orphans. A master, instead of the town, became responsible for their personal and occupational needs (Barlow, 1967).

In general, apprenticeship agreements provided food, clothing, and shelter; religious training; general education as needed in the trade; knowledge, understanding, and experience in the trade skills; and finally, for the "mysteries" of the trade, or the techniques that had some elementary scientific basis. These were the traditional elements. Both boys and girls were apprenticed for periods of time varying from five to ten years. Girls usually served until they were eighteen or were married. Apprenticeship started in many instances at the age of eight or nine. Apprenticeship was not a scheme of exploitation, but was essentially an educational institution (Seybolt, 1917).

The Apprenticeship Indenture

When a master took an apprentice, he entered into a contract (usually written) with the apprentice or the overseer. This contract or indenture when properly witnessed and recorded became a public document. As a public record it provided protection to both the apprentice and his master. The following apprenticeship indenture made in 1676 illustrated the type of contract used in the New England colonies:

> *This Indenture witnesseth that I, Nathan Knight . . . have put myself apprentice to Samuel Whidden, of Portsmouth, in the county of Portsmouth, mason, and bound after the manner of an apprentice with him, to serve and abide the full space and term of twelve years and five months . . . during which time the said apprentice his said master faithfully shall serve . . . He shall not . . . contract matrimony within the said time. The goods of his said master, he shall not spend or lend.*

He shall not play cards, or dice or any other unlawful game, whereby his said master may have damage in his own goods, or others, taverns he shall not haunt, nor from his master's business absent himself by day or by night, but in all things shall behave himself as a faithful apprentice ought to do.

And the said master his said apprentice shall teach and instruct, or cause to be taught and instructed in the art and mystery as mason; finding unto his said apprentice during the said time, meat, drink, washing, lodging, and apparel, fitting an apprentice teaching him to read, and allowing him three months toward the latter end of his time to go to school to write, and also double apparel at end of said time . . . (Erden, 1991, p.30).

When the apprenticeship was completed, this fact was acknowledged by the master at a town meeting and duly entered into the minutes of the meeting. If the apprentice had given satisfaction, he was permitted to follow his trade. However, if the master was not satisfied with the progress made, the apprentice was forbidden to practice the trade and could, if all parties agreed, continue his apprenticeship program.

Reasons for the Decline of Apprenticeship in America

Following 1807, an industrial revolution similar to that which England had experienced took place in America. As a result of the Industrial Revolution, the apprenticeship program lost its most important characteristics—the personal guidance and instruction by the master. This change in apprenticeship was due to the heavy increases in the demand for manufactured goods that were met by the use of experienced machine operators who did not need a long period of apprenticeship.

Apprenticeship declined in importance in the colonial period and was dealt its heaviest blow by the factory system in the nineteenth century. The reasons for its decline included the following: (1) large groups succeeded small forces of labor. Each group was trained to work in a specific task or operation, (2) scattered industries became centralized, (3) industry developed so many subdivisions that training was both expensive and useless, (4) indenture laws gradually became ineffective, (5) many trades became overcrowded because of the large numbers of apprentices who were allowed to learn them, (6) wages were kept very low, (7) young helpers were taught not simply by the technique of some single process but by the "arts and mysteries of a craft", and (8) the development of the free public elementary schools.

Apprenticeship served as the major source of education and training for the masses. New systems of education and training were beginning to surface in a progressive America that would regulate apprenticeship to serve only a small number of people. While a small number of workers continued to be thoroughly trained through apprenticeship, most workers learned job skills from parents or through on-the-job training—learning job skills through observation, trial and error, and imitation.

Apprenticeship Today

In 1934, a federal committee on apprentice training was created by executive order of the president of the United States (Roberts, 1957). However, it was not until the passage of the Fitzgerald Act in 1937 that statutory provision was made for the establishment and continuing development of a program of apprenticeship. This act authorized the secretary of labor to establish standards to guide industry in employing and training apprentices. The act also provided plans to bring management and labor together to formulate programs for training apprentices, appointing national committees, and promoting acceptance of apprenticeship standards.

By 1940, eleven states had enacted apprenticeship laws and in thirteen others apprenticeship councils had been formed. Recommendations adopted by the International Labor Organization during the summer of 1939 were given wide publicity in the United States both by labor and the U.S. Office of Education. These recommendations included provisions for (1) written agreements showing the terms of the agreements and the terms of the apprentice's relationship, (2) learning schedules in various aspects of the trade, (3) a scale of wages with periodic increases, (4) attendance in classes for related instruction, (5) continuous employment, and (6) approval by joint committees of employers and employees (Byer, 1940).

During the thirteen-year period 1941 to 1953, a cumulative total of 687,605 persons registered with authorized apprenticeship agencies to receive training as apprentices. During this period a total of 192,473 registered apprentices completed training, 328,332 left before completion, and 166,800 were still in training at the close of the period. The number of registered apprenticeship systems increased from 760 in 1941 to 50,220 in 1953. This increase was due to newly established systems of apprenticeship and to the registration of previously established nonregistered systems (Roberts, 1957).

Although today's apprentices still work under the terms of formal apprenticeship agreements, they work regular work weeks, reside in their own homes, and earn real wages instead of the "meat, drink, washing, lodging, and apparel" promised to young Nathan Knight.

Apprenticeship in America today is a government credentialing system for developing and recognizing specific skills, competencies, and accomplishments. Credentialing is handled in a manner similar to that of schools and colleges. An individual's registration in a specific program is documented. The apprentice's day-to-day progress toward learning all facets of the target occupation is recorded and matched against the approved, written training outline that describes what functions must be learned, for how long, and where. Apprentices who complete all phases of the prescribed training earn a certificate of completion.

Apprentices are usually high school graduates with manual dexterity or other characteristics directly related to the occupation they want to enter. The average age of beginning apprentices is twenty-five years old. About

A State Director for the U.S. Department of Labor Bureau of Apprenticeship and Training is shown here addressing the state Joint Apprentice Training and Advisory Council. This state has Youth Apprenticeship programs.

two-thirds of the apprenticeable occupations are in the construction and manufacturing trades, but apprentices also work in such diverse fields as electronics, service industries, public administration, and medical and health care. The length of an apprenticeship varies depending on the occupation and the standards adopted by the industry. The minimum term of apprenticeship is one year.

On-the-job apprentice training takes place under close supervision of a skilled and experienced craft worker. It is on the job that apprentices learn the practical skills they will need to become skilled craft workers. Apprentices learn the theoretical side of their jobs in technical classes that they usually attend after work. Related training may cover such subjects as mathematics, blueprint reading, and applied English, as well as more technical courses required for specific occupations.

Wages paid to apprentices begin at approximately half those paid to fully trained craft workers. The wages advance rapidly at six-month intervals until the training is completed and apprentices qualify for the full craft worker wage.

Because apprenticeship combines learning and earning, many different groups must work together to coordinate successful programs. Apprenticeship programs depend on the cooperation of private sector organizations that control jobs and employers (individually and through trade associations) and who sponsor the nation's apprenticeship programs often in partnership with organized labor unions.

INDUSTRIAL REVOLUTION

In the late 1700s, colonial leaders could no longer maintain their Renaissance-based philosophy especially with the beginnings of the Industrial Revolution in Great Britain. According to Walter (1993), the arrival of the Industrial Revolution in the United States was delayed until after 1800, largely by restrictive trade laws. Roberts (1957) points out that in 1803 there were only four cotton mills operating in the entire country. Industrial craftsmen and their apprentices continued to dominate manufacturing in the United States until 1807, when the situation dramatically changed (Walter, 1993). Hawkins, Prosser, and Wright (1951) cite the Embargo Act, the Non-Intercourse Act, and the War of 1812 as the three events that generated the American version of the Industrial Revolution. The combined effects of the three effectively sealed the marketplace to foreign manufactured goods and guaranteed a return on any money invested in U.S. production facilities. Spurred by the no-risk situation, businessmen quickly sought to apply new technology to their manufacturing operations and to switch to large-scale production. Since the apprenticeship system was unable to supply the subsequent demand for trained workers, the stage was set for new forms of education to emerge.

Among the disadvantages that technology brought were (1) increased accidents, (2) poor working conditions, (3) layoffs when production was not in line with demand, (4) blacklisting workers who protested the system, and (5) economic chaos for those families who lost their breadwinner. These situations were largely due to the inability of the industrial and political leaders to recognize and to meet the changing conditions of the worker.

Charitable groups and societies of mechanics initiated efforts to establish schools to provide factory workers with educational opportunities formerly supplied by the apprenticeship system (Walter, 1993). Bennett (1926) cites the Farm and Trade School, founded in Boston in 1814, as one of the first of this type of institution. Its purpose was to provide orphans the benefits of both academic and vocational preparation.

Generally, 1826 is recognized as the beginning of the **American lyceum movement,** a device for popular adult education through lectures; "scientific farming" was a frequently heard topic (Venn, 1964). In 1823, the first school devoted entirely to practical studies, the Gardiner Lyceum in Maine, was opened. According to Roberts (1957), by 1833 there were about one thousand lyceums in the United States. However, most of them, lacking an adequate financial basis and facing the distrust of farmers and mechanics, did not last long.

In 1824, the second of this type of school addressed the problem of providing the populace with information on the application of technology in the workplace from another angle. The purpose of the Rennselear School in Troy, New York, was to provide teachers of science with the opportunity to apply the scientific principles as they were studying on actual farms and in production-oriented workshops. The school's mission continued to expand with the addition of Mathematical Arts in 1835, which led to its evolution into the first school of engineering in the United States (Bennett, 1926).

THE MANUAL TRAINING MOVEMENT

General Samuel Chapman Armstrong, the son of American missionaries to Hawaii, had headed an African American regiment during the Civil War. He had been selected for the position due to extensive experience in educating the illiterate people of Hawaii. Both experiences proved valuable when, in 1866, he was appointed the superintendent of education for African-Americans of Virginia. Immediately, he began the development of what became Hampton Institute (Barlow, 1976). Hampton Institute opened in 1868 based on the philosophy that there was dignity in all forms of work and that human beings, regardless of race, could only truly appreciate that which they had earned. Therefore, students at Hampton were expected to work for the school to earn their tuition. This marked the beginning of the manual labor school movement in America. The idea was not original with Armstrong, who personally had been educated in such a way. While in Hawaii, he had attended the Royal School for Hawaiian Chiefs where some manual labor was required of everyone (Hall, 1973).

The first school designed to provide this type of education was the Worcester Polytechnic Institute at Worcester, Massachusetts, which opened in 1868 (Bennett, 1926). The curriculum combined theoretical classes with production work in laboratories, so that students completing the program would be ready for jobs without an apprenticeship period (Walter, 1993).

In 1870, Calvin Woodward introduced shopwork at Washington University as a means of providing his applied-mechanics students with a visual representation of the problems they were attempting to solve (Bennett, 1937). The success of this technique led to the development of specific projects to provide students with practice in the use of tools and machinery (Walter, 1993).

The greatest stimulus to the manual training movement, however, was the Russian exhibit at the Centennial Exposition in Philadelphia in 1876. Victor Della Vos, Director of the Imperial Technical School of Moscow, exhibited a system of tool instruction based on the construction of models from plans designed and drawn by students (Wirth, 1972).

John Runkle, president of the Massachusetts Institute of Technology, saw the Russian system of tool instruction as the answer to a problem he had been attempting to solve. Graduates of his engineering program were well schooled in theory and principles, but industries often required them to complete an apprenticeship period because they needed employees who also possessed tool and machinery skills. Runkle was successful in persuading his institution to develop both laboratories to provide engineering students with mechanical skills, in 1877, and a secondary level program, called the School of

Mechanic Arts, in 1878. The success of both convinced Runkle that such opportunities should be provided for boys in public schools (Bennett, 1937).

As the manual training movement grew, pressure to increase its availability to all students as part of the public schools also grew. The 1884 convention of the National Education Association in Madison, Wisconsin, became a forum for both advocates and opponents of manual training (Bennett, 1937). Educators in favor of including manual training in the public high schools stressed the general nature of the skills developed and the relationship to academic study of the basic sciences. Those opposed stressed that it was a vocationally oriented substitute for apprenticeship and thus should be limited to separate schools (Walter, 1993).

Despite the continued oppositions, by the end of the decade manual training as envisioned by Woodward and Runkle had won its prominence in the schools. The shop system, which at once claimed to be a democratic recognition of the importance of the industrial classes and of the learning-by-doing theories of Rousseau and Pestalozzi, was adopted by Woodward as the pedagogical heart of his manual arts program (Venn, 1964). Today, the shop system remains an important part of the legacy of manual arts to vocational education.

In what could be regarded as a compromise institution, the Baltimore Manual Training High School was opened in 1884 as the first separate manual training school. The mission of this school was to provide both manual and academic training for students. The curricula offered by this school was replicated in many other cities in America.

The Sloyd (Swedish) System and The Russian System

The Sloyd system advocated that manual labor in a prevocational sense should be taught as part of a general education. Selected principles of this system were that the work should be given by a trained teacher, not an artisan; students should make useful articles and not articles of luxury or parts of articles; and the articles were to be made starting with the simple and progressing to the more complex, using models as a guide (Salomon, 1906). In 1888, Gustaf Larson a teacher of Sloyd in Sweden, came to America and established sloyd instruction in Boston. Before long, Larson had to make changes in traditional sloyd methodology to make it work in America. Several of these changes were:

- Swedish models that were first used had no appeal to American youth and had to be replaced with models of interest to students.
- Traditional sloyd emphasized working from models, but American industry developed products from drawings and drawing was already a school subject of importance in general education. The practice of students working from models was replaced with students working from teacher-prepared drawings and later from student-developed drawings.

• The mostly individualized method of instruction was broadened to include more group instruction, which had become successful in American schools. These adaptations of Swedish sloyd led to the term "American sloyd" (Smith, 1981).

The Russian System, introduced by Victor Della Vos, was essentially a laboratory method of teaching. The method was quite similar to other laboratory work involving a given set of exercises. These exercises were arranged in what was considered to be a logical order for teaching purposes (Struck, 1930).

The major difference between manual training and American sloyd was based on the focus sloyd had on the development of the learner rather than the development of skill in the use of hand tools, and the use of trained teachers rather than the use of skilled craftworkers to teach tool skills. Manual training focused on teaching the use of specific tools by completing exercises or making incomplete objects without sufficient attention directed to the individual needs and capacities of youth. Sloyd, on the other hand, placed careful attention on developing capacities of the individual in the selection of graded models and projects, which were interesting to youth and on the sequence of instructional tasks based on the capacity of each youth leading to the completion of useful objects. Other advantages of sloyd over the Russian system of manual training were:

• prominence of form study of the object,
• greater variety of tasks,
• importance of using completed models, and
• importance of the teacher being a trained educator.

The sloyd movement lasted only a few years but it did change the way practical art subjects were taught and encouraged the use of trained teachers (Smith, 1981).

Perhaps the greatest contribution of the manual training movement, from the vocational education viewpoint, was its effect on the perception of what could or should be taught in public schools. This spread of manual training signaled the beginning of a shift from the belief that the ideal high school curriculum was one which was devoted solely to college preparation, to one which also reflected the need to prepare students for a variety of career options requiring less than college-level preparation. Coupled with the growing specialization of jobs, this broadening of the high school curriculum also pointed out that young people needed assistance in choosing which of the many career paths to follow (Walter, 1993).

More than anything else, manual training changed the conception of what might legitimately be taught in the schools; once this was accomplished, the shift to vocational purposes seemed a logical development.

PHASES OF TECHNOLOGY DEVELOPMENT

Many vocational educators equate the development of technology with the Industrial Revolution. However, technology affected not only industrialization, but also had an impact on social, economic, and educational institutions. According to Thompson (1973), most early historians of vocational education were concerned how the Industrial Revolution affected vocational education programs for production.

In the development of technology it is possible to describe five major phases that occurred during the growth of vocational education in America.

Phase One: Application of Power to Machines

This phase of development was characterized by the dominance of the application of power to machines. Thompson (1973) cites inventions such as the loom, the steam engine, and the spinning frame as basic to this era. These inventions were responsible for the establishment of a factory system in America. During this phase, craftsmen developed a cooperative institute to maintain craftsmanship. However, the craftsmen were not economically viable to purchase the power supply and the power-driven machines.

Phase Two: Introduction of Mass Production

The mid-1800s marked the beginning of the second phase. Factors such as population growth and the Civil War placed increasing demands on production. During this phase, production was characterized as too slow and too costly. A craftsman role in the factory was reduced to producing only a single item.

Manufactured goods increased trade, which in turn created additional demands for improvements and new inventions (Thompson, 1973). The profit motive was the major concern of those who controlled business and industry. Therefore, this phase had an influence on the development of mass production through some form of assembly line techniques. This era of technology development in vocational education elevated the craftsman to the status of a technician. Industrial growth resulted in more and better-quality goods.

There was no social consciousness on the part of an employer during this phase. Since education was not needed to perform simple work tasks, no "vocational education" was provided to those who performed such tasks (Thompson, 1973).

Phase Three: Influence of Automation

This phase of technological development was often referred to simply as automation (Buchingham, 1961). The beginning of this era was probably during the time frame when Henry Ford introduced automation. The basic pattern of commonality during this era was multiconnected machines. This phase produced more demands for vocational education and, therefore, an increase in the level of preparation needed by workers in America.

Phase Four: Miniaturization

The fourth phase of the development of technology can be traced to the early 1970s. This phase was characterized by the development of the miniaturization of electronic techniques. The prominence of plastics and synthetics replaced a majority of materials.

Phase Five: Global Network/Technological Explosion

This phase of technology evolved during the 1980s–1990s. During the 1980s the videocassette recorder gained prominence as a teaching device in many vocational classrooms. Rapid manufacturing of personal computers was also on the increase. Business and industry saw the introduction of automated teller machines and answering machines as linkage to the "new industrial revolution" in the workplace.

Technology has invaded our vocational schools in the 1990s. Vocational educators are purchasing new equipment, hooking up to computer network systems such as Internet and Global Schoolhouse, and developing curricula focusing on new technologies. In many school districts, vocational teachers are leading the technological invasion in the hope of preparing students for the computerized, information-based world in which they will work.

Implications for the Workplace

- Technology will provide the flexibility necessary to meet the escalating client requests for specialized, custom-designed products and services. As a result, workers will need both wider varieties of skills and higher levels of technical competence.
- Market mandates for fast turnaround and quick response will force further decentralization in management and decision-making skills—fueling an increased demand for production teams who can work together to solve problems, inspect for quality, maximize production and quality, and minimize costs.
- Workers will need to handle extreme pressure: they will be required to know more about the company and its products or services, to interface frequently with the end users, to take initiative and make decisions based on many more unknowns, and to be dedicated team players.
- Mechanics, technicians, and other "fixers" will need to understand complicated manuals and follow complex systems of repair and maintenance. Advances in microprocessors and electronics will make existing equipment obsolete in shorter periods of time. As a result, workers will need to

continually upgrade their technical expertise and broaden the scope of their interpersonal skills to function effectively.

SUMMARY

- The foundations of the American educational system were built on the types of education that evolved in Europe. The eighteenth century, or Age of Reason, was an age of democratic liberalism, benevolence, and tolerance. Among the noted exponents of these ideas were Jean Jacques Rousseau and Johann Heinrich Pestalozzi. In the nineteenth century, positive gains of lasting significance were made in the utilization of the elements of industry in education. Pestalozzi's ideas about the importance of vocational component in the school curriculum spread across Europe and into the United States.

- The apprenticeship laws of the Massachusetts colonies demonstrated their commitment to the concept of public support for both academic and vocational instruction. For more than 150 years colonial America used an American version of apprenticeship as the chief source of education for training the masses. However, as the factory system of production developed, the interest in apprenticeship declined.

- The Industrial Revolution created not only a working class demanding new educational opportunities but also jobs requiring an entirely new type of education. Engineers, designers, and managers needed education that provided both scientific theory and practical applications of the theory.

- The greatest stimulus to the manual training movement was the Russian exhibit at the Centennial Exposition in Philadelphia in 1876. Manual training was not without its critics. Technical education was called a "deceptive farce" by zealous guardians of liberal education who considered it a threat to the intellect and unacceptable in the public schools. In some ways these fundamental arguments are indicative of the problems faced by vocational education in today's society.

- During the 1980s and 1990s world competition increased rapidly, leading to a surge in consumer-driven styles and services; these phenomena will continue to escalate the pace of change and the unpredictability in technology and markets. Hence, mass production, standardization, and assembly-line routinization will no longer assume profits through economics of scale. Customers—weary of sameness of clothes, cars, and even home styles—are demanding distinctiveness, quality, and diversity demands that mass-production techniques cannot meet.

DISCUSSION QUESTIONS AND ACTIVITIES

1. Justify the reasons for the five major phases of technology development during the growth of vocational education in America.

2. Distinguish between the characteristics of apprenticeship in colonial America and present-day apprenticeship programs.

3. Differentiate between the principles of the Sloyd and the Russian system.

4. Discuss the effects of technology and changing lifestyles on vocational education in today's society.

5. Interpret the meaning of the term "indentured apprenticeship" and what functions did it serve?

6. Justify what factors caused the decline of apprenticeship in colonial America and what were the effects of the decline.

7. Explain what influenced the American Lyceum.

8. Debate the following: "Advantages and disadvantages of technology in vocational education."

9. Extrapolate on the key concepts and ideas of work education proposed by the early educational reformers of Europe.

For Exploration

10. What were some of the arguments for and against including vocational subjects into the elementary and secondary schools of America?

11. Compare and contrast the educational principles and methods of instruction of Johann Pestalozzi with present-day vocational education programs in America.

12. Extrapolate on how the *lineage* of Rousseau, Pestalozzi, and General Armstrong, influenced the Manual Training movement.

REFERENCES

Barlow, M.L. (1967). *History of industrial education in the United States.* Peoria, IL: Chas. A. Bennett Co., Inc.

Barlow, M.L. (1976). Independent action. *American Vocational Journal, 51(5),* 31–40.

Benavot, A. (1983). The rise and decline of vocational education. *Sociology of Education, 56,* 63–76.

Bennett, C.A. (1926). *History of manual and industrial education up to 1870.* Peoria, IL: Manual Arts.

Bennett, C.A. (1937). *History of manual and industrial arts 1870–1917.* Peoria, IL: Manual Arts.

Buchingham, W. (1961). *Automation: Its impact on business and people.* NY: Harper & Row.

Byer, C.M. (1940). Labor's interest in apprenticeship and vocational education. *AVA Journal and News Bulletin, 15*(1), 30–31.

Culver, S.M. (1986). Pestalozzi's influence on manual training in nineteenth century Germany. *Journal of Vocational and Technical Education, 2*(2), 37–43.

Davidson, T. (1900). *A history of education.* NY: AMS.

Erden, J.V. (1991). Linking past & present, students & jobs. *Vocational Education Journal, 66*(7), 30–32, 69.

Grubb, N. and Lazerson, M. (1975). Rally round the workplace: Continuities and fallacies in career education. *Harvard Education Review, 45,* 451–474.

Hall, C.W. (1973). Black vocational technical and industrial arts education: Development and history. Chicago: American Technical Society.

Hawkins, L.S., Prosser, C.A., & Wright, J.C. (1951). *Development of vocational education.* Chicago, IL: American Technical Society.

Report of the commission appointed to investigate the existing systems of manual training and industrial education (1893). Boston, MA: State of Massachusetts.

Roberts, R.W. (1957). *Vocational and practical arts education* (1st ed.). NY: Harper & Row.

Roberts, R.W. (1971). *Vocational and practical arts education* (3d ed.). NY: Harper & Row.

Salomon, O. (1906). *The theory of educational Sloyd.* Boston: Silver, Burdette.

Seybolt, R.F. (1917). *Apprenticeship and apprenticeship education in colonial New England and New York.* Teachers College Press, Columbia University.

Silber, K. (1965). *Pestalozzi: The man and his work.* London: Butler and Tanner Limited.

Smith, D.F. (1981). Industrial arts founded. In T. Wright & R. Barella (Eds.), *An interpretative history of industrial arts: The relationship of society, education and industrial arts.* 30th Yearbook. American Council on Industrial Arts Teacher Education. Bloomington, IL: McKnight Publishing Company.

Struck, F.T. (1930). *Foundations of industrial education.* New York: John Wiley and Sons.

Thompson, J.F. (1973). *Foundations of vocational education: Social and philosophical concepts.* Englewood Cliffs, NJ: Prentice-Hall, Inc.

Venn, G. (1964). *Man, education and work.* Washington, DC: American Council on Education.

Walter, R.A. (1993). Development of vocational education. In C.A. Anderson and L.C. Ramp (Eds.), Vocational education in the 1990's, II. A sourcebook for strategies, methods, and materials (pp. 1–20). Ann Arbor, MI: Prakken Publications, Inc.

Wirth, A.G. (1972). *Education in the technological society: The vocational liberal controversies in early twentieth century.* Scranton, PA: Intext Educational.

2

LEADERS INFLUENCING VOCATIONAL CURRICULUM DEVELOPMENT

From early apprenticeship programs to the present day, various forms of curriculum and instructional systems have been planned, developed, and implemented. The struggle to introduce vocational education into all educational curricula was identified with Booker T. Washington, an educator and leader; David Snedden, an educational administrator; Charles Prosser, a lawyer; and John Dewey, a philosopher.

Washington emphasized both cognitive and problem-solving skills as essential educational goals. Snedden argued for social efficiency and the need for all students to prepare for useful employment. Prosser was an advocate for integrating vocational education into the general curriculum. Dewey saw vocational education as a means of liberalizing education. He contended that traditional liberal education did not provide the skills and attitudes necessary for living in an age of science.

This chapter presents an overview of selected leaders who have made significant contributions to the foundation and structure of vocational curriculum development in America.

HISTORICAL ROLE OF BOOKER T. WASHINGTON

Perhaps less generally recognized than his leadership skills are the important contributions that Washington made to the theory and practice of education—contributions that transcend their time and remain relevant today (Wolfe, 1981). Hampton Institute's most famous graduate was Booker T. Washington who, in 1881, was recommended by General Samuel Chapman Armstrong to become principal of a new school in Tuskegee, Alabama (Thornbrough, 1969). With only $2,000, Washington founded Tuskegee Institute based on the same principles that his mentor had established for Hampton Institute. In the years that followed, both Washington and Tuskegee grew in fame and national acclaim. Vocational programs were developed for foundry, electricity, machine shop and stationary engineering, painting, plumbing, carpentry, blacksmithing, basket making, harness making, brick laying, brick making, wheelwrighting, and tinsmithing. By the time of Washington's death in 1915, Tuskegee owned 2,300 acres of land, 123 buildings, and more than $1,000,000 worth of equipment (Hall, 1973).

Washington defined an educated person as one possessing (1) both cognitive and problem-solving skills, (2) self-discipline, (3) moral standards, and (4) a sense of service. His recognition that true learning is more than memorization was unusual in his day. Only since the twentieth century have we begun to define cognitive learning as the acquisition of knowledge and those thinking skills that enable us to use knowledge to solve problems (Wolfe, 1981). Washington's writings are replete with evidence of his concern for real understanding, not merely book learning:

> *Happily the world has at last reached the point where it no longer feels that in order for a person to be a great scholar he has got to read a number of textbooks and that he has got to master a certain number of foreign languages; but the world has come to the conclusion that the person who has learned to use his mind . . . that the person who has mastered something, who understands what he is doing, who is master of himself in the classroom, out in the world, master of himself everywhere, that person is a scholar. (Washington, 1938, p. 18)*

The requirement that every Tuskegee student do some manual labor was intended not only to develop self-discipline but also to develop healthy respect for honest labor. In his emphasis on learning by doing, Washington foreshadowed John Dewey and the Progressive education movement by nearly two decades. Dewey used this principle as curricular focus when he established his laboratory school at the University of Chicago in 1896 (Wolfe, 1981). Of his own emphasis on learning by doing, first at Hampton Institute in Virginia (1879–1881) and then at Tuskegee, Washington (1901) wrote:

> *Students were admitted to the night school only when they had no money with which to pay any part of their board in the regular day school. It was further required that they must work for ten hours during the day at some trade or industry and study academic branches for two hours during the evening . . . There could hardly be a more severe test of a student's worth than this branch of the Institute's work. It is largely because it furnishes such good opportunity to test the backbone of a student that I place such high value upon our night school . . . No student, no matter how much money he may be able to command, is permitted to go through school without doing manual labor. (p. 125)*

Washington also believed that he could not develop a truly educated person without stressing moral developments:

"That education . . . That gives one physical courage to stand in front of a cannon and fails to give him moral courage to stand up in defense of right and justice is a failure." (Washington, 1938, p. 17)

Washington's personal devotion to Tuskegee Institute and to its program exemplified his belief that people must lose themselves in significant, selfless causes in order to find themselves. He lived this ideal by precept as well as by example:

Education is meant to make us give satisfaction and to get satisfaction out of giving it. It is meant to make us get happiness out of service to our fellows. And until we get to the point where we can get happiness and supreme satisfaction of helping our fellows, we are not truly educated. (Washington, 1938, p. 25)

VIEWS OF BOOKER T. WASHINGTON AND W.E.B. DUBOIS*

It was in 1895 that Booker T. Washington delivered his famous "Atlanta Compromise" speech. Washington's philosophy paved the way for the widely acclaimed Washington and DuBois debates. Washington, a true scholar and leader, was considered to be the major voice in the movement for Black advancement. His beliefs are criticized for having encouraged Black people to cultivate a spirit of "peaceful coexistence" with White Southerners. An

*Source: Moore, G. E. (1993). *An informal conversation with Booker T. Washington and W. E. B. DuBois.* Raleigh, NC: North Carolina State University. University Council for Vocational Education.

excerpt from the "Atlanta Compromise" speech reveals some of Washington's beliefs:

> *Our greatest danger is that in the leap from slavery to freedom we may over-look the fact that the masses of us are to live by the production of our hands, and fail to keep in mind that we shall prosper in proportion as we learn to dignify and glorify common labor, and put brains and skill into common occupations of life; shall prosper in proportion as we learn to draw the line between the superficial and the substantial, the ornamental gewgaws of life and the useful. No race can prosper till [sic] it learns that there is as much dignity in tilling a field as in writing a poem. It is at the bottom of life that we must begin and not at the top. (Moody, 1980, p. 32)*

Washington's speech was widely acclaimed by many, including the president of the United States, as a blueprint for Black advancement.

However, Washington's speech and philosophy on Black progress was not totally supported by Dr. W.E.B. DuBois of the same era. DuBois, born in Great Barrington, Massachusetts, in 1868, was a scholar, author, and historian with a Ph.D. from Harvard. DuBois believed that it was more important for Blacks to press for the immediate implementation of their civil rights. He believed that Blacks should cultivate personal, aesthetic, and cultural values in the struggle for social emancipation (Moody, 1980). DuBois is credited for having been a central figure in the founding of the NAACP. As a leader of the Niagara Movement (the first Black protest organization of the twentieth century), DuBois said, "We want full manhood suffrage and we want it now . . . We want the constitution of the country enforced . . . We are men! We will be treated as men and shall win." (Moody, 1980, p. 33)

It is difficult to assess the impact of the Washington and DuBois debates on shaping Black involvement in vocational education. However, there is a shared belief among Blacks that those debates did influence, to some unquantifiable degree, the attitudes of Blacks toward vocational education.

DuBois favored a more traditional academic education, but respected Washington as the greatest Black leader of the period. Washington believed that industrial education would build economic self-reliance and help Blacks become better integrated into industrial America. However, DuBois believed that Washington's program practically accepted an alleged substandard living for the Black race (Moody, 1980).

The following excerpt taken from *American Education and Vocationalism, a Documentary History,* reflects Booker T. Washington's belief that the future of his race lay in pursuing manual occupations in the South:

> *I believe that we are going to reach our highest development largely along the lines of scientific and industrial education. For the last fifty years, education has tended in one direction, the cementing of mind to matter. Most people have the idea that industrial education is opposed to literary*

training, opposed to the highest development. I want to correct this error. I would choose the college graduate to receive industrial education. The more mind the subject has, the more satisfactory would be the results in industrial education. It requires a strong mind to build a Corliss engine as it does to write a Greek grammar. (Lazerson and Grubb, 1974, p. 67)

Lazerson and Grubb (1974) further emphasized how important it was for the Black race to learn the following:

As a race there are two things we must learn to do—one is to put brains and skill into the common occupations of life, and the other is to dignify common labor. If we do not, we cannot hold our own as a race. Ninety percent of any race on the globe earns its living at the common occupation of life, and African Americans can be no exception to this rule. (p. 68)

It seems as though Booker T. Washington and W.E.B. DuBois were trailblazers for the pattern of philosophical distinction between vocational and academic education. Washington felt that for the masses of African Americans, the route to success in the financial and social spheres was through the acquisition of the vocational skills that are in demand by today's society. DuBois felt success would come through the development of those mental faculties that would result in African Americans being competitive at the managerial or executive levels. Unfortunately, both of these arguments still exist today with the resultant dichotomy. Even members of minority groups tend to view vocational training as inferior to academic education. For those from the minority middle class, vocational education continues to be something for someone else's children. School-to-Work Transition is one means currently being tested that may finally lead to a merging of distinctions. See Appendix A to obtain more information on the Washington and DuBois debates. Selected quotations of Washington are listed in Appendix C.

Although vocational education has continuously targeted special populations for access since 1963, both practitioners and researchers have increasingly cited the lack of attention to the vocational education needs of the African American community. This lack of attention was the subject of a national conference in 1977 that sparked the formation of the National Association for the Advancement of Black Americans in Vocational Education with the goal, in part, of promoting research on problems in vocational education idiosyncratic to this community (Porteous, 1980).

The principles that Washington enunciated over a century ago still have validity for vocational educators today. Washington believed that the total environment should be conducive to learning. Based on Washington's views of education, Wolfe (1981) cites the following guidelines for classroom practice in today's society:

- Motivation is essential to genuine learning. There can be no successful learning without persistent, selective, purposeful effort. Therefore, the

goals of schooling must be clearly defined, and both faculty and students must be committed to attaining them.
- Because learning is a goal-directed activity, students learn best when education meets their felt needs or purposes.
- Learning is enhanced when the material has meaning to the learner.
- Learning is facilitated when the learner participates in planning the learning experience.
- The holistic nature of learning suggests that learning is always influenced—positively or negatively—by emotions.

From these guidelines, certain principles of skill development emerge:

- Students should never be required to memorize by rote any material that they fail to understand; drill is best when it grows out of practical, real-life situations.
- Skill acquisition involves two stages: integration and refinement. During the first stage, we should give students many contracts with a given skill in a variety of practical situations. During the refinement stage, the student develops precision through repetitive practice (Wolfe, 1981).
- Skills should be taught when they can be mastered efficiently by students; that is, students must first have the experiential background that gives meaning to the material to be learned. The level of mastery varies between learners and their different learning styles.

As we advance to the twenty-first century, we are confronted with challenges in preparing students for the world of work. Each generation has debated the question of what should be taught in schools. However, the words of Booker T. Washington, written over a century ago, continue to define the mission of education today:

> There never was a time in the history of the country when those interested in education should more earnestly consider to what extent the mere acquiring of the ability to create and write, the mere acquisition of a knowledge of literature and science, makes men producers, lovers of labor, independent, honest, unselfish, and above all good. Call education by what name you please, if it fails to bring about these results among masses it falls short of its highest end. (Fant, 1940, p. 69)

VIEWS OF DAVID SNEDDEN, CHARLES PROSSER, AND JOHN DEWEY

Education for all was foremost in the early arguments for establishing vocational education. The public secondary schools were serving fewer than 15 percent of the school-age population at the turn of the century, and vocational education was intended to provide programs for those not being served by the public education system. The liberal education of the early 1900s, especially at the secondary level, was neither liberal nor liberating for the masses who did not attend school beyond the sixth grade (Miller, 1985).

Advocates of vocational education in the public schools believed that vocational education would make the schools more democratic. Snedden, Prosser, and Dewey were among those who held that vocational education had the potential to make public education more democratic.

Snedden and Prosser

Despite his impoverished childhood, Snedden moved rapidly up the social and economic ladder. His doctoral work at Columbia University convinced him of the important mission of school in society and of the integral part played by vocational education in schooling. As a faculty member of educational administration at Teacher's College, Columbia University, Snedden greatly influenced his student, Charles Prosser. Therefore, Prosser's philosophy evolved from the teachings of his mentor (Camp and Hillison, 1984).

Snedden was a powerful advocate of the social efficiency doctrine. He believed that schools should prepare individuals for the occupations at which they excelled. After graduate study in 1910, Snedden was appointed Commissioner of Education for Massachusetts. His appointment came about largely through the influence of powerful industrialists who liked his criticism of literacy education and his advocacy of social efficiency. Frederick P. Fish, founder and president of American Telephone and Telegraph, vocal foe of trade unions and chairman of Massachusetts Board of Education, was most influential in getting Snedden appointed commissioner (Wirth, 1972).

When Snedden had the opportunity to appoint an Associate Commissioner of Education for Massachusetts, he turned to his former student and disciple, Charles Prosser. After serving in that role for two years, Dr. Prosser went to the National Society of the Promotion of Industrial Education (NSPIE) as Executive Director. The purpose of the Society was to facilitate the passage of federal legislation for vocational education (Camp and Hillison, 1984).

The importance and need for occupational experience in vocational education were stressed early in the century. Snedden (1910) was clear about his position regarding the role that occupational experience should play in the education of the worker. As one of the early writers on vocational education, Snedden gave prominence to the desirability of occupational experience.

Prosser (1913) had much the same point of view as Snedden. Prosser felt that successful vocational education required the combining of two elements: (1) practice and thinking about the practice, and (2) doing and thinking about the doing. Prosser's view was that in vocational education practice and theory must go hand in hand; the more intimately they are related to each other, the more the school will contribute to the learner's immediate success in the shop and equip the person for mastery of one's calling.

Practical experience and financial incentives were two areas of emphasis in the writings of Snedden and Prosser. Whether the occupational experience occurred in the workplace or in the shop was not critical to either writer. It was, however, important that the productive experience be as much like the actual workplace as possible. In addition, Snedden believed that the student should benefit from some form of remuneration (Miller, 1985).

Charles Prosser's early work and vision for vocational education were crucial to its development. His pragmatic philosophy made sense to other educators, industrialists, and politicians. Largely because of this work, vocational education gained its first legislation as well as its early operating philosophy. Prosser established sixteen theorems (see Appendix D) based on his philosophy, which were instrumental in the formation of vocational education. Snedden and Prosser worked closely in promoting vocational education. Together, their influence was important in providing direction for the development of vocational education.

The conditions needed to improve society have changed rapidly since the inception of Prosser's sixteen theorems. In today's society the emphasis is on schooling today for skills tomorrow. These skills are classified as workplace competencies and foundation skills.

Workplace Competencies

- **Resources**—Knowing how to allocate time, money, materials, space and staff.
- **Interpersonal skills**—Knowing how to work on teams, teach others, serve customers, lead, negotiate, and work well with people from cultural diverse backgrounds.
- **Information**—Knowing how to acquire and evaluate data, organize and maintain files, interpret and communicate, and use computers to process information.
- **Systems**—Understanding social, organizational, and technological systems; knowing how to monitor and correct performance; and knowing how to design or improve systems.
- **Technology**—Knowing how to select equipment and tools, apply technology to specific tasks, and maintain and troubleshoot equipment.

Foundation Skills

- **Basic skills**—Reading, writing, arithmetic, mathematics, speaking and listening.
- **Thinking skills**—The ability to learn, to reason, to think creatively, to make decisions, and to solve problems.
- **Personal qualities**—Individual responsibilities, self-esteem and self-management, sociability, and integrity.

Dewey

Dewey (1916) saw occupations as central to educational activity. He did, however, express concern about any form of vocational education that would tend to continue the present forms of education for those whose economical status would allow such education while giving the masses a narrow education for specialized occupations under the control of industry.

Lakes (1985) points out that Dewey described youth as adequately prepared if they began to study occupations. By occupation, Dewey (1900) said, "I mean a mode of activity on the part of the child which reproduces, or runs parallel to some form of work carried on in social life" (p. 82). At his experimental elementary school at the University of Chicago, the occupations were represented in part by shop work, cooking, sewing, textiles, and gardening. Dewey felt that these studies would best prepare students to understand the science of tools and processes used in work, develop an appreciation for the historic evolution of industry, instill favorable group dynamics of shared discovery and communal problem solving, and plan and reflect on the entire process (Lakes, 1985).

Dewey believed that education needed change. Vocational education could, according to him, be the means to induce changes that would improve education. According to Dewey, a right educational use of vocational education:

> —*would react upon intelligence and interest so as to modify, in connection with legislation and administration, the socially obnoxious features of the present industrial and commercial order. It would turn the increasing find of social sympathy to constructive account, instead of leaving it a somewhat blind philanthropic sentiment. It would give those who engage in industrial callings desire and ability to share in social control, and ability to become masters of their industrial fate. It would enable them to saturate with meaning the technical and mechanical features which are so marked a feature of our machine system of production and distribution. (1916, p. 320)*

According to Miller (1985) considerable argument, frequently public, existed among Dewey, Snedden, and Prosser. Wirth (1972) treats this controversy in detail and labels Prosser's and Snedden's economic philosophy as Social Darwinism.

Origin and Justifications of the Dual System

Early leaders of the vocational education movement viewed vocational education as part of the public system of education in America. However, who should administer such programs under what organizational arrangement was of concern to educational leaders and others in the early part of the twentieth century.

One of the main tenets of Charles Prosser's vision of vocational education was that of a dual system with two clearly separated components, one part being academic and the other vocational. David Snedden also had a similar perspective. Hillison and Camp (1985) argued that David Snedden's advocacy of social efficiency was twofold. This doctrine held that it was the responsibility of members of society to contribute to the good of that society by working efficiently and by conforming to social norms. Both perspectives led Snedden, and eventually Prosser, to be strong proponents of the industrialist view of education and separate or dual system of education.

As early as 1916, Snedden was giving serious consideration to separate vocational facilities (Dutton and Snedden, 1916):

> *But the ends of vocational education cannot be achieved merely through courses of general instruction. More and more, in view of the social industrial needs of the time, the demand is that some special fitness be given to those who are to follow a special calling. (p. 143)*

Typewriting, stenography, bookkeeping, bricklaying, electrical wiring, plumbing, tailoring, millinery, and some aspects of machine operations were used as examples of separate vocational instruction provided in commercial and trade schools. Snedden further argued that teachers from "regular" schools would be totally unacceptable teaching in vocational school. He contended that the vocational teacher should be selected from the industry or trade concerned (Barlow, 1967).

The early advocacy of the dual system of education had its critics. For example, the National Education Association believed the concept a serious enough threat to demand alteration of the Smith-Hughes Act (Hillison and Camp, 1985). "The Association favors amending the Smith-Hughes Act to prevent the possibility of establishing a dual system of schools in any state" ("A War Platform," 1918, p.11, cited in Hillison and Camp, 1985).

A second major critic of the dual school system was John Dewey. In *The New Republic,* Dewey (1915a) succinctly stated one of his criticisms:

> *I argued that a separation of trade education and general education of youth has the inevitable tendency to make both kinds of training narrower, less significant and less effective than the schooling in which the material of traditional education is recognized to utilize the industrial subject matter active, scientific and social—of the present day environment. (p. 42)*

Dewey (1915b) noted further criticism in a second article published in *The New Republic* in 1915 when he wrote about a vast and costly duplication of buildings, environment, teachers, and administrators. He also noted that the dual educational system would segregate the children of well-to-do and cultured families from those children who would have to work for wages in manual and commercial employment. He continued:

> *It is self-evident that under the divided plan either the public must meet the expense of a vast and costly duplication of buildings, equipment, teachers*

and administrative directors; or else the old schools will have to strip them-
selves of everything but the rudiments of a traditional bookish education;
and the new schools confine themselves to a narrow trade preparation that
the latter will be ineffective for every industrial end except setting up a con-
gested labor market in the skilled trades and a better grade of labor at pub-
lic expense—for employers to exploit. (p. 284)

Hillison and Camp (1985) reported that Prosser and Snedden did not
want vocational education to be contaminated by the mistakes or the philosophy of general education. The position advocated by Prosser and Snedden
was not universally implemented. Vocational high schools, area vocational
centers, and vocational magnet schools resulted directly from that advocacy.

A REDEFINITION OF MANUAL TRAINING

Dewey viewed the potential misuse of occupations as purely sensory experiences in skill development. He suggested that nineteenth-century pedagogical theory advocated a complete isolation of the child's learning potential.
Dewey believed that faculty psychology programmed the development of the
child's abilities into independent training or exercise of separate components.
In *Manual Training Magazine*, Dewey (1901) wrote:

The idea of formal discipline, of the value of isolated and independent train-
ing of the so-called faculties of observation, memory, and reasoning, has
invaded both physical culture and manual training. Here also we have been
led to believe that there is a positive inherent value in the formal training
and eye quite apart from the actual content of such training—apart from its
social relations and suggestions. (p. 195)

Dewey was aware that one could easily misconstrue educational means
(technical proficiency) for educational ends (intelligence). Without an intellectual base, the study of occupations could become primarily utilitarian, as
did the ill-fated birdhouse project fad of the 1930s, for example (Barlow,
1967):

In such cases the work is reduced to a mere routine or custom, and its edu-
cational value is lost. This is the inevitable tendency wherever, in manual
training for instance, the mastery of certain tools, or the production of cer-
tain objects, is made the primary end, and the child is not given, wherever
possible, intellectual responsibility for selecting the materials and instru-
ments that are most fit, and given an opportunity to think out his own
model and plan to work, led to perceive his own errors, and find out how to
correct them—that is, of course, within the range of his capacities. (Dewey,
1900, pp. 82–83)

The project would not necessarily emphasize the development of a cultural perspective. For example, the creation of a simple breadboard requires more than just the task of planning a board (Diamond, 1936). It might involve an analytical assessment of the role of work in society. According to Lakes (1985), tangential areas of study could include energy conservation, quality of work life, ecological waste, human resource management, and the consumer ethic.

Vocational education's stigma has developed because of the separation that has been evident in the operation of many programs throughout the decades. Leighbody (1972) cites that many persons reject vocational education for their children not because of a snobbish prejudice but because they fear that when their children enroll in a vocational curriculum they will be cut off from further education and deprived of future educational and career opportunities.

If parental concerns about vocational education are not erased, vocational education cannot serve all of the persons who it can benefit. A major thrust of the workforce education reform movement is to eliminate the meaningless high school "general" curriculum that moves students to graduation with no clear purpose or promise. In its place would be an academically rigorous vocational–technical education curriculum that will produce graduates with a grounding in academic basics, plus job skills, and a focus on a sound career or further education.

DIFFERENCES IN EDUCATIONAL PHILOSOPHIES: JOHN DEWEY AND CHARLES PROSSER

John Dewey (1916) argued that education should use a critical democratic approach to raise student consciousness about values, attitudes, and worker responsibilities. He stated that the primary purpose of education in the United States was to foster the growth of democratically minded citizens, and Dewey made no distinction in the education of those who would manage the companies and those who worked on the shop floors. Dewey strongly advocated vocational exploration as a means to acquire practical knowledge, apply academic content, and examine occupational and societal values. However, he adamantly opposed the use of vocational education as merely trade education because it would overemphasize technical efficiency. If this occurred, and some would argue it has, Dewey warned "education would then become an instrument of perpetuating unchanged the existing industrial order of society, instead of operating as a means of its transformation" (p. 316). Dewey believed that it was education's role to combat social predestination, not contribute to it (Gregson and Gregson, 1991).

In contrast, Charles Prosser advocated an indoctrinational approach for teaching work values and attitudes; students should learn, without question, the ethical standards of dominant society and the professional ethics of the

TABLE 2.1   Comparison of the Educational Philosophies of John Dewey and Charles Prosser

Philosophical Criteria	Prosser	Dewey
Teaching Styles and Methodologies	Sequential, begins with basic facts. Instructors have strong industrial experience.	Begins with problem solving—results in knowledge base. Instructors have strong educational experience.
Administrative Structure	Seeks advice from industrial leaders, planner, implementer, cost-effective.	Facilitator of personal choices, advisor.
Personal/School Philosophies	Accents the needs of industry.	Accents the needs of individuals.
Benefits of the Program	Students gain marketable skills to become productive society members.	Students gain life skills and adapt ability skills.
Prosser-Dewey Dichotomy		
Transferability of Skills	Transfer occurs naturally between similar tasks. Transfer is not a focus.	Transfer is the focus of a broad education.
Training to Work Transition	Facilitated through current equipment and instructors with industrial background.	Facilitated through focus on transfer.
Development of Problem-Solving Skills	Acquiring a base of knowledge precedes problem-solving skills.	Instruction begins with problem-solving skills.
Continuation of Prosser Philosophy		
Major Goal of the School	To meet the needs of industry and prepare people for work.	To meet the needs of individuals and prepare people for life.
Influencing Factors on School Success	Follow Prosser's sixteen theorems.	Follow guidelines in Dewey's *Democracy and Education*.
Social and Economic Factors		
School Climate	Individualized differences are recognized, and all people and types of work are seen as having value.	Individual differences are equalized.
Adequate Supplies, Space, and Equipment	Schools must have adequate supplies, space, and equipment.	Schools need to have adequate supplies, space, and equipment, but students may use transfer skills to cover deficiencies.
Personal Motivations	Vocational education should be reserved for those who are motivated and can benefit.	Vocational education is for everyone and everyone can benefit.

Source: Griffin, D., and Herren, R.V.(1994). *North Carolina's first postsecondary technical institution:* Past, present, and future. Unpublished doctoral dissertation. University of Georgia, Athens, GA.

desired occupational area (Prosser, 1939). Supporters of this approach believed the primary purpose of public education was the development of human capital for the success of the industrial economy. To accomplish this, they argued that scientific management principles, drawn from the industrial sector, were employed in the public school setting, creating a hierarchically structured and production-oriented educational system (Spring, 1990). Prosser's sixteen theorems on vocational education support this vision of schooling. Table 2.1 provides a summary of the educational philosophies of John Dewey and Charles Prosser as they relate to vocational education.

SUMMARY

- The struggle to introduce vocational education into all educational curricula was identified with the careers of Booker T. Washington, an educator and leader; David Snedden, an educational administrator; Charles Prosser, a lawyer; and John Dewey, a philosopher.

- Washington defined an educated person as one possessing (1) both cognitive and problem-solving skills, (2) self-discipline, (3) moral standards, and (4) a sense of service. His recognition that true learning is more than memorization was unusual in his day.

- Washington's philosophy paved the way for the widely acclaimed Washington and DuBois debates. Concerned with the practical education of the masses recently freed from slavery, Washington advocated taking what was immediately available: industrial education in a segregated setting.

- DuBois was convinced that equality required developing a highly educated African American leadership, a "talented tenth" on an intellectual, social, and political par with Whites.

- Snedden was a powerful advocate of the social efficiency doctrine. He gave prominence to the desirability of occupational experience.

- Prosser's view was that in vocational education, practice and theory must go hand in hand; the more intimately they are related to each other, the more the school will contribute to the learner's immediate success in the shop and equip the person with mastery of one's calling.

- Dewey was a strong advocate for vocational education. He was critical of the existing traditional liberal education of the time and felt that it did not provide the skills and attitudes that individuals needed to live in an age of science. He believed that the curriculum should include a series of situations in which students are involved in solving problems of interest to them, such as the "project method" employed in some manual training schools that engaged students in activities that required thinking as well as doing.

DISCUSSION QUESTIONS AND ACTIVITIES

1. Select one vocational course you have taught or that you plan to teach and develop a statement of philosophy for that particular course.

2. Explain and generalize why it is important for a teacher, an educational department, and a school to have a philosophy of education.

3. Conduct an interview of vocational and nonvocational educators regarding their philosophy of vocational education. What are the similarities? Explain how they are different.

4. Critique the film *Washington-DuBois Debate*. See Appendix A for more information.

5. Debate the following: "The Integration of Academic and Vocational Education."

6. Compare and contrast the educational philosophies of John Dewey and Charles Prosser.

7. Critique the film *Dewey-Snedden Debate: A Recreation*. See Appendix A for more information.

8. Examine critically and justify the relevancy of Prosser's theorems in today's society (see Appendix D).

For Exploration

9. Discuss how our diverse school population influenced the philosophy of vocational education.

10. Formulate a statement of philosophy for each of the following educators based on their perception of vocational education:
    a. Booker T. Washington
    b. David Snedden
    c. Charles Prosser
    d. John Dewey
    e. W.E.B. DuBois

11. Explain the meaning of the term "Social Darwinsism."

12. Justify that "Social Darwinism" is important for workforce education (in the form of vocational education) to the curriculum of the American high school.

REFERENCES

Barlow, M.L. (1967). *History of industrial education in the United States*. Peoria, IL: Chas. A. Bennett Co.

Camp, W.G., and Hillison, J.H. (1984). Prosser's sixteen theorems: Time for reconsideration. *Journal of Vocational and Technical Education, 1* (1), 13–15.

Dewey, J.C. (1900). Psychology of occupation [Monograph]. *Elementary School Record,* No. 3 (April), 82–85.

Dewey, J.C. (1901). The place of manual training in the elementary course of study. *Manual Training Magazine* (4), 193–199.

Dewey, J.C. (1915a). Education vs. trade-training. *The New Republic* (28), 42.

Dewey, J.C. (1915b). Splitting up the school system. *The New Republic* (24), 283–284.

Dewey, J.C. (1916). *Democracy and education,* p. 316. New York: The Macmillan Co.

Diamond, T. (1936, March). Responsibility of industrial arts teacher in social problems. *AVA Journal, 25,* 104–106.

Dutton, S.T., and Snedden, D. (1916). *The administration of public education in the United States.* New York: The Macmillan Co.

Fant, C. (1940). *Tuskegee Institute yesterday and today,* p. 69. Tuskegee, AL: Tuskegee Institute Press.

Gregson, J.A., and Gregson, P. (1991, December). *Secondary trade and industrial education work values instruction: Emancipatory or indoctrinational?* Paper presented at the annual meeting of the American Vocational Educational Research Association, Los Angeles, CA.

Griffin, D.A., and Herren, R.V. (1994). *North Carolina's first postsecondary technical institution: Past, present, and future.* Unpublished doctoral dissertation. University of Georgia: Athens, GA.

Hall, C.W. (1973). *Black vocational technical and industrial arts education: Development and history.* Chicago, IL: American Technical Society.

Hillison, J.H., and Camp, W.G. (1985). History and future of the dual school system of vocational education. *Journal of Vocational and Technical Education, 2* (1), 48–50.

Lakes, R.D. (1985). John Dewey's theory of occupations: Vocational education envisioned. *Journal of Vocational and Technical Education, 2* (1), 41–45.

Lazerson, M., and Grubb, W.N. (1974). *American education and vocationalism,* pp. 67–68. New York: Teachers College Press, Columbia University.

Leighbody, G.B. (1972). *Vocational education in America's schools.* Chicago, IL: American Technical Society.

Miller, M.D. (1985). *Principles and a philosophy for vocational education.* Columbus, OH: The National Center for Research in Vocational Education.

Moody, F.B. (1980). The history of blacks in vocational education. *Vocational Education, 55* (1), 30–34.

Porteous, P.L. (1980). NAABAVE: New rallying point for black concerns. *Journal of Vocational Education,* 55(1), 44–48.

Prosser, C.A. (1913, May). The meaning of industrial education. *Vocational Education,* 401–410.

Prosser, C.A. (1939). *Secondary education and life.* Cambridge, MA: Harvard University Press.

Snedden, D. (1910). *The problem of vocational education.* Boston, MA: Houghton Mifflin Company.

Spring, J. (1990). *The American school 1642–1990.* White Plains, NY: Longman.

Thornbrough, E.L. (Ed.). (1969). *Booker T. Washington.* Englewood Cliffs, NJ: Prentice-Hall.

Washington, B.T. (1901). *Up from slavery,* p.125. Garden City, NY: Doubleday and Company.

Washington, E.D. (1938). *Quotations of Booker T. Washington,* p. 18. Tuskegee, AL: Tuskegee Institute Press.

Wirth, A.G. (1972). *Education in the technological society.* Scranton, PA: Intext Educational Publishers.

Wolfe, D.C. (1981, November). Booker T. Washington: An educator for all ages. *Phi Delta Kappan, 63* (3), 205, 222.

3

IMPACT OF LAND-GRANT INSTITUTIONS ON THE PROFESSIONAL GROWTH OF VOCATIONAL EDUCATION

In mid-nineteenth-century America, President Barnard of the University of Alabama indicated that the craft society and all that were vocationalism would never have a place in institutions of formal learning:

"While time lasts, the farmer will be made in the field, the manufacturer in the shop, the merchant in the counting room, the civil engineer in the midst of the actual operation of science." (Leslie, 1976, p. 237)

Such views, however, were not present in the earliest days of the university. The first universities specialized in preparing young men for professional callings (Leslie, 1976).

This chapter focuses on vocational education in the four-year college domain. It provides information on the following acts: First Morrill Act, Second Morrill Act, and the Smith-Lever Agricultural Extension Act.

When the university came to America with the founding of Harvard in 1636, it did not come to prepare professionals. Colleges such as Harvard and Yale were established to prepare persons for the ministry and other professions. This type of education was not viewed as particularly practical either by or for the general populace. Americans placed little faith in those things that were not practical. Commanger (1950) comments:

The American's attitude toward culture was at once suspicious and indulgent, where it interfered with the more important activities he distrusted it;

where it was the recreation of his leisure hours, or his women folk, he toler-ated it. For the most part, he required that culture serve some useful purpose. He wanted poetry that he could recite, music that he could sing, and paint-ings that told a story . . . Education was his religion, and to it he paid the tribute both of his money and his affection; yet, as he expected his religion to be practical and pay dividends, he expected education to prepare for life— by which he meant increasingly, jobs and professions. (p. 10)

These institutions, along with some twenty state universities that had been established by 1860, did not turn out graduates able to address them-selves to the practical problems of the day (Thompson, 1973). Agriculture and industry were the principal resources of the American economy and trained workers were needed to develop their potentials.

The demands for the development of vocational education occurred between 1820 and 1860. In general, the agricultural sector of the economy demanded vocational and practical education. The working individual did not want a totally skill-oriented training but, rather, an education more prac-tical than was commonly offered by secondary schools and colleges of the day. If the farmers' problems were to be met, there had to be a "practical" impetus from education. Developing the nation's great agricultural resources required leadership from technically trained persons in public education at the secondary and college level.

Industrial development faced a void of engineers able to deal with the more practical problems of plant layout, machine design, and machine parts. Traditional colleges prepared students for law, medicine, teaching, and the ministry. These four professions would provide gainful employment for only a portion of the population. Among American's expanding masses were thou-sands of young men who could benefit from advanced training, but who were not interested in the professional, traditional training available. Congress responded to some of these practical problems by passing the Morrill Act of 1862 (Thompson, 1973). With the beginning of the land-grant movement, the spirit of vocationalism could no longer be resisted by elitist universities. Leslie (1976) noted that the public universities only feigned resistance; most soon became willing partners in vocational education.

The land-grant mission that evolved was service to the people. It was, in the words of Lincoln Stevens of the University of Wisconsin, "Sending a state to college"; it was "teaching anybody—anything—anywhere" (Leslie, 1976, p. 240). The land-grant university was county agents and agricultural experi-ment stations; it was providing the expertise for anything the people needed or wanted to know. However, it was more than just direct service to the peo-ple. The land-grant university meant preparing all kinds of expert profession-als that the people might need. The land-grant mission also meant reacting to the immediate need of the people and anticipating their needs in advance.

Land-grant institutions were called "colleges of agriculture," "colleges of mechanic arts," or "colleges of agriculture and mechanic arts." Their purposes were primarily to educate the farmers and agricultural technicians in increased crop production; to educate the housewife-home economist and her supporting cast in better nutrition, childrearing, and homemaking; and to prepare the engineers and technicians for a soon-to-expand industrial society.

Other universities, both public and private, involved themselves in professional education. However, they limited their efforts to those professions that could be characterized as learned—medicine, law, theology. The somewhat tainted professions—the mechanic arts (engineering) and especially agriculture and home economics—were almost the exclusive domain of the land-grant institution.

FIRST MORRILL ACT (ADOPTED JULY 2, 1862)

Senator Justin A. Morrill of Vermont introduced the first Land-Grant Bill in 1857. The bill failed in the Senate, so he reintroduced it in 1859 (Walter, 1993). The bill passed both houses of Congress, but was vetoed by President Buchanan. In 1862, Senator Morrill, along with the support of Ohio Senator Benjamin Wade, again passed the Morrill Act for Land-Grant Institutions through both houses. The rationale was to support the legislation for the agrarian community farmer, but Wade took advantage of wartime concerns and illustrated that colleges would be ideal for training officers and engineers for the war effort (Miller, 1993). President Lincoln signed the legislation on July 2, 1862.

The primary purpose of this act was to promote the liberal and practical education of the industrial classes in pursuits and professions of living. Andrews (1918) reported that this act granted 30,000 acres of land to each state for each senator and representative in Congress to which the state was entitled by apportionment under the census of 1860:

> *All money derived from the sale of these lands was to be invested by the state in securities bearing interest at not less than 5 percent except that the legislature of the state might authorize the use of not more than 10 percent of capital for the purchase of sites for the college or experimental farm. The interest was to be used for the endowment, support, and maintenance of at least one college where the leading object should be to teach such branches of learning as are related to agriculture and the mechanic arts in order to promote the liberal and practical education of the industrial classes in the several pursuits and professions in life. (p. 10)*

It has been held that the Morrill Act authorized the purchase of apparatus, machinery, textbooks, reference books, and materials used for the purpose of instruction and for the payment of salaries of instructors in the branches of learning specified by the Land-Grant Act. In each case of machinery, such as boilers, engines, and pumps that were used to serve both instructional and other purposes, the fund could only be charged with an equitable portion of the cost of such machinery (Miller and Gay, 1914):

The act prohibited the expenditure of any portion of these funds for the purchase, construction, preservation, or repair of any building or buildings under any pretense whatever, and the salaries of purely administrative officers, such as treasurer, presidents, and secretaries. (p. 238)

The Morrill Act of 1862 was the first legislation passed by the national government to support vocational education. According to Calhoun and Finch (1982), institutions of higher education receiving support under the Morrill Act of 1862 were known as land-grant institutions because their financial support for vocational programs came primarily from the sale of land provided in the act. Table 3.1 lists the 1862 land-grant institutions.

Historians agree that neither Senator Justin Morrill, who sponsored the bill, nor the influential Senator Benjamin Wade, who guided it through Congress, had any clear idea of its educational implications. Venn (1964) argued that the implications of the Morrill Act were more extensive than Morrill and Wade had anticipated. Not only did the founding of these colleges enable higher education to be open to a broader public and improve agricultural techniques, but also the concept of integrated academics was first identified. Classical studies ranging from languages and mathematics were integrated for the first time into agricultural and science courses, that is, curriculum that was identified as vocational. The vocational and academic curricula were to be integrated without any superior rating, ranking, or qualitative judgment. Accompanying this integration of academics and the development of the experimental farms and extension programs, mechanical arts and agriculture were also given important status and, like science, were taught, "as an instrument for molding the societal envisonment" (Venn, 1964).

The primary difficulty the newly opened institutions encountered was the lack of adequately prepared students for higher education. The result of this perceived failure of public education permanently altered the secondary school curriculum. Leaders in the land-grant institutions realized the problems facing higher education and took it upon themselves to create university high schools. These high schools, run by the land-grant institutions, placed vocational preparation training at the forefront of their curriculum (Miller, 1993).

TABLE 3.1   List of Land-Grant Institutions in 1862

Institution	Date State Accepted Morrill Act	Date Institution Opened to Students	Location
Auburn University	1867	1872	Auburn, AL
University of Alaska	1929	1922	Fairbanks, AK
University of Arizona	1910	1891	Tucson, AZ
University of Arkansas	1864	1872	Fayetteville, AR
University of California	1866	1869	Davis, CA
Colorado State University	1879	1879	Fort Collins, CO
University of Connecticut	1862	1881	Storris, CT
University of Delaware	1867	1869	Newark, DE
University of Florida	1870	1884	Gainesville, FL
University of Georgia	1886	1801	Athens, GA
University of Idaho	1890	1892	Moscow, ID
University of Illinois	1867	1868	Urbana, IL
Purdue University	1865	1874	West Lafayette, IN
Iowa State	1862	1859	Ames, IA
Kansas State University	1863	1863	Manhattan, KS
University of Kentucky	1863	1880	Lexington, KY
Louisiana State University	1869	1874	Baton Rouge, LA
University of Maine	1863	1868	Orono, ME
University of Maryland	1864	1859	College Park, MD
University of Massachusetts	1863	1867	Amherst, MA
Michigan State University	1863	1857	East Lansing, MI
University of Minnesota	1863	1851	St. Paul, MN
Mississippi State University	1866	1880	Mississippi State, MS
University of Missouri	1863	1841	Columbia, MO
Montana State University	1889	1893	Bozeman, MT
University of Nebraska	1867	1871	Lincoln, NE

(Continued)

SECOND MORRILL ACT (ADOPTED AUGUST 30, 1890)

The intent of the 1890 Morrill Act was to provide educational opportunity for African American students. The act mandated that in the southern states where separate schools were maintained for Blacks that land-grant institutions be opened to both White and Black students or "separate but equal" facilities be established (Bell, 1987). It is interesting to observe, however, that in 1872 the state of Mississippi gave three-fifths of its land-grant funds from the 1862 Morrill Act to Alcorn State University (Moody, 1980). Braxton (1994) noted that Alcorn A&M University became the first Black land-grant institution established under the Morrill Act of 1862. Three other southern states (Virginia, South Carolina, and Kentucky) established land-grant colleges for African Americans as well as colleges for Whites. It was not until the Second

TABLE 3.1   (*Continued*)

Institution	Date State Accepted Morrill Act	Date Institution Opened to Students	Location
University of Nevada	1866	1874	Reno, NV
University of New Hampshire	1863	1868	Durham, NH
Rutgers State University	1863	1771	New Brunswick, NJ
New Mexico State University	1898	1890	Las Cruces, NM
Cornell University	1863	1868	Ithaca, NY
North Carolina State University	1866	1889	Raleigh, NC
North Dakota State University	1889	1891	Fargo, ND
Ohio State University	1864	1873	Columbus, OH
Oklahoma State University	1890	1891	Stillwater, OK
Oregon State University	1868	1865	Corrallis, OR
Pennsylvania State University	1863	1859	University Park, PA
University of Rhode Island	1863	1890	Kingston, RI
Clemson University	1868	1893	Clemson. SC
South Dakota State University	1889	1884	Brookings, SD
University of Tennessee	1868	1794	Knoxville, TN
Texas A&M University	1866	1876	College Station, TX
Utah State University	1888	1890	Logan, UT
University of Vermont	1862	1801	Burlington, VT
Virginia Polytechnic Institute and State University	1870	1872	Blacksburg, VA
Washington State University	1889	1892	Pullman, WA
West Virginia University	1863	1868	Morgantown, WV
University of Wisconsin	1863	1849	Platteville, WI
University of Wyoming	1889	1887	Laramine, WY

Source: Anderson, G.L. (1976). *Land-grant universities and their continuing challenge.* Michigan State University Press, East Lansing, MI.

Morrill Act of 1890 that all of the southern states established or designated land-grant institutions for African Americans (Baker, 1991).

In 1890, Congress passed the Second Morrill Act, which was an amendment to the Morrill Act of 1862. This act (also known as the Maintenance Act) authorized the application of a portion of the proceeds from sale of public lands under the first Morrill Act to the more complete endowment and support of the land-grant institutions, and for the benefit of agriculture and the mechanic arts. Each state and territory received an amount of $1,500 annually. This amount was to be supplemented by an automatic annual increase of $1,000 until the year 1900 (Hawkins, Prosser, and Wright, 1951).

Miller and Gay (1914) reported that the Second Morrill Act was similar to the original act, but it had the following provisions:

> *That in any state in which there has been one college established in pursuance of the act of July second, eighteen hundred and sixty-two, and also*

in which an educational institution of like character has been established, and is now aided by such state from its own revenue, for the education of colored students in agriculture and mechanic arts, however named or styled or whether or not it has received money hereto fore under the act to which this act is an amendment, the legislature of such state may propose and report to the Secretary of the Interior a just and adequate division of the fund to be received under this act between one college for white students and one institution for colored students established as if one said which shall be divided into two parts and paid accordingly, and thereupon such institutions for colored students shall be entitled to the benefits of this act and subject to its provisions, as much as it would have been if it had been included under the act of eighteen hundred and sixty-two and fulfillment of the fore-going provision shall be taken as a compliance with the provision in reference to separate colleges for white and colored students. (pp. 237–238)

The last institution to be organized as a Black land-grant college was Tennessee A&I State College in Nashville in 1912. The state of Tennessee accepted the provisions of the Second Morrill Act in 1891 and established an industrial department at Knoxville College, which it supervised and funded until 1912 (Hall, 1973).

Land-grant institutions for Blacks did not develop as rapidly as those for Whites in the 17 northern states where they were located. The retardation of these institutions can be greatly attributed to the misappropriation of federal funds entrusted to the states for distribution to these institutions. The Black schools received a fairly equitable share of funds made available under the Morrill Act of 1890, but were denied their equitable share of other federal funds based on population (Guzman, 1952).

A study by Wilkerson (1939) revealed that blacks constituted from 25 to 27 percent of the population of the southern region in the 1920s and 1930s, but their land-grant colleges received only 3 to 8 percent of all federal funds coming into the region for this type of education. A breakdown of these disparities between 1923 and 1936 is given in Table 3.2.

For many years Black land-grant institutions were largely secondary institutions. This was mainly due to inadequate public schools for Blacks and the lack of Black students prepared to do college work. Their industrial offerings prior to 1930 were confined mostly to manual training and subcollegiate trade courses in occupations that were in harmony with the then prevailing social and economic status of Black men in the South. A study of these schools in 1934 and 1935 revealed that auto mechanics and woodworking, including carpentry, were the most frequently offered trade courses and no course in professional engineering existed (Caliver, 1937).

Teacher education became the main function of the Black land-grant institutions when most of their curricula were elevated to the collegiate level in the 1930s. By 1934, eleven of the seventeen institutions offered industrial teacher education programs (Caliver, 1937). According to Hall (1973), these early pro-

TABLE 3.2   Percentage Distribution of Federal Funds to Black Land-Grant Institutions (1923–1936)

Year Ending (June 30)	All Funds (%)	1862 Land-Grant Funds (%)	Smith-Hughes Funds (%)	Second Morrill, Nelson Bankhead Jones Funds (%)
1923	6	10	16	29
1924	6	10	15	29
1925	7	7	23	29
1926	6	7	21	29
1927	6	7	31	29
1928	6	15	28	29
1929	5	—	36	29
1930	3	7	23	29
1932	5	10	27	29
1933	5	8	32	29
1934	8	8	16	29
1935	4	12	15	29
1936	5	12	17	29

Source: Wilkerson, D.A. (1939). *Special problems of negro education,* pp. 81–82. Washington, DC: Government Printing Office.

grams were extensions of the colleges' vocational trade courses combined with clusters of general and professional education courses, and they attempted to prepare persons to be vocational-industrial education teachers in a four-year sequence. This arrangement was prompted by the need for Black vocational teachers at the secondary level. With the apprenticeship programs closed to Blacks and no specialized vocational schools available to them, it became necessary for these institutions to develop programs to supply the public schools' manpower needs. However, it is obvious that the structure of these programs prevented satisfactory attainment of all their objectives, but they did produce a cadre of vocational-industrial education teachers who later pursued successfully advanced degrees at outstanding graduate schools in the North.

Table 3.3 lists the historically and predominantly Black land-grant institutions in 1890.

West Virginia State College is one of few predominantly Black institutions of higher education that has experienced reverse integration as a result of the U.S. Supreme Court's decision declaring racial segregation illegal. Until 1957, West Virginia State College was similar to the other institutions in 1890—receiving small appropriations from state and federal governments and training Black students in agriculture-related fields. But that year, responding to the U.S. Supreme Court's decision in *Brown v. Board of Education,* the West Virginia Legislature voted to move all land-grant activities to West Virginia University (Jaschik, 1994). However, all of the other states kept their land-grant institutions as such.

Over the years, West Virginia State's White enrollment grew, but most of the students were commuter students. Hall (1973) reported that by 1957 more

TABLE 3.3   List of Land-Grant Institutions in 1890

Institution	Date State Accepted Morrill Act	Date Institution Opened to Students	Location
Alabama A&M University	1891	1875	Huntsville, AL
University of Arkansas at Pine Bluff	1891	1882	Pine Bluff, AR
Delaware State College	1891	1892	Dover, DE
Florida A&M University	1891	1887	Tallahassee, FL
Fort Valley State College	1890	1891	Fort Valley, GA
Kentucky State University	1893	1887	Frankfort, KY
Southern University	1892	1881	Baton Rouge, LA
University of Maryland– Eastern Shore	1890	1886	Princess Ann, MD
Alcorn State University	1892	1872	Lorman, MS
Lincoln University	1891	1866	Jefferson City, MO
North Carolina A&T State University	1891	1891	Greensboro, NC
Langston University	1890	1898	Langston, OK
South Carolina State College	1868	1896	Orangeburg, SC
Tennessee State University	1868	1912	Nashville, TN
Virginia State University	1870	1868	Petersburg, VA
West Virginia State College[a]	1890	1891	Institute, WV

Source: Anderson, G.L. (1976). *Land-grant universities and their continuing challenge.* Michigan State University Press, East Lansing, MI

[a]West Virginia State had been a land-grant institution until the 1950s, when the designation was withdrawn. In 1991, the West Virginia Legislature returned land-grant status to the institution.

then 1,000 white students were attending integrated classes at the school. In 1994 its student body was 87 percent White and resident population was about 80 percent Black (Jaschik, 1994).

West Virginia State College has been redesignated as a land-grant institution, meaning the school will get $50,000 a year from the U.S. Department of Agriculture (Jaschik, 1994). In 1991, the West Virginia Legislature returned land-grant status to the institution. Although West Virginia State College has been redesignated as a land-grant institution, the college cannot participate in programs created after 1890 to support Black land-grant institutions. As of 1997, the university was focusing on creating new programs in agribusiness and economics that would help low-income students and state residents.

THE SMITH-LEVER AGRICULTURAL EXTENSION ACT

In 1914 the Smith-Lever Act was passed. This act completed the land-grant triumvirate—teaching, research, and extension. The Smith-Lever Act provided

West Virginia State College is one of the few predominantly Black institutions that has experienced reverse integration.

for a program of cooperative extension work in agriculture and home economics. Merriam and Cunningham (1989) cite several events that made the Smith-Lever Act possible: aggressive promotion by special interest groups, development of the agricultural sciences, and the creation of a method for knowledge dissemination.

The Smith-Lever Act also formally established the principle that while elementary and secondary education might remain the responsibility of the states, the national government would aid the expansion of higher learning to the "common individual." What this has meant for the land-grant colleges, over and beyond being trendsetters, is that they have enjoyed systematic treatment from Washington compared to other colleges and universities (Nichols, 1976).

Provisions of the Smith-Lever Agricultural Extension Act (38 Stat. 372)

A brief summary of the principal provisions of the act follows:

1. **Cooperative Character of the Work**

    a. It must be carried on in connection with the land-grant college in cooperation with the U.S. Department of Agriculture.
    b. It enables the use of plans that are mutually agreed upon by the Secretary of Agriculture and the land-grant college.

Procedure: The director of extension draws up, through the state extension staff, plans of work that include the estimated funds necessary for personnel, expenses, and materials to carry them out, subject to the approval of the dean and trustees, regents, or curators of the land-grant institutions. The plans are then forwarded to the administrator of extension, U.S. Department of Agriculture, who, with federal extension staff, checks them for final approval.

2. **Wide Scope of Work**

   a. It provides that work is to be with persons not attending or residents in land-grant colleges. There is no limitation as to age, sex, race, or business.
   b. The subject-matter scope is practically unlimited—"the giving of instruction . . . in agriculture, home economics, and subjects relating thereto."

3. **Educational Character of Work**

   a. Cooperative extension work is a function of a land-grant college. The Morrill Acts provide that these colleges are to teach.
   b. The act specifies that the "work shall consist of the giving of instruction."

4. **Emphasis on the Demonstration**

   a. The work "shall consist of the giving of . . . practical demonstrations."
   b. It shall impart "information . . . through demonstrations."

5. **Finance and Distribution Based on Rural and Farm Population**
   Congress is authorized to appropriate such sums as it deems necessary. Out of these sums each state, Puerto Rico, and the Federal Extension Service shall receive funds as indicated by the terms of the current authorizing amended act. These federal funds require some degree of offset from nonfederal funds by the states and Puerto Rico. Certain sums are available to states without offset; in general, the balance of the appropriated sums has to be duplicated by a like amount raised within the state. A small percentage is available to the Secretary of Agriculture to be allotted on the basis of special needs due to population characteristics, area in relation to farm population, or other special problems.
   The Federal Extension Service shall receive such amounts as Congress shall determine for administration, technical, and other services and for coordinating the extension work of the department and the several states, territories, and possessions.

6. **Limitations.** Funds may not be used for:

   a. Purchase, erection, preservation, or repair of buildings
   b. Purchase or rental of land
   c. College course teaching
   d. Lectures in college
   e. Other purposes not specified in the act

States determine which college or colleges shall administer the funds. Each college shall make, annually, a detailed report of operations, receipts, and expenditures to the governor of the state and the Secretary of Agriculture. The law gave the Secretary of Agriculture and the state agricultural colleges joint approval authority. It established a national system of cooperative extension education.

Implications for Vocational Education

The Morrill Act was the cornerstone for the development of land-grant institutions in America. These institutions have paved the way for leadership, training, and research in specialized fields. Land-grant institutions induced a major redirection in the pattern of higher education in America. Some of the implications for vocational education were as follows:

1. A liberal and practical education was prescribed.
2. The doors of higher education were opened to a wider public audience.
3. Prominent status was given to the mechanical arts, agriculture, and other disciplines.
4. The acceptance of vocationalism was extended to farmers, business professionals, public schools, and various community agencies.
5. The social efficiency of vocational education was widely recognized.
6. Land-grant institutions were perceived as models for solving urban and rural problems.

Today the historic land-grant institutions and their sister state universities address the large and demanding problems of the nation and all mankind—energy and the environment, inflation and recession, and the need for an adequate and nutritious food supply—and accept responsibility for helping to solve them.

The issues facing American society today call for greatly expanded efforts by all of higher education. Yet, no social institution is so uniquely equipped to meet this challenge as the land-grant college or university, an institution that was created to meet precisely this need, and an institution that has a long and distinguished record of such accomplishments.

SUMMARY

- When the university came to America with the founding of Harvard in 1636, it did not come to prepare professionals. Colleges such as Harvard and Yale were established to prepare persons for the ministry and other professions. This type of education was not viewed as particularly practical either by or for the general populace.

- The demands for the development of vocational education occurred between 1820 and 1860. In general, the agricultural sector of the economy demanded vocational and practical education.

- Land-grant institutions were called "colleges of agriculture," "colleges of mechanic arts," or "colleges of agriculture and mechanic arts." Their purposes were primarily to educate farmers and agricultural technicians for increased crop production; to educate the housewife—home economist and her supporting cast for better nutrition, childrearing, and homemaking; and to prepare the engineers for a soon-to-expand industrial society.

- The Morrill Act of 1862 was the first legislation passed by the national government to support vocational education. Proposed by Senator Justin Morrill of Vermont, the act granted 30,000 acres of land to each state for each senator and representative it had in Congress. Income from the sale of such lands by the states would be used to create and maintain agricultural and mechanical arts colleges.

- The Second Morrill Act (also known as the Maintenance Act) authorized the application of a portion of the proceeds from the sale of public lands under the first Morrill Act to the more complete endowment and support of the land-grant colleges, and for the benefit of agriculture and the mechanic arts. Each state and territory received an increase of $1,500 annually. This amount was to be supplemented by an automatic annual increase of $1,000 until the year 1900. The Second Morrill Act of 1890 gave new life to land-grant college education for Blacks and other minorities.

- The Smith-Lever Act, known as the Agricultural Extension Act, provided for a program of cooperative extension work in agriculture and home economics. The practice of 50-50 matching began with this act. The state was required to finance half of the cost of the extension programs and the federal government the other half. This act also provided farmers and homemakers with a program of cooperative extension work in agriculture and home economics.

DISCUSSION QUESTIONS AND ACTIVITIES

1. Discuss the role of the land-grant system in the development of vocational education.

2. Describe some of the vocational education programs that are conducted by the Cooperative Extension Service in your community.

3. Discuss the provisions of the Smith-Lever Agricultural Extension Act.

4. Compare and contrast the mission of land-grant institutions with that of non-land-grant institutions **(Library Research).**

5. Contrast the provisions of the First Morrill Act with the provisions of the Second Morrill Act.

6. List and discuss the tripartite system of the land-grant system **(Library Research).**

7. Debate the following topics:

    a. Will the land-grant institutions need to change their concepts or mission of goals in order to remain viable?

b. Should teacher education programs in agricultural education be limited to land-grant universities?

8. Who was Senator Justin A. Morrill? Explain his role in the development of vocational education.

REFERENCES

Andrews, B.F. (1918). The land-grant of 1862 and the land-grant colleges. *Bulletin No. 13,* p. 10. Washington, DC: U.S. Government Printing Office.

Baker, S.A. (1991). The impact of the civil war on vocational education. *Journal of Vocational and Technical Education, 7*(2), 56–60.

Bell, A.P. (1987, December). Commitment of 1890 land-grant institutions to teacher education in agriculture. *The Agricultural Education Magazine, 60*(6), 13.

Braxton, G.J. (1994). *Historically black colleges and universities in the United States.* Washington, DC: National Association of Foreign Students Affairs Publications.

Calhoun, C.C., and Finch, A.V. (1982). *Vocational education: Concepts and operations.* Belmont, CA: Wadsworth Publishing Company.

Caliver, A. (1937). *Vocational education and guidance of Negroes.* Washington, DC: Government Printing Office.

Commanger, H.S. (1950). *The American mind,* p. 10. New Haven: Yale University Press.

Guzman, J.P. (1952). *1952 Negro yearbook.* New York: William H. Wise and Co.

Hall, C.W. (1973). *Black vocational technical and industrial arts education: Development and history.* Chicago: American Technical Society.

Hawkins, L.S., Prosser, C.A., and Wright, J.C. (1951). *Development of vocational education.* Chicago: American Technical Society.

Jaschik, S. (1994, April, 27). West Virginia state college regains black land-grant status. *The Chronicle of Higher Education,* p. A22.

Leslie, L.L. (1976). Updating education for the profession: The new mission. In G.L.

Anderson (Ed.), *Land-grant universities and their continuing challenge* (pp. 237–265). Michigan State University Press, East Lansing, MI.

Merriam, S.B., and Cunningham, P.M. (1989). *Handbook of adult and continuing education.* San Francisco: Jossey-Bass Publishers.

Miller, K., and Gay, J.R. (1914). *Progress and achievements of colored people.* Washington, DC: Austin Jenkins Co.

Miller, M.T. (1993). *The historical development of vocational education in the United States: Colonial America through the Morrill legislation.* (ERIC Document Reproduction Service No. ED 360 481).

Moody, F. (1980). The history of blacks in vocational education. *Voc.Ed., 55* (1), 30–34.

Nichols, D.C. (1976). Land-grant university services and urban policy. In G.L. Anderson (Ed.), *Land-grant universities and their continuing challenge* (pp. 223–236). Michigan State University Press, East Lansing, MI.

Thompson, J.F. (1973). *Foundations of vocational education: Social and philosophical concepts.* Englewood Cliffs, NJ: Prentice Hall.

Venn, G. (1964). *Man, education and work.* Washington, DC: American Council on Education.

Walter, R.A. (1993). Development of vocational education. In C. Anderson and L.C. Rampp (Eds.), *Vocational education in the 1990's, II: A sourcebook for strategies, methods, and materials* (pp. 1–20). Ann Arbor, MI: Prakken Publishing Company.

Wilkerson, D.A. (1939). *Special problems of negro education.* Washington, DC: U.S. Government Printing Office.

4

SELECTED FACTORS THAT INFLUENCED VOCATIONAL EDUCATION DEVELOPMENT

From 1917 to 1918, efforts in vocational education were largely devoted to the needs of the nation in World War I. Participation of America in war activities made urgent the rapid and effective training of masses of inexperienced persons. Thousands of civilian workers in the war effort learned their skills in vocational education classes—skills they put to good use in the postwar economy.

As America approached the twentieth century, support for the use of state and federal funds to establish and operate a comprehensive system of vocational education began to increase. However, there was no universal agreement as to what form vocational education should take, but there was agreement that changes in the ways of preparing workers were required. Various agencies and organizations expressed an interest in providing additional opportunities for vocational education. These groups engaged in studies, passed resolutions, and petitioned legislative bodies to provide financial assistance in establishing programs of vocational education at public expense.

This chapter is concerned with a discussion of selected factors that influenced the development of vocational education. For convenience these factors are grouped under the following headings: Impact of War Activities, Study Panels, and American Vocational Association.

IMPACT OF WAR ACTIVITIES

Since 1917, the public vocational schools have trained large numbers of workers for occupations essential to the national economy in peacetime and wartime. It is not accurate to say that the Smith-Hughes Act was passed because of the possibility of war, but it is apparent congressional leaders saw a close relationship between the vocational education bill and national preparedness.

The war found America vocationally unprepared. The critical military and industrial shortage of trained workers became an emergency for the newly created Federal Board for Vocational Education. The Federal Board had the responsibility of building a permanent system of vocational education and its task was to train men in skilled occupations useful in combat conditions. Both the War Department and the U.S. Shipping Board requested assistance from the Federal Board in organizing and conducting war classes for various occupations after the actual military training (Bauder, 1918). "Thus for the first time in the history of the United States the schools of America were called upon by the Federal Government to undertake vocational training" (Federal Board for Vocational Education, 1917, p. 10).

Shortly after the approval of the Smith-Hughes Act in 1917, America became involved in World War I. Other major wars that have influenced vocational education include World War II, the Korean War, and the Vietnam War.

World War I

This was a war of various mechanical forces. To fight a mechanical war, highly trained mechanics, technicians, and experienced supervisory forces were needed, in addition to troops. Efforts of World War I created and expanded industries. For the production of the necessary equipment and supplies, industry required increasing numbers of trained crafts personnel. The War Industries Board and the Federal Board for Vocational Education took the necessary challenges and lead in providing this trained manpower. The Federal Board for Vocational Education stated in 1918 that at the request of the United States Army it had "undertaken to aid the Army to secure proper training of conscripted men before they are drafted . . . This bulletin is issued for the purpose of supplying information to school authorities who will undertake this work as a patriotic duty" (p. 3).

The Federal Board for Vocational Education worked with the army to determine that it needed 200,000 mechanics. In addition, a need for radio operators, radio repairmen, automobile drivers, gasoline engine repairmen, and others was discerned. The board then formulated a plan to train personnel. Its major effort was to establish classes in specialized subjects for training men prior to their induction into the service. Training was eventually provided at 125 local induction centers (Federal Board for Vocational Education, 1919).

Beginning July 1, 1917, and continuing until the conclusion of World War I, 62,161 persons were trained for war production jobs. This was in the early stages of the federally aided program of vocational education of less than college grade. After World War I, an upsweep in economy carried America through a period of high-level prosperity that ended with the 1929 economic crash. The industrial activity, which followed the 1937 depression, proved to be the initial industrial effort for World War II (Seidel, 1951).

World War II

The participation of America in World War II necessitated the rapid and effective training of masses of inexperienced persons. According to Dennis (1950), an unprecedented feat of training on such a vast scale and in such short time was made possible through close cooperation between the federal government and those vocational schools equipped to handle the problem. Thompson (1973) reported that Vocational Training for War Production Workers (VTWPW) and Vocational Education for National Defense (VEND) were initiated to expand the vocational training programs.

The objective of VTWPW was the immediate employability of the trainee for a specific job. In a large number of instances, new workers received instruction but in other cases, workers employed in civilian production were given "conversion training" for jobs in war industry (Siedel, 1951). VEND was initiated and administered through the same process as the Smith-Hughes Act. A commonality of VEND and VTWPW is that both were largely urban centered and operated to train industrial workers. Several pieces of federal legislation were enacted for vocational training during World War II. It was estimated that the total appropriation was more than $370 million.

Effects of Korean and Vietnam Wars

The effects of the Korean and Vietnam Wars on vocational education involvement included the following:

1. A greater need for food and industrial production.
2. A large number of draftees.
3. A decline in unemployment.
4. A rise in unemployment due to returning veterans entering the labor market.
5. An increased labor supply.
6. An expansion of existing programs and creation of new programs to assist veterans entering the labor market.

Benefits of War Training on Vocational Education

Foreman training was perhaps the largest direct result of vocational education involvement during the wars (Thompson, 1973). Hawkins, Prosser, and Wright (1951) list ten benefits from the effects of war training on vocational education. Among the ten are:

1. America became conscious of the need for vocational education.
2. Adults need training even after they are employed.
3. Women can be trained to do men's work.
4. The need for short, intensive, teacher-training courses.
5. The philosophy was advanced that vocational education was part of the preparation for living needed by all individuals.

Servicemen's Readjustment Act of 1944 (Public Law 78-346)

In June 1944, President Franklin D. Roosevelt signed into law the Servicemen's Readjustment Act of 1944, known as the GI Bill of Rights. The purpose of this act was to assist World War II veterans in readjustment to civilian life. Few requirements were placed on the veterans; they simply were to select the kind of training and/or education they wanted, apply for admission to a recognized training program, and maintain the academic standards necessary to continue in the program. In addition to the direct participants in vocational education, a large number of veterans in college majored in vocational teacher education and taught in vocational programs. The veteran was allowed time for participation in accordance with the time he or she had been in service. Subsequent legislation passed along these benefits to veterans of the Korean and Vietnam Wars.

Implications

The future will be determined to a great extent by how vocational education, defense, and industry accept the challenge and work together toward the short- and long-range goals for reducing the shortage of skilled and technical workers for the defense industrial base. Defense industry leaders need to take positive action to improve their industry's image if they want more young people to choose careers with them. The opportunity is there for leaders in defense industries to become more visible in community and school activities where bridges can be built and communications opened.

They might find it advantageous to participate actively in career days, in promoting occupational opportunities in industry, speaking at school events, arranging plant tours and, in general, exposing students, counselors, teachers, and administrators to their world in the same way that other business and industry leaders do. They need to serve on advisory committees and on school boards, taking actions that make them important to students and administrators. Only in this way will they be assured that their points of view will be incorporated into local decision making.

One valuable lesson from this era of stress that must not be forgotten is that our final strength as a country in war or in peace lies in the effective cooperation, effort, and adaptability of our citizens. It is imperative that as a nation we continue to maintain our ability to produce and the faculty to adjust ourselves to sudden, unexpected demands on our manpower if we are to retain our position as a people confident of our destiny. However, we can no longer afford to waste any of our resources, especially our human resources.

STUDY PANELS

Before discussing the history and objectives of these national panels, it is important to obtain a perspective of the National Association of Manufacturers, Douglas Commission, and the National Society for the Promotion of Industrial Education.

The National Association of Manufacturers

The National Association of Manufacturers (NAM) was organized January 22, 1895, at a convention held in Cincinnati, Ohio (Roberts, 1971). The NAM was organized in response to a period of economic depression and was keenly interested in securing an adequate supply of trained workers and reducing the power of the growing labor movement. Their Committee on Industrial education issued a report in 1905 citing high dropout rates and the failure of the apprenticeship system as justification for the creation of a separate system of trade schools. The first report advocated that the schools be funded through corporate or private endowments rather than through public funds. Seven years later, however, the committee modified its position. Recommendations made in their 1912 report included:

- creation of German-style continuation schools;
- development of courses centered on the needs of local industry;
- administration of the schools by coalition of business and labor to ensure that industrial education not be corrupted by educators the way manual training had been; and
- the use of federal funds to improve industrial education as the Morrill and Hatch Acts had improved Agricultural Education (Wirth, 1972).

Douglas Commission of Massachusetts

Various vocational historians have suggested that the present vocational programs began in Massachusetts with the report of the Douglas Commission. This commission was also called the Commission on Industrial and Technical Education (the term used then for vocational education). This commission was directed to investigate the present facilities and needs for vocational education. McCarthy (1950) points out that:

It must be remembered that the Douglas Commission was created not only because of the inadequacy of manual training programs in the public schools, but because the land-grant colleges failed to serve the needs of agriculture or industry on the workers' level. (p. 5)

As provided for by the legislature, in 1905 Governor William Douglas of Massachusetts appointed a commission composed of representatives of manufacturing, agriculture, labor, and education (Walter, 1993). The Douglas Commission criticized existing manual training programs and called for a more industrially oriented educational system. The commission's most controversial proposal, however, was for the establishment of public trade schools independent of the existing educational system.

The Douglas Commission Report concluded that lack of industrial training for workers increased the cost of production. The report stated that workers with general intelligence, technical knowledge, and skill would command the world market. The Douglas Commission emphasized that the foundation for technical success required a wider diffusion of industrial intelligence and that this foundation could only be acquired in connection with the general system of education in which it would be an integral part of the curriculum from the beginning (Barlow, 1976). The Douglas Commission Report was an instrumental landmark in the development of vocationalism in the public schools. Venn (1964) notes that the recommendations of the Douglas Commission Report were enacted into law in 1906.

The initial formation of national groups, such as the National Society for the Promotion of Industrial Education and the national study panels, had the benefit of this report which served as a model to guide them. The report was also influential in the passage of the Smith-Hughes Act of 1917.

National Society for the Promotion of Industrial Education (NSPIE)

Labor and management could not agree on urban programs and had little interest in rural programs. Rural dominated state legislatures were not going to vote money for vocational programs because most of the eligible schools would be in the cities (Venn, 1964).

In 1906 the National Society for the Promotion of Industrial Education brought its study of vocational education needs to the public's attention. According to Barlow (1976), two leaders of manual training, Dr. James P. Hanly and Professor Charles R. Richards, assembled a group of thirteen representative leaders at the New York City Engineers Club on June 9. This gathering was followed by another meeting of about 250 persons on November 16 (Thompson, 1973). As a result of this meeting, the National Society for the Promotion of Industrial Education was organized on November 16, 1906.

The major objectives of the National Society for the Promotion of Industrial Education were:

1. To bring to public attention the importance of industrial education as a factor in the industrial development of America to provide opportunities for the study and discussion of the various phases of the problem.
2. To make available the results of experiments in the field of industrial education.
3. To promote the establishment of institutions of industrial training.

The members of the society consisted of educators, manufacturers, mechanics, businessmen, and representatives of other occupations.

Dr. Charles Prosser served as executive secretary of NSPIE in 1912 (Roberts, 1957). Subsequently this organization and its successor, the National Society for Vocational Education, served as a means of discussing issues of vocational education. The society was instrumental in advocating the appointment in 1914 of the National Commission on National Aid to Vocational Education.

Various national panels were appointed to study vocational education intensively. These panels were responsible for recommending changes that would permit the growth of vocational education. During the period from 1914 to 1968 there were six national panels responsible for reporting on vocational education. Five of the six panels were appointed by the president of the United States. The six panels were:

1. Commission on National Aid for Vocational Education, 1914.
2. Committee on Vocational Education, 1928–1929.
3. National Advisory Committee on Education, 1929–1931.
4. Advisory Committee on Education, 1936–1938.
5. Panel of Consultants on Vocational Education, 1961–1962.
6. National Advisory Council on Education, 1967.

Commission on National Aid to Vocational Education, 1914

President Woodrow Wilson responded to a joint resolution of Congress in 1914 and appointed a special nine-member commission to study the issue of federal aid to vocational education. The Commission on National Aid to Vocational Education included Senator Hoke Smith of Georgia, who served as chair; Representative Dudley Hughes of Georgia; and Charles Prosser, secretary of NSPIE. Dr. Prosser was regarded as the guiding figure of the national commission.

The commission had various meetings that involved the gathering of information to answer six basic questions: (1) What is the need for vocational education, (2) Was there a need for a federal grant (assuming a need for vocational education), (3) What vocational programs required federal grants, (4) To what extent should the federal government extend federal grants for vocational education to the states, (5) What amount of money was needed (the proposed legislation), and (6) What standards are required for the federal government to grant monies to the states for vocational education. (See Appendix A for more information.)

Individuals as well as representatives of national organizations and the various departments of the federal government submitted replies to the commission's questionnaire, both in person and by mail. Barlow (1976) cites Captain Douglas MacArthur (destined for later fame in World War II and Korea) as one of the respondents.

In less than sixty days the commission had created a two-volume report of nearly 500 pages on the six basic questions (Commission on National Aid, 1914). The report included the following recommendations:

1. Funding support for precollege level programs in public schools.
2. Federal aid designed to prepare students more than fourteen years old for employment.
3. Support for three types of schools: full-time schools, with 50 percent of the time in vocational instruction; part-time schools for employed youth; and evening schools for adult workers.
4. Federal grants should be used for training vocational teachers.
5. Grants should be available for paying part of the salaries of vocational teachers.
6. Funds should be available for vocational teachers to conduct research activities.
7. Schools receiving federal funds should be under public supervision.
8. Schools receiving federal grants should be less than college grade.
9. Some form of administrative structure should be developed to supervise grants on a statewide basis.
10. Federal grants should be distributed under the discrepancies of a federal board.

Committee on Vocational Education, 1928–1929

This was the only national committee during that time period not appointed by the president of the United States. The committee did not function as its sponsors intended it should, and soon after its appointment it was phased out.

National Advisory Committee on Education, 1929–1931

This committee was appointed by President Hoover and the Department of Interior. The major result of the first meeting was the creation of a conference. The following recommendations were made by this committee:

1. The Smith-Hughes Act of 1917 and all acts subsequent to it dealing with vocational education would be amended by repealing those provisions that require state matching of federal funds.

2. Abolish the Federal Board for Vocational Education, transfer its remaining functions and staff to the proposed Department of Education.

Advisory Committee on Education, 1936–1938

President Roosevelt appointed a group of twenty-four members to work on this committee. Dr. Floyd W. Reeves served as the committee chairperson. The President requested that the committee conduct a study focusing on the following three areas:

- the experience under existing programs for federal aid to vocational education;
- the existing relationship of training to academic education and to prevailing economic and social conditions; and
- the extent to which there was a need for expanded programs in vocational education.

This advisory committee made six recommendations: (1) to review the basic statutes with the specific intent of removing restraining provisions, (2) to consolidate all federal funds for vocational education of less than senior college grade into a single fund, (3) that the determination of educational activities deemed vocational be transferred to the states, (4) that plant training programs be continued and expanded, (5) to provide for those states that have separate schools for Blacks to receive a just and equitable share of federal funds, and (6) to establish a minimum age of seventeen for instruction designed to prepare for a specific trade and the age of fourteen should be established for participation in all special fields of education, but this could be waived for club work for rural boys and girls (National Advisory Committee on Education, 1938, pp. 206–207).

Panel of Consultants on Vocational Education, 1961–1962

Each year a committee of the Congress of the United States conducts hearings on appropriations for all government agencies. These are held to decide if adjustments of appropriations for any activity of the federal government are necessary and the committee's conclusions are embodied in a recommended budget. During the hearings on the federal budget for the fiscal year 1961, there was a recommendation to reduce the amount of funds allocated to vocational education. According to Roberts (1971), the proposed reduction for vocational education was $2,000,000.

Vocational education did have major issues to resolve, but reduction in expenditure of federal funds was scarcely an appropriate aid toward meeting the required vocational adjustments. Roberts (1971) suggested that federal aid for vocational education was ill-timed because of social, economic, and technological changes. The reduction in the appropriation was adjusted to be inconsistent with the needs of the nation, and the committee restored the $2 million to the budget (Barlow, 1976). However, this led to the appointment of a task force to make a comprehensive study of vocational education.

During the presidential election year of 1960 the American Vocation Association sought the opinions of the candidates about vocational education. Barlow (1976) reported that both John F. Kennedy and Richard M. Nixon cited their support for the area of vocational education.

President Kennedy, in a special message to Congress on February 20, 1961, empowered the creation of a panel of consultants to study vocational education. His message said:

> *The National Vocational Education Acts first enacted by Congress in 1917 and subsequently amended have provided a program of training for industry, agriculture, and other occupational areas. The basic purpose of our vocational education effort is sound and sufficiently broad to provide a basis for meeting future needs. However, the technological changes which have occurred in all occupations call for a review and reevaluation of these acts, with a view toward their modernization.*
>
> *To that end, I am requesting the Secretary of Health, Education and Welfare to convene an advisory body drawn from the educational profession, labor, industry, and agriculture as well as the lay public together with representatives from the Departments of Agriculture and Labor to be charged with the responsibility of reviewing and evaluation the current National Vocational Education Acts, and making recommendations for improving redirecting the program. (U.S. Congress, 1961, 107, Part 2, 2391)*

This panel consisted of twenty-five members representing vocational education, business, labor, education, government, and the press. The panel was chaired by Dr. Benjamin C. Willis, superintendent of schools for the city of Chicago. The panel was responsible for reviewing and evaluating vocational education with the objective of improving and redirecting the programs offered. The panel released its report in the spring of 1963 in "Education for a Changing World of Work." This report served as a basis for modernizing and improving job training, and it set the stage for the passage of the Vocational Education Act of 1963.

The panel's general recommendations were that in a changing world of work, vocational education must:

1. Offer training opportunities to the 210 million noncollege graduates who would enter the labor markets in the 1960s.
2. Provide training or retraining for the millions of workers whose skills and technical knowledge must be updated as well as those whose jobs will disappear due to increasing efficiency, automation, or economic change.
3. Meet the critical need for highly skilled craftsmen and technicians through education during and after the high school years.

4. Expand the vocational and technical programs consistent with employment possibilities and national economic needs.
5. Make educational opportunities equally available to all regardless of race, sex, scholastic aptitude, or place of residence (Panel of Consultants on Vocational Education, 1963).

The panel suggested that federal aid to specific occupational categories be discontinued and support increased for five clientele groups and services:

1. High school youth. Expansion of present occupational programs.
2. High school-age youth with academic, socioeconomic, or other handicaps.
3. Post-high school opportunities.
4. The unemployed or underemployed youth.
5. Services to assure quality (instructional materials, occupational counseling, and various forms of research).

National Advisory Council on Vocational Education, 1967

This council grew out of the 1963 Vocational Education Act and was required by that act to make a report on vocational education every five years. The National Advisory Council on Vocational Education was appointed in 1967 by President Lyndon B. Johnson. The focus of this committee was the enlargement of the concept of vocational training and the necessity to integrate more effectively the poor, unemployed, and underemployed into the economic system. Dr. Martin Essex of Ohio chaired the twelve-member advisory council, and its report was released in 1968.

The first report of the National Advisory Council on Vocational Education stated that the majority of Americans felt vocational education was designed for somebody else's children. It further accused the nation of intellectual snobbery where vocational education was concerned (Calhoun and Finch, 1982). "Clearly, in the minds of some," Leighbody (1972) states, "the goal of vocational education is to meet the needs of those who are less fortunate economically, socially, and intellectually" (p. 9).

The report of the 1967 Advisory Council on Vocational Education concluded that vocational education is not a separate discipline within education; rather, it is a basic objective of all education and must be a basic element of each person's education (Leighbody, 1972).

AMERICAN VOCATIONAL ASSOCIATION (AVA)

The National Society for Vocational Education met in Cleveland, Ohio, December 3–5, 1925, for its nineteenth annual convention. The name of the society was changed to the American Vocational Association, the new constitution was adopted, and the proposed amalgamation with the Vocational Education Association of the Middle West was endorsed. As president of the newly formed American Vocational Association, the Cleveland convention elected Edwin A. Lee, Director of the Division of Vocational Education, University of California, whose plan had stimulated the new union. The American Vocational Association (1926) stated that:

> *Lee's vigorous acceptance of the responsibility inspired confidence among those who did not know him before. They know now that they have a vital force at the head of the new organization; and those who have known him longer can vouch for the fact that he is an efficient administrative officer. (p. 208)*

The spirit and morale of the convention delegates seemed suddenly to be lifted by their act of amalgamation. Dennis (1926) who was to become executive secretary wrote:

> *We find ourselves in a situation where leaders in vocational education have a fine faith in each other and a greater belief in the great work in which we are all endeavoring to do our part. (p. 4)*

The final step in the amalgamation awaited only the action of the Vocational Association of the Middle West. This action was taken unanimously at the Des Moines Convention, March 17–20, 1926. No regret was expressed concerning the demise of the old organization; only the hope and promise of the future occupied the attention and thoughts of the delegates. Charles A. Prosser addressed the convention on the topic "The Magic Chance of Vocational Education."

> *If you want the magic chance get in on the new movement. That's the chance in manual training; that's the chance in vocational education. Manual training, vocational education and art education have made more progress than any other departments of education. (Bennett, 1926, p. 353)*

The first convention of the new organization—the American Vocational Association—was held December 2–4, 1926, in Louisville, Kentucky.

Objectives and Purposes of AVA

The American Vocational Association (AVA) is a national organization for vocational education professionals with state affiliates representing some 40,000 members composed primarily of vocational education teachers, supervisors, teacher educators, counselors, administrators, special support personnel, and graduate students. The mission of the AVA is to provide educational leadership in developing a competitive workforce.

The major objectives of the AVA include the following:

1. To assume and maintain active national leadership in the promotion of Vocational Education.
2. To render service to state or local communities in stabilizing and promoting Vocational Education.
3. To provide a national open forum for the discussion of all questions involved in Vocational Education.
4. To unite all the Vocational education interests of the country through membership representative of the entire country (American Vocational Association, 1986).

The purpose of the AVA includes:

1. *Professional development*—Encourage career development, professional involvement, and leadership among members.
2. *Program improvement*—Foster excellence in vocational technical education.
3. *Policy development*—Advocate national policy to benefit vocational technical education.
4. *Marketing*—Marketing vocational technical education (American Vocational Association, 1992; American Vocational Association, 1995).

The American Vocational Association is composed of the following divisions:

1. Administration
2. Agricultural Education
3. Business Education
4. Employment and Training
5. Guidance
6. Health Occupations Education
7. Family and Consumer Sciences
8. Marketing Education
9. New and Related Services (including an international division)
10. Special Needs
11. Technical Education
12. Technology Education
13. Trade and Industrial Education

The American Vocational Association holds an annual convention, usually in December. The convention city is selected on a rotating basis so that the meeting is held in various parts of the nation. The AVA publishes the *Techniques* (formerly the *Vocational Education Journal*) monthly, September through June with a combined November/December issue. The name change (*Techniques*) went into effect in September 1996. Other publications of AVA include: *Vocational Education Weekly, School-To-Work Reporter,* and *Legislative Update*.

The AVA maintains a national headquarters at 1410 King St., Alexandria, VA 22314 (http://www.avaonline.org). The leadership of AVA includes: an executive director, a president, vice president representing the divisions of AVA, and vice presidents from regions 1–5. Each state is entitled to send office delegates to the annual convention from its state association. The number sent is based on the state's percentage of national membership. Official business of delegates is consummated in the meeting of the house delegates at the annual convention.

SUMMARY

- Shortly after the approval of the Smith-Hughes Act in 1917, America became involved in World War I. Other major wars that have influenced vocational education include World War II, the Korean conflict, and the Vietnam War. Two major benefits from the effects of war training were: (1) the country became conscious of the need for vocational education and (2) the philosophy was advanced that vocational education was a part of preparation for living needed by all normal individuals rather than a device for keeping youth in school or for taking care of delinquents.

- The National Association of Manufacturers (NAM) was organized in response to a period of economic depression. The NAM was keenly interested in securing an adequate supply of trained workers and reducing the power of the growing labor movement.

- Public discussion and interest in the educational needs of the labor force were stimulated by the report of the Douglas Commission. Governor Douglas of Massachusetts, responding to a legislative mandate, appointed a Commission on Vocational Education composed of nine representatives from manufacturing, agriculture, education, and labor to investigate the need for vocational education, to determine the extent of existing programs meeting this need, and to make recommendations regarding how to modify existing programs to serve a vocational purpose.

- A number of separate national panels, committees, and commissions were appointed to study vocational education intensively. Most of these groups were created to find ways of improving the status of vocational education. The panels were to study the existing condition of vocational education and recommend what changes were needed.

- Founded in 1926, American Vocational Association (AVA) is committed to helping members grow personally and professionally . . . to improving vocational-technical programs nationwide. AVA's mission is to provide educational leadership in developing a competitive workforce. AVA seeks to provide the kind of foresight and direction America needs to develop a productive, competitive workforce and to position our nation as a leader in the global marketplace.

DISCUSSION QUESTIONS AND ACTIVITIES

1. Extrapolate on the activities of the Federal Board for Vocational Education in the training of persons for World War I.

2. Explain how the War Production Training Program of World War II was organized.

3. Justify the need for the types of training that were provided in the World War II War Production Training Program.

4. Compare and contrast the activities of the following organizations:
   a. Douglas Commission
   b. National Society for the Promotion of Industrial Education (NSPIE)
   c. Commission of National Aid to Vocational Education.

5. Extrapolate on the recommendations of the Advisory Committee on Education.

6. Explain the role of the American Vocational Association in the development and growth of vocational education.

7. View the following videocassette: *The Commission on National Aid to Vocational Education: A Re-enactment of the 1914 Hearing.* See Appendix A for more information.

8. Discuss the impact of study panels in the development of vocational education.

For Exploration

9. Appraise the influence war training had on vocational education.

10. Assess the impact of the Servicemen's Readjustment Act on the development and growth of vocational education.

REFERENCES

American Vocational Association. The A.V.A. *Industrial Education Magazine, 27*(7), 208.

American Vocational Association (1986). AVA at 60: The past is prologue. *Vocational Education Journal, 61*(8), 23.

———. (1992). American Vocational Association annual report 1991. *Vocational Education Journal, 67*(1), 31.

———. (1995). Inside AVA. *Vocational Education Journal, 70*(2), 13.

Barlow, M.L. (1976). 200 years of vocational education 1776–1976. *American Vocational Journal, 51*(5), 21–108.

Bauder, W.T. (1918, September). Training the fighting mechanics. *Manual Training Magazine, 20*(1), 1–10.

Bennett, C.A. (1926). The merger wins unanimously at Des Moines. *Industrial Education Magazine, 28*(11), 353.

Calhoun, C.C. and Finch, A.V. (1982). *Vocational Education: Concepts and operations.* Belmont, CA: Wadsworth Publishing Company.

Commission on National Aid to Vocational Education. (1914). *Annual report.* Washington, DC: Government Printing Office.

Dennis, L.H. (1926, February). The Cleveland convention. *American Vocational Association, 1*(1), 4.

———. (1950, February). Vocational education for American youth. *American Vocational Journal, 25*(2), 5.

Federal Board for Vocational Education(1917). *First annual report,* p. 20. Washington, DC: Government Printing Office.

———. (1918). *Bulletin number 2,* p. 3. Washington, DC: Government Printing Office.

———. (1919). *Third annual report.* p. 66. Washington, DC: Government Printing Office.

Hawkins, L.S., Prosser, C.A., and Wright, J.C. (1951). *Development of vocational education.* Chicago: Harper and Row.

Leighbody, G.B. (1972). *Vocational education in America's schools: Major issues of the 1970s,* p. 9. Chicago: American Technical Society.

McCarthy, J.A. (1950). *Vocational education: America's greatest resource,* p. 15. Chicago: American Technical Society.

National Advisory Committee on Education. (1938). *Annual report,* pp. 206–207. Washington, DC: Government Printing Office.

Panel of Consultants on Vocational Education. (1963). *Education for a changing world of work.* Washington, DC: Office of Education, U.S. Department of Health, Education, and Welfare.

Roberts, R.W. (1957). *Vocational and practical arts education.* 1st ed. New York: Harper and Row.

———. (1971). *Vocational and practical arts education.* 3rd ed. New York: Harper and Row.

Seidel, J.J. (1951, May). Vocational education in the national mobilization. *American Vocational Journal, 26*(5), 5, 7.

Thompson, J.F. (1973). *Foundations of vocational education: Social and philosophical concepts.* Englewood Cliffs, NJ: Prentice Hall, Inc.

U.S. Congress. (1961). *Journal of Proceedings,* 107, Part 2, 2391. Washington, DC: Government Printing Office.

Venn, G. (1964). *Man, education and work.* Washington: American Council on Education.

Walter, R.A. (1993). Development of vocational education. In C. Anderson and L.C. Rampp (Eds.), *Vocational education in the 1990s, II: A sourcebook for strategies, methods, and materials* (pp. 1–20). Ann Arbor, MI: Prakken Publishing Company.

Wirth, A.G. (1972). *Education in the technological society.* Scranton, PA: Intext Educational.

5

LEGISLATIVE HISTORY AND THE CHANGING WORKFORCE

In the last quarter of the nineteenth century as America moved to establish public secondary schools, there were battles over the role of classical and practical education programs. With more students going to school, the narrow classical curriculum did not satisfy the proponents of an expanded practical education curriculum.

In 1905, proponents of vocational education argued that a broader curriculum was needed to prepare people for the new industrial age. They wanted youth and adults to have a chance for better careers. They were unhappy that only 8 percent of youth graduated from high school, and almost all male graduates went to college while female graduates went into white-collar work (Plawin, 1992). These advocates also were concerned about America's ability to compete in world agricultural and industrial markets. Eventually they developed a coalition to press for federal legislation.

Chapter five is organized according to the legislative history of vocational education and today's changing workforce.

PRE-1917 LAWS AND BILLS

Vocational education has a long history in America. Since the Land Ordinance of 1785 and Northwest Ordinance of 1787, the federal government has demonstrated continued interest in the education of citizenry. Although 1917 marked the first significant legislation relating to vocational education, several pieces of supportive legislation were passed earlier. The most significant of these pre-1917 laws include the following:

Ordinance of 1785. In the ordinance of 1785, Congress required that certain western lands be divided into thirty-six sections, with the sixteenth section set aside for the support of education (Fitzpatrick, 1933).

Ordinance of 1787. In the Northwest Ordinance of 1787, Congress specified (Thorpe, 1909): "Religion morality, and knowledge being necessary to good government and the happiness of mankind, schools and the means of education shall be forever encouraged"(p. 961). By the time that Ohio, the first state in these new western territories was admitted to the Union, the practice of setting aside the sixteenth section of each township to support education was firmly established. Without entering directly into education of various states, the federal government through these two acts expressed an interest in the education of the nation's citizens (Calhoun and Finch, 1982).

1887 Hatch Act. Provided $15,000 to each state for the development of agricultural experiment stations.

The Davis and Dolliver-Davis Bills. In 1907 Representative Charles R. Davis of Minnesota introduced his first bill providing federal aid for industrial education. This bill proposed to allocate federal funds to agricultural high schools for teaching agriculture and home economics and to secondary schools in urban communities for the teaching of mechanical arts and home economics. Senator Dolliver introduced a revised version of the Davis Bill into the U.S. Senate in 1910. However, the National Society for the Promotion of Industrial Education voiced objections to the Dolliver-Davis Bill. Senator Dolliver died in 1910, and friends did not seek its passage but concentrated on the Page Bill of 1911 (Roberts, 1957).

The Page Bill. Carol S. Page, a U.S. Senator from Vermont, was prominent among the early federal supporters of vocational education. According to True (1929), in March 1911, Senator Page introduced a bill proposing federal appropriations to the states. Roberts (1971) points out that the Page Bill provided for a division of funds in states that maintained separate schools for Blacks in proportion to the population of the two races. The bill also provided for evening schools. The Page Bill was amended in the Senate in 1912.

Page felt keenly that the actual preparation for the majority of farm, shop, and home tasks should begin in the high school. Page was unsuccessful in getting congressional action on his proposed legislation. When it became evident that the Page Bill would not pass, the National Society for the Promotion of Industrial Education and other interested individuals suggested that Congress establish a commission on national aid for vocational education (Miller, 1985).

AUTHORS OF FEDERAL LEGISLATION
FOR VOCATIONAL EDUCATION

Smith, Hughes, George, Perkins . . . the names read like a roster of vocational education's hall of fame. Their leadership has led to some of the most important pieces of legislation in vocational education in this country.

Hoke Smith and Dudley Hughes

In January 1914, Congress authorized the president to appoint a commission to study national aid for vocational education. Senator Hoke Smith of Georgia was elected chairman. On December 7, 1915, Smith introduced Senate Bill 703 to provide the promotion of vocational education; to provide cooperation with the states in promotion of such education in agriculture, trades and industries; to provide cooperation with the states in the preparation of teachers of vocational subjects; and appropriate money and regulate its expenditure (Plawin, 1992).

On February 10, 1916, Representative Dudley M. Hughes of Georgia, also a member of the commission, introduced similar legislation in House Bill 11250. The House Committee on Education, which quickly approved it, filed a report that stated:

> It is especially designed to prepare workers for the most common occupations in which great mass of our people find useful employment . . . to give training of a secondary grade to persons more than 14 years of age for . . . employment in the trades and industries, in agriculture, in commerce and commercial pursuits, and in callings based upon . . . home economics. (Plawin, 1992, p. 31)

President Woodrow Wilson signed the Smith-Hughes Vocational Education Act into law on February 23, 1917. Thus, these two Georgians became partners, sponsored the Smith-Hughes Act, and gave the nation what has proved to be one of its greatest assets, vocational education.

Walter F. George

It is significant in the legislative history of vocational education that in six Senate terms, Walter F. George sponsored every federal act for vocational education since the Smith-Hughes law of 1917. These are the George-Reed, George-Ellzey, George-Deen and George-Barden Acts. Senator George's efforts culminated in vocational education funds totaling more than $40,000,000 for fiscal 1958 alone. According to Mobley (1957), "When George of Georgia spoke his fellow senators—and the world—listened with respectful attention."

Senator George suggested that he never thought vocational training should interfere with a well-rounded academic course of study, but that the two could well be brought together, beginning at the secondary level . . . For, after all, he added, most of our people do not go to college anyhow. He then continued:

> *I don't mind saying that I got very great inspiration from reading about the work of Booker T. Washington, a famous African American educator. Booker T. Washington had advanced knowledge of the practical, purely utilitarian side of schooling. His method and his pretty [sic] well-grounded belief was that practical education was the way up for his race. (Williams, 1950, p. 3)*

Carl D. Perkins

The 1950s experienced the baby boomers entering school and the race for space. The turbulent 60s were pockmarked by civil rights marches, drug addicts, assassinations, and the Vietnam War. During this time Representative Carl D. Perkins of Kentucky emerged as a strong advocate for vocational education. He served as the primary force in writing, introducing, and supporting legislation that became the Vocational Acts of 1963 and 1984. The latter was named the Carl D. Perkins Act (Baker, 1991).

MAJOR VOCATIONAL LEGISLATION 1917–1984

The Constitution of the United States makes no provision for federal support or control of education. However, the federal government has considered vocational education in the national interest to provide federal legislation in support of vocational education. Beginning with the Morrill Act in 1862, which established land-grant colleges aimed at preparing people for the "agricultural and mechanical arts," the federal government has had an enduring interest in vocational education (Wrench, Wrench, and Galloway, 1988). The following descriptions highlight the major provisions of these important pieces of legislation.

Smith-Hughes Act (Public Law 64-347)

The Smith-Hughes Act of 1917 was the first vocational education act, and it contained several specific elements that contributed to the isolation of vocational education from other parts of the comprehensive high school curriculum. For example, in order to receive federal funds under Smith-Hughes, each state was required to establish a state board for vocational education. This requirement led, in some states, to the establishment of a board separate from the State Board of Education. Thus, two separate governmental structures could exist at the state level. This in turn fostered the notion of vocational education as separate from academic education.

The Smith-Hughes Act tended to promote a segregated curriculum, with Agriculture, Homemaking, and Trade and Industrial Education segments separated not only from academic programs, but all other vocational programs as well. The impact of this separation has been felt through subsequent decades in the development of separate training programs, separate teacher organizations, and separate student organizations.

The Federal Board for Vocational Education, which was created by the Smith-Hughes Act, consisted of the following members:

- secretaries of commerce, agriculture, and labor
- the commission of education
- three appointed citizens (Plawin, 1992)

Situation—World War I.
        —Germans had demonstrated superior vocational preparation.
Study Group—Commission on National Aid to Vocational Education, 1914.

The Smith-Hughes Act was a grant in perpetuity. However, during July of 1997, the Smith-Hughes Act was repealed.

George-Reed Act of 1929 (Public Law 70-702)

The George-Reed Act, introduced by Senator George and Representative Daniel A. Reed of New York, authorized an increase of $1 million annually for four years (1930–1934) to expand vocational education in agriculture and home economics. The administration of agricultural education and home economics were similar to the provisions of the Smith-Hughes Act with the following exceptions: (a) agricultural education finds were allotted on the basis of farm population rather than rural population, (b) home economics education funds were allotted on the basis of rural population rather than urban, and (c) the George-Reed Act was an authorization for funds whereas Smith-Hughes Act was an appropriation. The George-Reed Act was approved by President Calvin Coolidge on February 5, 1929.

George-Ellzey Act of 1934 (Public Law 73-245)

The George-Ellzey Act was sponsored by Senator George and Representative Lawrence F. Ellzey of Mississippi. The act authorized $3 million annually for three years, to be apportioned equally in agriculture, home economics, trade, and industrial education. In a sense, it replaced the temporary George-Reed Act. The George-Ellzey Act was signed by President Franklin D. Roosevelt on May 21, 1934.

George-Deen Act of 1936 (Public Law 74-673)

The George-Deen Act authored by Senator George and Representative Braswell Dean of Georgia, authorized approximately $14 million a year for vocational education in agriculture, home economics, trade, and industrial education. The George-Deen Act was significant because marketing occupations were recognized for the first time. Money was also authorized for teacher education programs. Unlike the Smith-Hughes Act, it was an authorization, not a permanent act. Mobley (1956) cites the late Dr. Lindley H. Dennis, then American Vocational Association Executive Secretary, for planning the strategy and organizing the support for this legislative victory. The George-Deen Act was signed by President Franklin D. Roosevelt on June 8, 1936.

Situation—Trying to come out of the Great Depression.

Study Group—Advisory Committee on Education 1936–1938.

George-Barden Act of 1946 (Public Law 79-586)

The George-Barden Act was authored by Senator George and Representative Graham A. Barden of North Carolina, as an amendment to the George-Deen Act. It authorized a larger appropriation from $14 million to $29 million annually. One of the major factors contributing to this legislation was the need to provide a means for thousands of returning World War II veterans to acquire employable skills in a rapidly expanding economy (Calhoun and Finch, 1982). Mason, Furtado, and Husted (1989) cite the following major provisions of the George-Barden Act:

1. This act authorized $10 million for agricultural education, to be allocated among the states on the basis of farm population.
2. Authority was given in the act for the expenditure of funds in support of two youth organizations in agriculture: the Future Farmers of America and the New Farmers of America.
3. The act authorized $8 million for home economics, the basis of allotment being the rural population of the state.
4. It also authorized $8 million for trade and industrial education, to be allocated among the states on the basis of nonfarm population.
5. Funds for marketing occupations were limited to support for part-time (cooperative) and evening courses for employed workers—no preparatory courses in other fields were authorized.

The act provided that after June 30, 1951, not more than 10 percent of these funds could be used for the purchase or acquisition of equipment. The George-Barden Act was signed by President Harry S. Truman on August 1, 1946.

Situation—Boom period. Needed cars, not tanks.

George-Barden Amendments of 1956
(Public Law 84-911)

In 1956 the George-Barden Act was amended to add practical nursing ($5 million) and fishery occupation ($375,000) to a list of approved areas of instruction (Venn, 1964). Area vocational programs were provided with an annual authorization until 1962.

Situation—Nurse shortage.

National Defense Education Act of 1958
(Public Law 85-864)

The National Defense Education Act of 1958 was passed following the Soviet Union's placement of Sputnik I, the first man-made earth satellite, into space in 1957. Sputnik created an intensity to reform the educational system particularly in the sciences.

This was the first act to stress the importance of science, mathematics, foreign language, and technical competencies. The focus of this act was providing vocational training for youths, adults, and older persons, including related instruction for apprentices, designed to fit them for employment as technicians or skilled workers in scientific or technical fields.

The following is a summary of the major provisions of the National Defense Education Act:

1. Provided assistance to state and local school systems for strengthening instruction in science, mathematics, foreign languages, and other critical subjects.
2. Improvement of state statistical services.
3. Improvement of guidance counseling, testing services, and training institutes.
4. Provided funds for higher education, student loans, and fellowships.
5. Provided funds for experimentation and dissemination of information on more effective use of television, motion picture, and related media for educational purposes.
6. Provided funds to maintain vocational education for technical occupations, such as data processing, necessary to the national defense.

Situation—Sputnik, Russians surpassed the United States in space.
—Recession.

Manpower Development Training Act of 1962
(Public Law 87-415)

In 1962 there was fear that technological change would cause unemployment among heads of families. Evans and Herr (1978) reported that the Manpower

Development Training Act was created to ease this dislocation by authorizing funds for training and retraining of unemployed and underemployed adults. A large sum of money ($370,000,000) was authorized to be spent over a three-year period.

This act was a milestone in providing training for those who were economically disadvantaged and were not being served in regular vocational programs. Eligible trainees and potential job openings were identified by the state employment service. State vocational education departments contracted for the courses and experiences that matched the identified needs. Preference for retraining was given to unemployed and underemployed workers who had at least three years experience in gainful employment. A unique feature was the provision for payment of subsistence benefits during training.

Situation—Automation and technological changes.

Vocational Education Act of 1963
(Public Law 88-210)

The year 1963 was very significant in the legislative history of vocational education since the 1917 Smith-Hughes Act. The Perkins-Morse Bill, known better as the Vocational Education Act of 1963 was signed into law by President Lyndon B. Johnson, marking a new era for vocational education.

The purposes of the act were varied. However, the major ones were to maintain, extend, and improve existing programs of vocational education and to provide part-time employment for youth who needed the earnings to continue their schooling on a full-time basis. The intent of the act was to ensure that persons of all ages in all communities would have ready access to vocational training or retraining of high quality, suited to their personal needs, interests, and abilities. The law also stipulated that funds be used for persons who have academic, socioeconomic, or other handicaps that prevent them from succeeding in the regular vocational education program. Mason, Furtado, and Husted (1989) reported that for the first time, vocational education was mandated to meet the needs of individual students and not just the employment needs of industry.

This legislation did not stipulate funds for the various vocational education services; instead it stipulated them for particular types and ages of persons. Ninety percent of the authorized funds were to be allotted to the states on the basis of formulas. According to Calhoun and Finch (1982), the formula that was used required that 50 percent of the allotted funds be used for the 15 to 19 age group, 20 percent for the 20 to 25 age group, 15 percent for the 25 to 65 age group, and 5 percent for all groups regardless of age. See Appendix G for vocational education appropriations for fiscal years 1952 to 1966.

Situation—A reaction to too much emphasis on service and unemployment.
Study Group—Panel of consultants on vocational education.

Vocational Education Amendments of 1968
(Public Law 90-576)

The Vocational Education Act of 1963 was amended in October of 1968; these changes are referred to as the Vocational Education Amendments of 1968. The Vocational Education Amendments of 1968 replaced all previous federal legislation for vocational education except the Smith-Hughes Act, which was retained for sentimental reasons as the first legislation passed by the federal government for secondary vocational education.

The purpose of the 1968 amendments was to provide access for all citizens to appropriate training and retraining, which was similar to the Vocational Education Act of 1963. The major differences were that the 1968 amendments emphasized vocational education in postsecondary schools and broadened the definition of vocational education to bring it closer to general education. The Vocational Education Act of 1963 authorized the appropriation of millions of dollars for vocational education in an attempt to find solutions to the nation's social and economic problems.

Under the amendments, federal funds could be used for:

1. High school and postsecondary students.
2. Those who have completed or left high school.
3. Those in the labor market in need of retraining.
4. Those who have academic, socioeconomic, or other obstacles.
5. Those who are mentally retarded, deaf, or otherwise disabled.
6. Construction of area vocational school facilities.
7. Vocational guidance for all persons mentioned.
8. Ancillary services (preparation of state plans, administration, evaluation of programs, teacher education, etc.)
9. Training in private schools under contract with public schools.

Situation—Violence, unrest.

Study Group—Advisory Council on Vocational Education.

Table 5.1 provides a distribution of authorized appropriations of the Vocational Education Amendments of 1968.

Comprehensive Employment Training Act of 1973
(Public Law 93-203)

After a decade, the Manpower Development Training Act was replaced by the Comprehensive Employment Training Act (CETA). The principal effect of this new act was to transfer decision making from Washington to local and state governments (Evans and Herr, 1978).

One of the unique features of CETA was its funding pattern. The act established the delivery concept of a prime sponsor. The occupational education,

TABLE 5.1 Distribution of Authorized Appropriations of the Vocational Education Amendments of 1968

Program	Funds Authorized
Grants to the States for Vocational Education, including Research and Training	
FY 1969	$355,000,000*
FY 1970	$565,000,000
FY 1971	$675,000,000
FY 1972	$675,000,000
Each year thereafter	$565,000,000
Programs for the Disadvantaged	
FY 1969	$ 40,000,000
FY 1970	$ 40,000,000
Work-Study	
FY 1969	$ 35,000,000
FY 1970	$ 35,000,000
Exemplary Programs	
FY 1969	$ 15,000,000
FY 1970	$ 57,500,000
FY 1971	$ 75,000,000
FY 1972	$ 75,000,000
Cooperative Work-Study	
FY 1969	$ 20,000,000
FY 1970	$ 35,000,000
FY 1971	$ 50,000,000
FY 1972	$ 75,000,000
Demonstration Residential Schools	
FY 1969	$ 25,000,000
FY 1970	$ 30,000,000
FY 1971	$ 35,000,000
FY 1972	$ 35,000,000
Grants to States for Residential Schools	
FY 1969	$ 15,000,000
FY 1970	$ 15,000,000
Consumer and Homemaking Education	
FY 1970	$ 25,000,000
FY 1971	$ 35,000,000
FY 1972	$ 50,000,000
Curriculum Development	
FY 1969	$ 7,000,000
FY 1970	$ 10,000,000
Vocational Education Professions Development	
FY 1969	$ 25,000,000
FY 1970	$ 35,000,000

* Note: 10 percent set aside for research and training activities.

training, and other employment services programs were conducted in conjunction with local units of government known as CETA prime sponsors. Prime sponsors provided a variety of employment and training services by contracting with approved public and private agencies.

In general, the special provisions of the Comprehensive Employment Training Act included the following:

1. consolidated previous labor and public service programs;
2. authorized funds for employment counseling, supportive services, classroom training, training on the job, work experience, and public service employment; and
3. incorporated essential principles of revenue sharing, giving state and local governments more control over use of funds and determination of programs.

Vocational Education Amendments of 1976 (Public Law 94-482)

Congress added several new clauses to its declaration of purpose in the 1976 vocational amendments. One new purpose for the authorization of funds was to ensure that states improve their planning by involving a wide range of interested agencies and making use of all available resources for vocational education. Another purpose was to assist states in overcoming sex discrimination and sex stereotyping in their vocational education programs.

The Vocational Education Amendments of 1976 extended and increased funding of the Vocational Education Act of 1963 and the Vocational Education Amendments of 1968. The major thrusts of the Vocational Education Amendments of 1976 were to:

1. extend, improve, and where necessary, maintain existing programs of vocational education;
2. develop new vocational education programs; and
3. provide part-time employment for youths who need the earnings to continue their training on a full-time basis.

With these purposes identified for a major portion of the legislation, the Vocational Education Amendments of 1976 revised the preceding acts to provide for continued support in the form of state grants, supplemented by additional categories that reflect priorities identified by Congress. These added categories included vocational guidance and counseling, preservice and inservice training for personnel, renovation and remodeling of facilities, and grants to overcome sex bias.

See Table 5.2 for the funding categories and sums authorized.

Situation—Women's liberation, threat to funds of teacher education.

TABLE 5.2 Authorizations for Vocational Education Under Title II, Education Amendments of 1976 (Vocational Education Act of 1963 as Amended 1976)

Program	FY 78	FY 79	FY 80	FY 81	FY 82
Basic State Grants (Sec. 120)	$704,000,000	$824,000,000	$944,000,000	$1,060,000,000	$1,188,000,000
Sex Bias Monitoring Personnel (Sec.104b) ($50,000 per state)					
Work-Study (Sec.121), Cooperative Education (Sec. 122), Energy Education (Sec. 123), Residential Schools (Sec. 124)					
Program Improvement And Supportive Services (Sec. 130), Research (Sec. 131) Exemplary and Innovative (Sec. 132) Curriculum Development (Sec. 133) Guidance and Counseling (Sec. 134) Preservice and Inservice Training (Sec. 135) Grants to Reduce Sex Bias (Sec. 136)	176,000,000	206,000,000	236,000,000	265,000,000	297,000,000
State Planning Grants	25,000,000	25,000,000	25,000,000	25,000,000	
Special Disadvantaged (Sec. 140)	35,000,000	40,000,000	45,000,000	50,000,000	50,000,000
Consumer and Homemaking (Sec. 150)	55,000,000	65,000,000	75,000,000	80,000,000	80,000,000
Bilingual Training (Sec. 181)	60,000,000	70,000,000	80,000,000	90,000,000	80,000,000
Renovation and Remodeling (Sec. 191) (Urban and Rural)	25,000,000	50,000,000	75,000,000	100,000,000	
State Advisory Councils (Sec. 105)	8,000,000	8,500,000	9,000,000	10,000,000	8,000,000
National Advisory Council (Sec. 162)	450,000	475,000	500,000	500,000	500,000
Totals	1,088,450,000	1,288,975,000	1,489,500,000	1,680,500,000	1,703,500,000

Job Training Partnership Act of 1982 (Public Law 97-300)

The Job Training Partnership Act (JTPA) replaced CETA, which expired September 30, 1982. JTPA was intended to establish programs to prepare youth and unskilled adults for entry into the labor force and to afford job training to economically disadvantaged individuals facing critical barriers to employment.

The statute enlarged the role of state governments and private industry in federal job training programs, imposed performance standards, limited support services, and created a new program of retraining displaced workers (Mason, Furtado, and Husted, 1989). The following can be regarded as duties of the state governor in implementing the statute:

1. designate local service delivery areas (SDAs);
2. pass judgment on plans drawn up for the local training programs; and
3. draw up a plan for coordinating job training programs with other human services in the state.

Service delivery areas are the districts in a state through which direct job training services are delivered. SDAs may include more than one general purpose local government, but may not split local political jurisdictions. Each SDA has a private industry council (PIC). States must pass 78 percent of their allocations to SDAs (National Alliance of Business, 1983).

The PIC represents local business leaders, who must make up a majority of its members. Fifty percent of the business majority should represent small businesses. The other PIC members represent:

- education
- organized labor
- rehabilitation agencies
- community-based organizations
- economic development agencies
- local employment agencies

The Job Training Partnership Act identifies the following list of activities for which funds may be used:

1. Job counseling and job search assistance
2. Remedial education in the basics
3. Work experience and on-the-job training
4. Vocational exploration
5. Bilingual education
6. Job development
7. Customized industry training

8. Supportive services including payments to persons who are economically disadvantaged (those receiving public assistance or with family income below poverty level)
9. Preemployment skills training for 14- and 15-year-old youths

Implications of JTPA for Vocational Education Teachers and Administrators

Griffin (1983) cites the following implications of JTPA policies for vocational education teachers and administrators:

1. Added funds to reach out and serve more disadvantaged individuals and groups.
2. Additional services to those disadvantaged individuals currently in the programs.
3. New programs offered by vocational educators and by professionals not formerly part of the school system.
4. More active interest from private sectors in the workings of vocational education.
5. More local planning for vocational education.

As compared to CETA policies, JTPA policies require that vocational education be involved as an integral component of the job training activities. JTPA requires that 8 percent of the funds a state receives for youth and adult training be set aside for state education coordination grants. The state education agency and the local education agency (LEA) must provide a 50/50 match for at least 80 percent of the monies in this program. The remaining 20 percent may be used for technical assistance, program improvement, or coordination activities. No match is required for this amount.

Carl D. Perkins Vocational Education Act of 1984 (Public Law 98-524)

The Carl D. Perkins Vocational Education Act of 1984, amended the Vocational Education Act of 1963, and replaced the amendments of 1968 and 1976. The act consisted of two major goals, one economic and one social. The economic goal of the act was to improve the skills of the labor force and prepare adults for job opportunities. The social goal was to provide equal opportunities for adults in the vocational education. The act changed the emphasis of federal funding in vocational education from primarily expansion to program improvement and at-risk populations.

REFORM AND VOCATIONAL EDUCATION

Education reforms began in the early 1980s and have focused on secondary education, prompted by concern by the nation's declining competitiveness in the international market, the relative poor performance of American students on tests of educational achievement (both nationally and internationally), and complaints from the business community about the low level of skills and abilities found in high school graduates entering the workforce.

A review of the literature on education reforms finds a consensus that there have been two waves of reform since 1980—both focused on secondary education (Asche, 1993). The first wave, sometimes characterized as academic reform, called for increased effort from the current education system: more academic course requirements for high school graduation, more stringent college entrance requirements, longer school days and years, and an emphasis on standards and testing for both students and teachers.

Beginning in the mid-1980s, a second wave of school reform arose, based in part on the belief that the first was not thorough enough to improve education for all students. Sometimes referred to as "restructuring," the second wave called for changes in the way schools and the educational process were organized.

The reform movement—and particularly its first phase—received major impetus from the publication in 1983 of *A Nation at Risk,* the report of the National Commission on Excellence in Education (1983). This report observed that the United States was losing ground in international economic competition and attributed the decline in large part to the relatively low standards and poor performance of the American educational system.

The publication of other reports such as *America's Choice: High Skills or Low Wages, Workforce 2000,* and reports from the Secretary's Commission on Achieving Necessary Skills (SCANS) have shifted the debate away from a narrowly defined set of academic or general competencies, technical and specific job skills, interpersonal abilities, and behavioral traits, including motivation. These reports and the attention given to them have lifted vocational education from relative obscurity to a place of prominence in the ongoing debate surrounding school reform. Each of the reports stressed issues such as:

1. Lengthening the school day and the school year.
2. Increasing the number of units (credits) required for high school graduation by specifying additional units in English, mathematics, science, and social studies.
3. Raising the entrance requirements for state colleges and universities.
4. Restructuring the high school curriculum by prescribing five "new basics"—four years of English, three years of mathematics, three years of social studies, and one-half year of computer science, and requiring college-bound students to have two years of a foreign language.

VOCATIONAL EDUCATION IN THE 1990S

In this section, various pieces of legislation that had an influence on the growth of vocational education in the 1990s are discussed.

TABLE 5.3 Authorized Appropriations of the Carl D. Perkins Vocational and Applied Technology Act of 1990

Total Authorization	$1.6 Billion
Basic State Grant	$1.258,150 billion
Community-Based Organizations	$15 million
Consumer/Homemaking Education	$38.5 million
Career Guidance and Counseling	$20 million*
Business/Labor/Education Paternerships	$10 million*
Tech-Prep	$125 million
Supplementary State Grants for Facilities and Equipment	$100 million
Bilingual Vocational Education	$10 million
State Councils	$9 million
National Council	$350,000
Community Education–Lighthouse Schools	$10 million*
Tribally Controlled Postsecondary Institutions	$4 million

Source: American Vocational Association, Inc. (1990). *The AVA to the Carl D. Perkins Vocational and Applied Technology Act of 1990.* Author.

Note: Appropriation for a basic grant must be at least $1 billion before this program is funded.

Carl D. Perkins Vocational and Applied Technology Education Act of 1990 (Public Law 101-392)

On September 25, 1990, President George Bush signed into law the Carl D. Perkins Vocational and Applied Technology Act. The new name—Vocational and Applied Technology Education—signaled congressional interest in emphasizing the application of the academic and vocational skills necessary to work in a global technologically advanced society. The Carl D. Perkins Vocational and Applied Technology Education Act of 1990 amends and extends the Carl D. Perkins Vocational Education Act of 1984.

Table 5.3 depicts authorized appropriations of the Carl D. Perkins Vocational and Applied Technology Education Act of 1990.

For the first time, the act was directed toward "all segments of the population." Congress, in enacting Perkins II, set the stage for a three-pronged approach for better workforce preparation. Perkins II emphasizes (1) integration of academic and vocational education, (2) articulation between segments of education engaged in workforce preparation—epitomized by congressional support for Tech Prep, and (3) closer linkages between school and work.

All these changes represent a major shift in the ways vocational education has historically been provided in America. Earlier provisions, initiated and promulgated by Congress and accepted by vocational educators since the days of the Smith-Hughes Act, tended to separate and isolate vocational teachers, students, and curriculum from the rest of the school community.

In addition, there are two more components of the Perkins Act marking serious departures from past practice. They deal with funds distribution and accountability. As a result of problems perceived to exist under prior legislation, Congress, in Perkins II, bypassed the state agency decision makers by allocating the vast bulk of the funds directly to local education agencies, thus removing virtually all distributional discretion from state officials. In addition, the act explicitly requires states to develop systems of performance measures and standards for secondary and postsecondary vocational education.

Congress has thus provided a template for the vocational education portion of the merging strategy for preparing the workforce of the future. Its three core approaches mark a significant departure from past vocational education acts by emphasizing not the separation and segregation of vocational education but its integration with academic instruction, between secondary and postsecondary institutions, and with business and labor. The historical separation of vocational and academic education is a powerful barrier to integration and the ultimate success of this initiative will depend on the willingness of policy makers and practitioners at the federal, state, and local levels to stay the course.

Major Flaws of the Carl D. Perkins Vocational Applied Technology Act of 1990

Swanson (1991) cites at least five major flaws in the Carl D. Perkins Vocational Applied Technology Education Act of 1990. The five flaws are summarized as follows:

1. **Purpose/funding doesn't match.** The act's formulas for implementation and funding are addressed to a totally different purpose. The act does more to erect barriers than to remove them.
2. **Micromanagement.** Members of Congress have not been prepared, either professionally or by experience, to manage these tasks they have mandated. Conducting hearings is not an adequate way to acquire this training or experience.
3. **Legislated learning.** Learning is as difficult to legislate as morality. Congress should leave both to more competent hands. Legislated learning appears to be an attempt to guarantee tracking.
4. **Legislated methodology.** With its legislated instructional methodology, Congress makes curricula easy to "McDonaldize"—a precondition for curricula to become marginal, even trivial. If teaching quality is declining, Congress should begin to take the blame as it continues to legislate methodology.
5. **Mistrust democracy.** State legislative functions are ignored in the act. The act appears to assign most of its implementation to congressionally prescribed entities and to reduce the ability of state and local government to administer whatever remains.

**TABLE 5.4 Funding for Vocational Education (FY95, FY96, FY97)
(In Millions)**

Program	FY95	FY96	FY97
Perkins			
Basic State Grant	972.8	972.8	1015.6
Tech Prep	108.0	100.0	100.0
National programs	29.9	5.0	13.5
State Councils of Vocational Ed.	8.9		
Tribally Controlled Postsecondary			
Vocational Institutions	2.9	2.9	2.9
School-to-Work	245.0	350.0	400.0
Smith Hughes	7.1	7.1	7.1

Source: Personal communication with Bridget Brown of AVA's Office of Government Relations, on May 21, 1997.

School-to-Work Opportunities Act (STWOA) of 1994 (Public Law 103-239)

The School-to-Work Opportunities Act was passed to address the national skills shortage by providing a model to create a highly skilled workforce for our nation's economy through partnerships between educators and employers. The STWOA emphasized preparing students with the knowledge, skills, abilities and information about occupations and the labor market that will help them make the transition from school to postschool employment through school-based and work-based instructional components supported by a connecting activity's component. Key elements of STWOA included (a) collaborative partnerships, (b) integrated curriculum, (c) technological advances, (d) adaptable workers, (e) comprehensive career guidance, (f) work-based learning, and (g) step-by-step approach.

This act promises to play a key role in the educational reform of our nation's secondary schools and is expected to expand postsecondary programs and services to include a wider audience. It is hoped that the school-to-work transition programs will redirect the focus of high schools toward integration of academic and vocational course work, teaching all aspects of an industry, integrating school-based and work-based learning, and establishing functioning partnerships among elementary, middle, secondary, and postsecondary schools (Brustein & Mahler, 1994). This legislation is authorized through 1999 with a sunset provision effective October 1, 2001. At the sunset of this legislation, states will be required to continue their school-to-work systems with nonfederal funds. A summary of vocational funding for 1995, 1996, and 1997 is provided in Table 5.4. These data will be useful in observing trends in funding vocational education programs. See Appendix E for a

TABLE 5.5 Percentage of Adults Served by Vocational Technical Education: Welfare Original Law Versus New Provisions

	Original Law			New Provisions	
Fiscal Year	% Required to Work	% Served by Education	% Adults Served*	% Adults Served by Vocational-Technical Education	
1997	25	20	14	7.5	(30% of 25%)
1998	30	20	14	9.0	(30% of 30%)
1999	35	20	14	10.5	(30% of 35%)
2000	40	20	14	6.0*	(30% of 40%)
2001	45	20	14	7.5*	(30% of 45%)
2002	50	20	14	9.0*	(30% of 50%)

Source: Personal communication with Bridget Brown of AVA's Office of Government Relations on August 8, 1997.

*6 % for teen parents subtracted from % served by education.

summary of major events concerning the growth of vocational preparation and retraining.

Personal Responsibility and Work Opportunity Act of 1996 (Public Law 104-193)

President Clinton signed the new welfare reform bill, the Personal Responsibility and Work Opportunity Act of 1996, into law on August 22, 1996. While vocational education is by no means a welfare program, some policy makers argued that there were opportunities for linkages with other agencies. Therefore, it was important that vocational educators participate in the state's decision-making process to ensure an appropriate role for vocational education.

As part of the enacted Personal Responsibility and Work Opportunities Act of 1996, recipients of welfare were required to work within two years of receiving federal assistance. This work requirement was expected to be phased in over a six-year period. Welfare recipients were allowed to count up to twelve months of vocational education training as "work" and teenage parents were allowed to use high school attendance as part of their work requirements.

Under the original law, a state could allow 20 percent of its welfare population to count vocational education as work; subtracting the 6 percent of teen parents under the cap, 14 percent of those receiving vocational education would be adults. Under the new agreement, the 1997 percentage of adults served by vocational education drops to 7.5 percent, or 30 percent of the 25 percent of recipients required to work (see Table 5.5). The percentage of adults who can count vocational education as work increases through FY 1999 as the percentage of people required to work goes up, but dips when teen parents come back under the cap in FY 2000. This action taken by Congress reduces vocational education's role to serve adult welfare recipients.

Suggestions for Teaching Welfare Clients

Welfare clients have several needs. Many are severely deficient in basic skills and unfamiliar with the world of work. Years of dependency have contributed to a loss of self-esteem and confidence. Following are some suggestions for meeting these needs in your classroom or programs:

- Make learning relevant.
- Adjust to different learning styles.
- Make your expectations clear.
- Maintain frequent contact.
- Establish a peer support network.
- Emphasize co-op and apprenticeship programs. Help strengthen the connection between learning and employment.

IMPLICATIONS FOR TODAY'S GLOBAL WORKFORCE

Federal support for vocational education is a critical element in meeting students' and employers' needs. Since the passage of the Smith-Hughes Act in 1917, the federal government has provided funding to states and localities to bolster the improvement and expansion of occupationally oriented education. Congress also has recognized the need for leadership and cost-effective information sharing by providing support for those activities at the national level to assist educators and students.

Federal legislation directing this funding has evolved through the years to reflect the needs of students, the changing economy, and the diversification of the workforce. At times, more national activities have been needed to determine how needs are changing. At other times, greater emphasis has been placed on the needs of states and localities to address growing student populations, the need to infuse new technologies into the classroom, or other demands of local business and industry to meet workforce needs.

The demand for new technologies, the changing demographics of the workforce reflecting increasing numbers of minorities and women, and the increase in academic and technical skill levels needed in almost every employment sector require that Congress carefully consider the need for greater federal support for vocational-technical education. This authorization will have an influence on the growth of American society as we enter the next millennium.

To keep America's place in the global economy secure, the federal investment in vocational education must support the improvement of academic and occupational skills and the expansion of access for all students in these programs. To meet these needs of students and the workplace, it is imperative that integration of core academic and vocational education continue. To ensure emphasis on this priority, governance of vocational education must remain within the purview of education and not segregated from other education reform efforts.

Vocational education provides the initial opportunity for students to explore career options in a setting that takes into account the broad range of every student's needs—from career guidance and counseling to course work that stresses the academic and occupational applications of the subject matter. Strong vocational education as part of effective education reform efforts will significantly reduce the need for "second chance" job training efforts, increase the earning power and educational achievements of its students, and improve our nation's ability to compete in the global marketplace.

SUMMARY

- Although 1917 marked the first significant legislation relating to vocational education, several pieces of supportive legislation were passed earlier. Some of the most important pieces of legislation in America started with the leadership of Hoke Smith, Dudley Hughes, Walter F. George, and Carl D. Perkins.

- The primary unifying force for vocational education in America has been federal legislation. Since federal vocational dollars were the only education funds that flowed from federal government to the states until the 1958 National Defense Education Act, federal policy played a primary role in shaping current programs.

- A broad education reform movement began in the early to mid-1980s, prompted by concerns about America's competitiveness in the international economy and the poor performance of American students on international tests. The movement called for greatly improved academics, to be achieved primarily through increased education standards and accountability (both teacher and student).

- In the mid-to late-1980s, a second wave of reform sought to go beyond academics and accountability. Unlike the first wave, it tended to focus on nonacademics and college-bound students and to emphasize restructuring secondary curricula and organizations. The movement also included many educators and researchers intent on reforming vocational education.

- The Carl D. Perkins Vocational and Applied Technology Education Act Amendments of 1990 spurred significant changes in vocational education. The emphasis of this act was on increasing the links between academic and occupational skill development, secondary and postsecondary education, and business and education.

- The School-to-Work Opportunities Act was passed to address the national skills shortage by providing a model to create a highly skilled workforce for our nation's economy through partnerships between educators and employers.

- President Clinton signed the welfare reform bill, Personal Responsibility and Work Opportunity Act of 1996, into law on August 22, 1996. As part of the enacted Personal Responsibility and Work Opportunities Act of 1996, recipients of welfare were required to work within two years of receiving federal assistance.

- Quality programs depend on qualified educators with access to continuous professional development activities, state-of-the-art technology, and student support services; equity in access to programs; integrated academic and occupational curricula based on industry approved standards; and opportunities for work site learning experiences for all students. As the evolution toward higher technology in the workplace continues, the focus of federal support for vocational education must be on redoubling efforts to strengthen these links.

DISCUSSION QUESTIONS AND ACTIVITIES

1. Name the legislative ordinances prior to 1900 that had an impact on vocational education.

2. What was the first major legislation appropriating funds for vocational education programs at secondary schools?

3. Name the members of the Federal Board of Vocational Education as designated by the Smith-Hughes Act.

4. What were the principal provisions of the Smith-Hughes Act?

5. In what way did the George-Reed, George-Ellzey and George-Deen Acts differ from the Smith-Hughes Act?

6. What were the major differences between the George-Barden Act and the Smith-Hughes Act?

7. Under which act was marketing education (formerly distributive education) first appropriated?

8. Prepare brief biographical sketches of the following authors of federal legislation:
    a. Hoke Smith
    b. Dudley Hughes
    c. Walter George
    d. Carl D. Perkins

9. Read at least three articles on federal legislation pertaining to vocational education.

10. What was the impact of the National Defense Education Act on vocational education?

11. State the purpose of the Manpower Development Training Act of 1962. What were the conditions that led to the manpower legislation?

12. State the principal provisions of the Vocational Education Act of 1963.

13. What are the differences between the Vocational Education Act of 1963 and the 1968 Vocational Education Amendments? How are they similar?

14. What was the purpose of the Comprehensive Employment and Training Act?

15. What was the difference between the Comprehensive Employment Training Act and the Manpower Development Training Act?

16. In what way did the Job Training Partnership Act affect vocational education? Why do you believe these programs were established? Whom are they intended to serve? Do they relate at all to the regular vocational program?

17. State the major differences between the 1984 Carl D. Perkins Vocational Education Act and the 1976 Vocational Education Amendments.

18. Debate the following topics:
    a. Resolved, that the Carl D. Perkins Vocational and Applied Technology Education Act is not the worst piece of federal legislation ever passed.
    b. Resolved, that the Smith-Hughes Act is the most significant federal legislation passed affecting the development and growth of vocational education.

19. Interview a vocational teacher and a vocational director. Ask both of them which of the following vocational education needs most: funds, better equipment and facilities, community support, or business and industry support. Then ask the vocational director how federal legislation can help with these needs.

20. What are the principal provisions of the School-to-Work Opportunities Act?

21. How does the School-to-Work Opportunities Act affect vocational education in your community? State? Invite an official to discuss this legislation with your class.

22. View and critique the film: *Jobs: The class of 2000.* See Appendix A for more information.

REFERENCES

Asche, M. (1993). *The impact of educational reform on vocational education.* Berkeley, CA: National Center for Research in Vocational Education.

Baker, S.A. (1991). The impact of the civil war on vocational education. *Journal of Vocational and Technical Education, 7*(2), 56–60.

Brustein, M. and Mahler, M. (1994). *AVA guide to the school-to-work opportunities act.* Alexandria, VA: American Vocational Association.

Calhoun, C.C. and Finch, A.V. (1982). *Vocational education: Concepts and operations.* Belmont, CA: Wadsworth.

Evans, R.N., and Herr, E.L. (1978). *Foundations of vocational education. 2nd ed.* Columbus, OH: Charles E. Merrill Publishing Company.

Fitzpatrick, J.C. (Ed.) (1933). *Journals of the Continental Congress, 1774–1789.* Vol. 2, pp. 373–386. Washington, DC: Government Printing Office.

Griffin, D. (1983). A new partnership becomes law. *Vocational Education Journal, 58*(1), 32–34.

Mason, R.E., Furtado, L.T., and Husted, S.W. (1989). *Cooperative occupational education and work experience in the curriculum.* 4th ed. Danville, IL: The Interstate Printers and Publishers, Inc.

Miller, M.D. (1985). *Principles and a philosophy for vocational education.* Columbus, OH: The National Center for Research in Vocational Education.

Mobley, M.D. (1956). History of federal funds for vocational education. *American Vocational Journal, 31*(9), 99.

———. (1957). Walter F. George. *American Vocational Journal, 32*(7), 3.

National Alliance of Business. (1983). *A pocket guide to the Job Training Partnership Act of 1982*. Washington, DC: National Alliance of Business.

National Commission on Excellence in Education (1983). *A Nation at Risk: The imperative for educational reform*. U.S. Department of Education.

Plawin, P. (1992). 1917–1992: A vocational education era. *Vocational Education Journal, 67*(2), 30–32.

Roberts, R.W. (1957). *Vocational and practical arts education*. 1st ed. New York: Harper and Row.

———. (1971). *Vocational and practical arts education*. 3rd ed. New York: Harper and Row.

Swanson, G.I. (1991). Vocational education and the United States Congress. *Vocational Education Journal, 66*(1), 30–31, 45.

Thorpe, F.N. (Ed.) (1909). *The federal and state constitutions, colonial charters, and other organic laws*. Vol. 2, p. 961. Washington, DC: Government Printing Office.

True, A.C. (1929). *A history of agricultural education in the United States*. Washington, DC: U.S. Department of Agriculture, Publication No. 36, Government Printing Office.

Venn, G. (1964). *Man, education and work*. Washington, DC: American Council on Education.

Williams, C. (1950). Vocational educators honor U.S. senator Walter F. George. *American Vocational Journal, 25*(4), 3.

Wrench, R.C., Wrench, J.W., and Galloway, J.D. (1988). *Administration of vocational education*. Homewood, IL: American Technical Publishers, Inc.

6

PARTICIPATION OF WOMEN IN VOCATIONAL EDUCATION

One of the remarkable phenomena of the last three decades has been the entrance of women in the workplace in record numbers. Their increased presence in the corporate world, government, and politics is the result of many factors including the changing attitudes of society toward working women. Whether for social, economic, or personal reasons, women have changed their roles in society through further education and increased participation in the labor market. This chapter addresses the historical work roles of women in vocational education, legislative breakthroughs affecting women, and selected problems associated with sex equity.

Historically, vocational education has consisted of practical and applied instruction aimed at matching students with work positions in industry and commerce (Benavot, 1983). Compared to other educational fields, vocational education more immediately satisfies Herzberg's (1966) notion that the primary function of any organization should be employment and the need for man [sic] to enjoy a meaningful existence. It is this purpose of connecting school and work that makes vocational education an important focus for equity work.

Vocational education is also a particularly useful field to examine because its framework has tended to be, and is presently, more responsive to political and economic factors than philosophical positions (Ray, 1968). As many writers have suggested, inequalities exist or are prolonged for economic and workplace reasons. In fact, economic factors have been used as reliable indicators of what areas of equity have been achieved (Harvey & Noble, 1985). The concept of equity corresponds in these terms to "the preferred shape of the distributional curve or the just distribution of economic resources in society" (Hewlett, 1977, p. 31). According to Osipow (1973):

> *Perhaps the most significant area of concern for advocates of equal rights for women lies in the topic of careers, especially as these rights concern equality of opportunity, treatment, remuneration and advancement, but also they concern the general social attitude toward women's careers, marriage, and family responsibility. (pp. 255–256)*

As Lewis (1985) has pointed out, years of schooling for women, especially minority, do not automatically translate into improved economic status. Rather, it is the link of "specialized schooling to career development" (p. 382) that makes a difference. In essence, developing sex equity in education through development of occupational skills and employment possibilities for women is a pragmatic, economic approach to equity that can be accomplished through vocational education (Burge and Culver, 1989).

HISTORICAL WORK ROLES OF WOMEN IN VOCATIONAL EDUCATION

Throughout the nineteenth and early twentieth centuries in the United States, vocational educators took their cues of what and whom to teach from the needs and desires of the workplace. Originally, this teaching, along with theories of career development and work, focused almost exclusively on men (Roby, 1976). However, as women's presence in the workplace increased, a movement for educating women in their new roles took place.

In the early part of the nineteenth century, thousands of women became part of the labor force in textile factories (Foner, 1987), or by selling or trading fruits and vegetables (Marshall and Paulin, 1987). Despite their growing numbers in the workforce, women were perceived as "better" if they stayed home, tending the family and house. Consequently, women during this time were trained in domestic instruction and ornamental instruction. It was seen as the duty of females to "regulate the concerns of every family" and so instruction geared toward making women good mothers or good "mistresses of families" was appropriate (Willard, 1987, p. 22). Ornamental instruction for the economically disadvantaged focused on drawing, painting, and "elegant penmanship, music, and grace of motion." Such instruction was important because it was not wise to allow female youth "to seek amusements for themselves" (Willard, p. 24).

Experimental learning was an important part of the curriculum in both the eighteenth and nineteenth centuries, after the publication of Rousseau's Emile in 1762. Emile, an orphan boy removed from society, discovers knowledge through things or objects (books are banned), and in this natural manner develops physically, intellectually, and morally until he is ready to take his place in society. As a consequence of such thinking, children were required to do manual training, to learn by doing. However, not all children learned to do the same things. Boys, for example, learned to saw and to dig and to cultivate gardens (Green, 1969). They also practiced bookbinding and other skills. Girls, however, were more likely to learn spinning, weaving, cooking, and sewing. Girls were also the more likely targets for moral instruction because for they were to be entrusted with maintaining "a moral home environment" (Gutek, 1968, p. 34).

It wasn't until the Civil War that women played an increasingly important role in industry and the production of goods. During World War I and World War II, the shortage of male workers and the industrial expansion necessitated by war created many new jobs for women in factories, sewing rooms, and munitions plants. Perhaps in recognition of new, limited opportunities for women, the Kansas State Agricultural College, as early as 1874, "allotted [women] to take courses in drawing and do shop work in scroll sawing, carving, and engraving." For most young women, however, there was a department of sewing, work in household economy, and "a very progressive course in household chemistry" (Bennett, 1937, p. 314). For young men, ship work was the emphasis, with importance also attached to mathematics, science, and drawing (Bennett, 1937). Ten years later, at Toledo Manual Training School in Toledo, Ohio, there was a clearly defined system of vocational training for girls that differed from that offered to boys. Boys' shop work included carpentry, wood turning, forging, welding, chipping, and the study of machinery and gas engines. The "domestic economy" outlined for girls included light carpentry; wood carving; clay modeling; instruction in preparing and cooking food; care of the sick; cutting, making, and fitting of garments; and household decorations (Clark, 1892).

During the Civil War women were employed as government clerks for the first time. As well as being trained differently from men, women would now be paid differently. Congress appropriated funds for the salaries of these women in 1864, but the appropriation set a cap of $600 a year for female government clerks, less than half the salary paid to male clerks (Baker, 1977). Taking the government cue, private industry also employed women for 50 percent of the wages men received for the same work. More than seventy years later, Westinghouse, maintaining this wage differential, stipulated in personnel manuals that the lowest paid male job was not to be paid a wage below that of the highest paid female job, regardless of the job content and value to the firm (Westinghouse Industrial Relations Manual: Wage Administration, Nov. 1, 1938, and Feb. 1, 1938, cited in Heen, 1984).

Not only was a wage differential the norm when doing the same job, but women were typically relegated to only a few jobs. For example, in 1870, 88 percent of women gainfully employed were in ten occupations, among them, domestic servant, seamstress, teacher, milliner, and nurse. By 1900, of 252 occupations listed by the U.S. Department of Labor, more than 90 percent of women were in twenty-five of them (Marshall and Paulin, 1987). This sex segregation was such a part of employers' and employees' perceptions that only after the equal opportunities legislation of the 1950s did it become illegal for

Technological advancements have created the need for training and retraining of women in nontraditional occupations.

employers to specify sex of applicants for job openings listed in the newspaper (Shaw and Shaw, 1987).

In the short history of our country, women have been limited in their labor force participation and in their wage earning potential, simply because of their gender. This lack of economic independence has done little to destroy inequitable policies and attitudes in all of society, and, in human capital terms, paints a dismal picture for all women, especially middle-aged and older (Shaw and Shaw, 1987). Young single mothers too are a group increasing in number and in economic disadvantage (Burge, 1987). Although improvements in breaking down barriers have been made, vocational education enrollments mirror limited labor force roles with narrow, sex-typed enrollment patterns. In 1980, females nationally represented 91 percent of student training as nursing assistants, 87 percent of those training for community health workers, and 92 percent of students in cosmetology and secretarial sciences. Similarly, 95 percent of students enrolled in electrical technology, 90 percent in electronics, 94 percent in appliance repair, 96 percent in carpentry, 95 percent in welding, and 96 percent in small engine repair, were males (Wells, 1983).

LEGISLATIVE BREAKTHROUGHS AFFECTING WOMEN

The Smith-Hughes Act of 1917 provided the first federal funding for public school programs in agriculture, trade, industrial, and home economics education. Reflecting the sex-role norm of the times, the first two programs were specifically designed for males and home economics was included to provide education for homemaking and occupations relating to the homemaker role.

With this beginning, vocational education programs were intentionally sex typed. This separation of training for males and females continued with no legislative direction for change until the Equal Pay Act of 1963 was passed. This act, considered the first significant legislation relating to vocational equity, called for the end of discrimination on the basis of sex in payment of wages for equal work. This law was soon followed by Title VII of the Civil Rights Act of 1964 prohibiting discrimination in employment on the basis of sex, race, color, religion, and national rights (Burge and Culver, 1989). The scope of Title VII was more extensive than the Equal Pay Act.

Title IX of the Educational Amendments of 1972 was the landmark legislation responsible for banning discrimination on the basis of sex in education. Title IX provided that "no person in the United States shall, on the basis of sex, be excluded from participation in, be denied the benefits of, or be subjected to discrimination under any educational program or activity receiving federal financial assistance." The Women's Educational Equity Act of 1974 (Public Law 93-380) provided for funding of projects to advance education between women and men (Burge and Culver, 1989). As Fishel and Potter (1977) noted, this act along with provisions for many aspects of education specifically provided for expansion and improvement of programs for females in vocational education and career education.

Despite the passage of Title IX and the Women's Educational Equity Act, the 1970s and 1980s did not experience much change in vocational enrollment patterns from the previous years. Legally required opportunities, or at least lack of discriminatory policies, were not sufficient to attract many students into programs considered nontraditional for their sex (Burge, 1990).

With an understanding that more dramatic efforts had to be implemented, Congress appropriated the first funds for sex equity in conventional programs through the Educational Amendments of 1976. These funds required the development and implementation of programs to eliminate sex discrimination, sex bias, and sex-role stereotyping. To comply with the 1976 directives, each state was required to employ a full-time sex equity coordinator to (a) provide specific leadership in eliminating those barriers that inhibit equal access to vocational education, (b) offer technical assistance to local educators, and (c) develop a public relations program. With limited funding, some small gains were made as a result, but enrollment patterns remained relatively unchanged because the gender-traditional influences of the cultural arena were pervasive and firmly established (Burge, 1990).

With the passage of the Carl D. Perkins Vocational Education Act in 1984, increased emphasis was placed on employing gender equity in vocational programs. In addition to the 1976 amendment requirements, states were directed to expend an 8.5 percent set-aside of their vocational federal funds to provide vocational education and training leading to marketable skills and support services for single parents, homemakers, and displaced homemakers. Another set-aside, 3.5 percent, was authorized for programs to eliminate sex bias and stereotyping and to increase sex equity in vocational programs. This money was the largest federal provision ever made for the vocational preparation of females (National Coalition for Women and Girls in Education, 1988) and for the support of males in nontraditional roles.

This legislation has resulted in many equity efforts nationwide. The efforts of these sex-equity programs, while considered successful by participants, are still largely unmeasured, and sex-segregated enrollment patterns still continue. The 1990 reauthorization of the vocational education amendments provided a similar significant amount of federal funding related to eliminating the problems of gender inequalities. Money for single-parent and homemaker programs and for efforts to increase the numbers of students in programs nontraditional to their gender will continue (U.S. Congress, 1990).

Equity Status in Vocational Education

While acknowledging the important role vocational education plays in our society, numerous studies, reports, and evaluations have repeatedly documented that sex segregation exists in the vocational education system (National Coalition for Women and Girls in Education, 1988). Among vocational programs, business, cosmetology, health occupations, and home economics have been the domain of women; agriculture, auto mechanics, building trades, and technology education have been areas considered appropriate for men. In fact, in the seven traditional vocational education program areas, six tend to be heavily sex typed (only marketing education is not) and nontraditional for one sex or the other. Yet, in spite of historically traditional workforce patterns and sex-related occupational stereotypes, vocational educators have been somewhat successful in attracting students into programs dominated by the other gender. Nontraditional students are those program enrollees, both male and female, who enroll in areas of study traditionally considered appropriate only for the opposite sex (Culver and Burge, 1985b).

Other groups often categorized as nontraditional vocational students are those females for whom paid employment is not a part of their self-perception. These women have been, or perceive their future roles to be, situated only in the domestic sphere. Any work for pay outside the home is viewed as a nontraditional option by this group. Examples of such women include displaced homemakers (displaced by death of a spouse, divorce, or separation), and many female single parents and teenage mothers. The number of women in these categories represents a significant portion of the total population, and they are a group in extreme economic need (Burge, 1990). Though education programs may provide some help, pregnant and parenting teens, as Cardenas and First (1985) have pointed out, are the young women most discriminated against in schools. These authors also note that a disproportionate number of these young women are minority students.

TABLE 6.1 Female Enrollment in Occupationally Specific Vocational Programs: 1971–1972 and 1981–1982

| Program | Year | | | | |
| | 1971–72 | | 1981–82 | | |
	Number	Percent of Students Who Are Women	Number	Percent of Students Who Are Women	Percent Change
Office Occupations	1,797,205	76.4	1,342,527	73.8	–2.6
Health Occupations	285,241	84.7	380,229	84.8	+0.1
Marketing Education	290,028	45.3	290,744	57.4	+12.1
Trade and Industry	279,510	11.7	296,702	18.5	+6.8
Home Economics	241,239	86.1	188,061	79.6	–6.5
Technical	33,007	9.8	93,384	22.3	+12.5
Agriculture	48,163	5.4	82,610	21.7	+16.3

Source: Vetter, L., and Hickey, D.R. (1985). Where the women are enrolled. *Vocational Education Journal*, *60*(7), 27–28.

Women Enrollment in Nontraditional Vocational Programs

Before the passage of Title IX of the Education Amendments of 1972, which prohibited sex discrimination in federally supported programs, little attention was given to providing women with occupational preparation offered by vocational education. In the 1971–1972 school year, nearly three million girls and women were enrolled in occupationally specific high school and post-secondary programs. Girls and women could be, and were, excluded from some vocational programs simply on the basis of their sex (Vetter and Hickey, 1985).

Relations implementing Title IX were not issued until 1975. During the interim three years, advocacy groups of vocational educators researched where women were being serviced in vocational education. Since women's enrollments were primarily in home economics, health occupations and office occupations, sex equity provisions were included in the vocational education section (Title II) of the Education Amendments of 1976 (Vetter and Hickey, 1985).

Table 6.1 provides an indication of the extent of change in women's enrollment patterns during the early 1970s and 1980s.

Despite the gains women have made in seeking employment, they continue to be segregated into a few occupations that require skills equal to those required in many male-dominated occupations (National Commission on Working Women of Wider Opportunities for Women, 1990). Yet these female-intensive areas continue to provide substantially lower pay. In the same patterns that occur in the workforce, females are at a disadvantage in selecting and completing gender-nontraditional, vocational programs that would train them for higher paying jobs. Yuen (1983) has noted that the results of much of the research about women suggest that even if discriminatory institutional barriers to career development are removed (and to some extent, this has occurred through federal legislation), most women need special support services to succeed in completing preparation for male-intensive employment. While the social and political climate presents significant limitations, the willingness of vocational educators to be innovative in their recruitment and retention activities can make a difference in individual lives. With adequate information about necessary support services, including emotional support, dependent care, self-esteem enhancement, skill assessment, basic skill development, and job-seeking strategies, vocational educators can better counteract tenacious beliefs about stereotypical workplace roles for women. Burge (1990) suggested that one way to make up for women's inequality in higher paying jobs (or in some cases, any job at all) is to learn more about the techniques for changing workplace inequalities and to develop strategies to improve Affirmative Action programs.

If a more equitable society is to be developed, a conscious effort must be made by parents, teachers, and counselors to liberate young people from many sex-role stereotypes prevalent in our society and help them to become independent human beings who choose their future vocational occupations after consideration of all available possibilities. Following are several strategies that could broaden the range of nontraditional opportunities for girls and women in vocational education:

- Provide career exploration activities.
- Provide information on nontraditional careers to families.
- Select texts and materials free from sex bias.
- Provide women students with role models.
- Treat students equally.
- Develop mentorship programs.
- Bring nontraditional students and nontraditional workers to the attention of all students through panel presentations and career day conferences.
- Recognize the achievements of nontraditional students.
- Include assertiveness training as part of an overall curriculum.
- Work with employers to assist them in obtaining highly skilled workers, regardless of gender.

SELECTED PROBLEMS ASSOCIATED WITH SEX EQUITY

There are three terms that need to be defined: sex bias, sex stereotyping, and sex discrimination. Sex bias is behavior, attitude, or prejudice resulting from the assumption that one sex is superior to another. Sex stereotyping is attributing behaviors, abilities, interest, values, and roles to an individual or group on the basis of sex. Sex discrimination is the denial of opportunity, privilege, role, or reward on the basis of sex (Butler, 1989).

According to Dykman (1997), when trainers are invited to schools or workplaces to do classes on sex equity, they may be working against the following attitudes:

- **Sex stereotyping.** Learned thought processes that place women into specific, often submissive, feminine roles and men into masculine, dominant roles.
- **Sex-role spillover.** Sometimes male workers will act out against female co-workers because they don't meet their expectation of "affectionate" female behavior.
- **Pack mentality.** The majority group often holds members of a minority to higher standards.
- **Somebody else's problem.** Male co-workers (or students) often fail to see any potential for harassment in their behavior because they believe only the behavior of supervisors can contribute to a sexual hostile environment.

Sex-role stereotyping is harmful to women, both economically and psychologically. Females in vocational education, as in the workplace, generally expect to have few fields of work to choose from and are segregated into a small number of occupational areas. These female-intensive areas are typically low paying and carry low prestige when compared to the areas of the occupational spectrum that are male-intensive (Biddlecombe et al., 1989). An important goal for vocational educators is to eliminate this clustering of women into a restricted range of occupations. Helping women broaden their occupational participation will assist development of a more equitable income distribution between men and women (Reider, 1977). In addition, traditionally female-intensive areas, while usually low paying, are often crucial for the well-being of our society. Efforts to increase the income potential and status of child- and health-care workers, for example, can provide another approach to enhancing the economic status of women (Burge, 1990).

Sex-role stereotyping is also harmful to males. Although workforce preparation and pay inequities controlled by a patriarchal system usually favor men, societal expectations place males in restrictive roles. Young boys learn early that they are expected to "prove" their masculine identity, typically by excluding certain natural human characteristics—nurturing others, being aesthetic, sensual, emotional—that have been labeled as feminine (Gordon, 1981). Stitt (1988) has described the destruction inherent in stereotyping males: "The price of defining masculinity as toughness, aversion to scholarship, devotion to business, and indifference to physical danger, however, is exorbitantly high. Ill-considered myths about what a man is, impair social relationships and compromise career development" (p. 12).

As men break traditional patterns and seek more active home and parenting roles, employers may lack sensitivity to males' potential conflicts between home and work, thus further compounding these problems (Couch, 1989).

Sex Bias and Sex Stereotyping

Sex bias and sex stereotyping in education and occupations in the late 1960s and 1970s were documented by Vetter, Sechler, Lowry, and Canora (1979). They concluded that, at the time, interests in occupations tended to be sex stereotyped, perhaps more for "real" choices than for "ideal" choices. Family members (parents, in particular), the mass media, and nearly every element of public education had been criticized in the literature for helping perpetuate rigid sex roles that limit people's vocational options to those traditional to their sex. Experimental studies had shown that sexist language and sexist instructional materials had affected the responses of students (Vetter, 1993).

At the high school level, studies of the High School and Beyond (HSB) database indicated that students in programs nontraditional for their sex (30 percent or fewer), whether male or female, held higher self-concepts than their counterparts in traditional programs (Culver and Burge, 1985b). On the whole, males were found to have more positive self-concepts than females. HSB students in traditional female programs had the highest job aspirations (measured by the Duncan Socioeconomic Index). Women students in male-intensive, female-intensive, and nonsex-intensive programs had higher aspirations than males in each of these groups (Culver and Burge, 1985a).

Employers of nontraditional vocational graduates indicated that sex stereotypes are a major barrier to such employment (Burge, 1983). Eighteen percent of the employers surveyed believed some jobs in their business could not be effectively filled by a man and 24 percent believed that some could not be effectively filled by a woman. Thus, while employers indicated the problem was that the clients or consumers would be uncomfortable with nontraditional workers, employers themselves were also uncomfortable (Vetter, 1993).

Harassment

In 1978, the largest problem identified by women students in nontraditional (fewer than 25 percent) high school vocational education programs was harassment by male classmates (Kane and Frazee, 1978). Fewer problems were reported in relation to teachers. Harassment was much diminished for women, which has obvious implications for policies of class assignment. When few women are enrolled in a nontraditional program, it would be helpful to assign them to the same class. Where only one or two women are enrolling in a program, support groups for women in different programs could be helpful. Teachers must be made responsible for combating the "turfism" expressed by traditional male students. When women are no longer a novelty in class, as is now the case in some nontraditional programs, this problem may fade as male students expect the women to be there, as evidenced in the New York City high schools (Schulzinger and Syron, 1984).

Between 1991 and 1996, the percentage of companies that reported at least one sexual harassment claim grew from 52 percent to 72 percent. Sexual harassment costs the typical Fortune 500 company $6.7 million a year in increased absenteeism, staff turnover, low morale, and low productivity (Dykman, 1997).

The same concerns can apply in the education arena. Sometimes a school's funding is tied to how well it improves gender equality. One example is the School-to-Work Opportunities Act, which requires state and local administrators to show how their plans will increase opportunities for women (and other groups) in careers that are not traditional for their gender (Dykman, 1997). These requirements and liabilities have increased awareness of gender equity between employers and vocational educators.

Following are several suggestions for vocational educators for dealing with the issue of sexual harassment:

1. Develop a comprehensive sexual harassment policy for dissemination to administrators, staff, students, and parents.
2. Parents, students, staff, and lawyers should participate in writing the policy.
3. Student support groups should be available for students in nontraditional vocational classes.
4. Develop a process to continuously monitor and evaluate your policy.
5. Provide workshops to train administrators, staff, and students about sexual harassment.

Lack of Support

A statewide study in West Virginia (Sproles, 1987) indicated that for nontraditional (less than 20 percent) completers of vocational programs, friends, parents, and school personnel were perceived as less helpful and as nontraditional choices. Vocational teachers were perceived as being more helpful than parents and friends by the traditional respondents, whereas parents were more helpful for the nontraditional respondents.

Houser and Garvey (1985), in studying California women in vocational education programs, found that nontraditional students differed from traditional students primarily in the support received from female friends and family members. Additionally, compared to a group of students who had considered nontraditional programs but then enrolled in traditional programs, nontraditional students reported receiving more encouragement from school personnel.

When students complete a vocational program, they should be ready for placement on the job. A major concern of students in nontraditional programs is whether they will find employment (Hollenback, 1985). Hollenback indicates that faculty members must encourage potential employers to hire nontraditional students at adequate salaries and with adequate opportunities for job advancement.

Recognizing these problems and others related to male sex-role stereotyping can help vocational educators identify equity as an area that benefits both sexes.

SUMMARY

- In the early part of the nineteenth century, thousands of women first became part of the labor force in textile factories. Despite their growing numbers in the workforce, women were perceived as "better" if they stayed home, tending family and house. It wasn't until the Civil War that women played an increasingly important role in the industry and the production of goods. During World War I and World War II, the shortage of male workers and the industrial expansion necessitated by war created many new jobs for women in factories, sewing rooms, and munitions plants.

- The Smith-Hughes Act of 1917 provided the first federal funding for public school programs in agriculture, trade, industrial, and home economics education. The first two programs were specially designed for males and home economics was included to provide education for homemaking. With this beginning, vocational programs were intentionally sex typed. This separation of training for males and females continued with no legislative direction for change until the Equal Pay Act of 1963 was passed. This act, considered the first significant legislation relating to vocational equity, called for the end of discrimination on the basis of sex in payment of wages for equal work.

- In the 1970s, Congress recognized the expanding role of women in the workforce. Congressional reports accompanying the 1976 Amendments to the Vocational Education Act noted that most women will work during at least some portion of their adult lives; that women constitute a large growing part of the labor force; that most women work out of necessity; and that in spite of all this, working women are concentrated in a few lower occupational areas.

- To remedy this situation, Congress included provisions in the 1976 amendments to eliminate sex bias and sex stereotyping in vocational education, and (later) to serve displaced homemakers. Recipients' responses to these provisions were initially very limited, promoting Congress to strengthen and expand the provisions in subsequent legislation.

  Other federal laws, including the Carl D. Perkins Vocational Act of 1984 and the Carl D. Perkins Vocational and Applied Technology Act of 1990, challenged business, industry, labor, and education to develop policy procedures and practices promoting racial and sex equity.

- Some of the problems associated with sex equity are as follows: sex bias, sex stereotyping, lack of support, and sexual harassment.

  Recognizing these problems and others related to male sex-role stereotyping can help vocational educators identify equity as an area that benefits both sexes.

DISCUSSION QUESTIONS AND ACTIVITIES

1. Discuss the differences between requirements of Title IX (Education Amendments of 1972) and the provisions of the Education Amendments of 1976 that pertain to sex discrimination and sex bias.

2. What are women's special vocational education needs? **(Library Research).**

3. What vocational training is currently available to women in your local community?
   a. How flexible are these courses in terms of time and place?
   b. To what extent are they concentrated on the traditional low-paying jobs?

4. In view of the important role of women in meeting the nation's need for trained workers, how can vocational training programs for women be strengthened and expanded to provide employment opportunities for women of *all* levels of educational attainment?

5. What programming is provided for minority women and for poor white women who live in rural areas and have less than a high school education? **(Library Research).**

6. Discuss the historical work roles of women in vocational education.

7. Differentiate between sex stereotyping and sex discrimination.

8. List and discuss some suggestions for vocational educators to utilize in addressing the issue of sexual harassment.

REFERENCES

Baker, R.K. (1977, July). Entry of women into federal job world at price. *Smithsonian, 8,* 83–85.

Benavot, A. (1983). The rise and decline of vocational education. *Sociology of Education. 56,* 63–76.

Bennett, C.A. (1937). *History of manual and industrial education. 1870 to 1917.* Peoria, IL: The Manual Arts Press.

Biddlecombe, L., Browne, J., Charlton, B., Dowden, H., Northcott, C., Onslow, J., Priestly, J., and Thompson, J. (1989). *Learning the hard way.* London: Macmillian.

Burge, P.L. (1983). Employers' perceptions of nontraditional vocational guidance. *Journal of Studies in Technical Careers, 5,* 299–306.

———. (1987). *Career development of single parents.* Information Series No. 324. Columbus, OH: ERIC Clearing house on Adult, Career, and Vocational Education. The National Center for Research in Vocational Education.

———. (1990). Vocational Education Gender-Equity Research Priorities for the 1990s. *The Journal of Vocational Education Research, 15*(3), 1–19.

Burge, P.L., and Culver, S.M. (1989). Vocational education: A pragmatic, economic approach to equity. *Journal of Vocational and Technical Education, 6*(1), 3–12.

Butler, D. (1989). *Title IX for cutting the tape to sex equity in education programs and activities.* Charleston, WV: West Virginia Department of Education.

Cardenas, J., and First, J.M. (1985). Children at risk. *Educational Leadership, 43*(1), 4–8.

Clark, I.E. (1892). *Art and industry.* Washington, DC: U.S. Bureau of Education.

Couch, A.S. (1989). Career and family: The modern worker's balancing act. *Vocational Education Journal, 64*(6), 24–27.

Culver, S.M., and Burge, P.L. (1985a). Expected occupational prestige of students in vocational programs nontraditional for their sex. *Journal of Studies in Technical Careers, 7,* 231–240.

Culver, S.M., and Burge, P.L. (1985b). Self-concept of students in vocational programs nontraditional for their sex. *The Journal of Vocational Education Research, 10*(2), 1–10.

Dykman, A. (1997, April). Taking aim at bias in school and the workplace. *Techniques, 72*(4), 19–21.

Fishel, A., and Potter, J. (1977). *National politics and sex discrimination in education.* Lexington, MA: Lexington Books.

Foner, P.S. (1987). Women and the American labor movement: A historical perspective. In K.S. Koziara, M.H. Moskow, and L.D. Tanner (Eds.), *Working women: Past, present, future* (pp. 154–186). Washington, DC: The Bureau of National Affairs, Inc.

Gordon, R. (1981). *Ties that bind: The price of pursuing the male mystique.* Washington, DC: Project on Equal Education Rights.

Green, J.A. (1969). *The educational ideas of Pestalozzi.* Originally published by W.B. Clive (1914). New York: Random House.

Gutek, G.L. (1968). *Pestalozzi and education.* New York: Random House.

Harvey, G., and Noble, E. (1985). Economic consideration for achieving sex equity through education. In S. Klein (Ed.), *Handbook for achieving sex equity through education* (pp. 17–28). Baltimore, MD: The Johns Hopkins University Press.

Heen, M. (1984). A review of federal court decisions under Title VII of the Civil Rights Act of 1964. In H. Remick (Ed.), *Comparable worth and wage discrimination: Technical possibilities and political realities* (pp. 197–219). Philadelphia: Temple University Press.

Herzberg, F. (1966). *Work and the nature of man.* Cleveland, OH: World Publications Company.

Hewlett, S. (1977). Inequality and its implications for economic growth. In I. Horowits (Ed.), *Equity, income, and policy* (pp. 29–48). New York: Praeger.

Hollenback, K. (1985). *Developing an equity handbook for community college personnel: A resource to increase female enrollment in nontraditional vocational education programs. Final report.* Pueblo, CO: Pueblo Community College (ERIC Document Reproduction Service No. ED 266 253).

Houser, B.B., and Garvey, C. (1985). Factors that affect nontraditional vocational enrollment among women. *Psychology of Women Quarterly, 9,* 105–117.

Kane, R.D., and Frazee, P.E. (1978). *Women in nontraditional vocational education in secondary schools.* Arlington, VA: RJ Associates.

Lewis, S. (1985). Achieving sex equity for minority women. In S.S. Klien (Ed.), *Handbook for achieving sex equity through education* (pp. 365–390). Baltimore, MD: The Johns Hopkins University Press.

Marshall, R., and Paulin, B. (1987). Employment and earnings of women: Historical perspective. In K.S. Koziara, M.H. Moskow, and L.D. Tanner (Eds.), *Working women: Past, present, future* (pp. 1–36). Washington, DC: The Bureau of National Affairs, Inc.

National Coalition for Women and Girls in Education. (1988). *Working toward equity: A report on implementation of the new equity provisions of the Carl D. Perkins Vocational Education Act.* Washington, DC: Displaced Homemakers' Network.

National Commission on Working Women of Wider Opportunities for Women. (1990). *Women and nontraditional work.* Washington, DC: Author.

Osipow, S.H. (1973). *Theories of career development.* Englewood Cliffs, NJ: Prentice Hall.

Ray, E.M. (1968). Vocational, technical, and practical arts education: Social and philosophical framework. *Review of Educational Research, 38*(4), 309–325.

Reider, C. (1977, April). *Women, work, and vocational education.* Occasional Paper No. 26. Columbus, OH: The National Center for Research in Vocational Education.

Roby, P.A. (1976). Toward full equality: More job education for women. *School Review, 84*(2), 181–212.

Schulzinger, R., and Syron, L. (1984). *Inch by inch: A report on equal opportunity for young women in New York City's vocational high schools.* New York: Center for Public Advocacy Research.

Shaw, L.B., and Shaw, R. (1987). From midlife to retirement: The middle-aged woman worker. In K.S. Koziara, M.H. Moskow, and L.D. Tanner (Eds.), *Working women: Past, present, future* (pp. 299–331). Washington, DC: The Bureau of National Affairs, Inc.

Sproles, E.K. (1987). Perceptions by nontraditional and traditional agricultural students toward their high school preparation and work barriers. *Journal of the American Association of Teacher Educators in Agriculture, 28*(2), 18–24.

Stitt, B.A. (1988). Male stereotyping isn't fair. *Vocational Education Journal, 63*(8), 12–14.

U.S. Congress. (1974). *Women's Equity Act of 1974 (P.L. 93-380).* Washington, DC: Government Printing Office.

———. (1990). *The Carl D. Perkins Vocational and Applied Technology Education Act (P.L. 101–392).* Washington, DC: Government Printing Office.

Vetter, L., Sechler, J., Lowry, C.M., and Canora, V. (1979). *Factors influencing nontraditional vocational education enrollments: A literature review.* Columbus, OH: State University, National Center for Research in Vocational Education.

Vetter, L., and Hickey, D.R. (1985). Where the women are enrolled. *Vocational Education Journal, 60*(7), 26–29.

Vetter, L. (1993). Sex equity programs and vocational education. In C. Anderson and L.C. Rampp (Eds.), *Vocational education in the 1990s, II: A sourcebook for strategies, methods, and materials* (pp. 225–242). Ann Arbor, MI: Prakken Publishing Company.

Wells, J. (1983). *Statement of the National Coalition for Women and Girls in Education.* Washington, DC: National Coalition for Women and Girls in Education.

Willard, E. (1987). *A plan for improving female education.* Originally published by Middleburg College (1918). Marietta, GA: Larlin Corporation.

Yuen, C.Y. (1983). Internal barriers for women entering nontraditional occupations: A review of the literature. *Occupational Education Forum, 12*(2), 14–39.

7

PARTICIPATION OF SPECIAL NEEDS POPULATIONS IN VOCATIONAL EDUCATION

The term *special needs populations* is generally used to describe individuals who are (1) members of minority groups; (2) limited-English speaking and physically and/or mentally disabled, economically and/or academically disadvantaged; or (3) gifted and talented.

Uniqueness of needs was recognized in the early development of vocational education. The Commission on National Aid to Vocational Education (1914) projected a special concern for persons leaving school at an early age. The figures cited by the commission are a clear representation of concern. One-half of the children who entered elementary schools in the United States of 1914 remained to the final elementary grade, and only one in ten reached the final year of high school. On the average, 10 percent of the children left school at 13 years of age; 40 percent left by the time they were 14; 70 percent by the time they were 15; and 85 percent by the time they were 16 years of age. On the average, the schools retained pupils as far as the fifth grade, but in some cities great numbers left below that grade.

Vocational education was intended to help change schools' inability to retain students. However, the commission's judgment was that special emphasis was needed on education for early leavers who were already employed. The commission responded to these special needs by recommending part-time schools. The purpose of such schools was twofold:

1. To increase the general intelligence of young workers and teach them to better understand their social and civic duties.
2. To increase their industrial intelligence and skill and develop capacity for advancement within a given trade if such opportunity exists, or if not, to

prepare for some skilled and remunerative work in another line (Commission on National Aid to Vocational Education, 1914).

In the 1960s and 1970s, much of the legislation passed by Congress dealt with providing equal education for *all*. Never before had there been such an emphasis on providing vocational education for all students, no matter what their race, sex, age, national origin, language, or economic level. Laws enacted during this period include the Civil Rights Act of 1964, the Economic Opportunity Act of 1965, the Elementary and Secondary Education Act of 1973, the Comprehensive Employment Training Act of 1973, the 1974 Education Amendments for the needs of limited-English proficient (LEP) students, the Education for All Handicapped Children Act of 1975, and the Vocational Act of 1976, which mandated changes designed to enable vocational education to better serve *all* people, including the special needs populations.

This chapter examines the historical relationship between ethnic groups and vocational education and also the participation of special education students in vocational education.

HISTORICAL RELATIONSHIP BETWEEN ETHNIC GROUPS AND VOCATIONAL EDUCATION

There is no doubt that minorities are inadequately represented in professional roles in vocational education. Vocational professionals who have worked with minority youth have noted that these youth seem to be less interested in vocational education than are nonminority youth. However, there is a paucity of data to substantiate this observation.

Ogbu (1986) argued that minorities who were incorporated into American society against their will are different from the White majority and from other minorities such as immigrants. He called these groups "castelike minorities" and gave as examples Blacks, Hispanics, and Native Americans. Boykin (1986) expanded on this theme by proposing the theory that minorities must cope within three areas. Everyone, including Whites, interacts within the "mainstream" or majority culture. Next, there is a separate minority culture that groups like Blacks, Hispanics, and Asian Americans contribute to and experience. Finally, each minority group has its own distinct actions, reactions, and experiences that fit into the majority culture with varying degrees of success.

Longstreet (1978) suggested that ethnic groups are unique according to several aspects of style: verbal and nonverbal communication, orientation modes, social value patterns, and intellectual modes. Longstreet used these aspects to conduct observations of minority and nonminority students in classroom settings. Studies by Marshall (1989), Metzger (1985), and Valverde (1988), which explored the underrepresentation of minorities and women in professional administrative jobs in education, suggest that stereotyping, discrimination, constraints imposed by self and family, low career aspirations, lack of confidence and initiative, and lack of sponsors are causes for low participation by these groups.

African Americans

African Americans have a long history and tradition of participation in American vocational education. Between 1619 and 1846 there were numerous apprenticeship programs for slaves. Manual labor schools for African Americans began to open in many parts of the South in the 1830s (Jennings, 1991). Several private industrial institutions, such as Tuskegee and Hampton, were founded. Leaders such as Frederick Douglas and Booker T. Washington spoke strongly in favor of expanding participation of African Americans in vocational education after the post–Civil War period. From 1910 to 1930 public secondary schools began to offer manual training for African Americans.

While the manual training movement had stressed the benefit to education of the integration of manual and intellectual training, a major purpose of industrial and vocational education was to meet the labor needs of industry. However, it also offered an educational response to two social and economic challenges: the huge influx of rural poor and newly free, uneducated, and unemployed African Americans in the South (DuBois, 1903; Lazerson and Grubb, 1974). Educators and industrialists were concerned about the immigrants' high attrition rate in secondary schools that left them uneducated, unskilled, and unprepared for life as industrial workers. For the urban immigrants and other poor, educators prescribed socialization and training in the values of hard work and proper homemaking, which in schools translated into woodworking or industrial arts for boys and sewing, cooking, or home economics for girls (Lazerson and Grubb, 1974).

During the first decade of the twentieth century, the educational opportunities of African American women slowly expanded. Local Black industrial training schools became public high schools and larger industrial training institutes were converted into colleges. Some of the new schools offered more academic work, and some expanded their vocational offerings as traditional trades became obsolete. For their daughters, African American families were interested in education that would ensure that the young women could avoid domestic work. Of the new vocational areas, African American women most often chose the field of nursing, cosmetology, or printing. Nursing and cosmetology were popular and open to African American women because these services were needed in the African American community, and the work fit into the accepted women's roles. Printing was opening up to women because print shops on campuses were expanding and men were choosing other fields of vocational work (Ihle, 1986).

After 1930, as industrial development demanded more skilled workers, a reversal occurred in vocational education as Whites claimed access to the better jobs. White schools began emphasizing industrial training while Black schools offered more academic education (Ogbu, 1978). In addition, the depression caused increased competition between Black and White schools for limited educational funds, so these public school systems, already separate, became even more unequal. By 1935, African Americans in the South were underrepresented in vocational education programs that received federal funds, and Black institutions were less likely to receive funds. While southern White students were equally likely to be enrolled in agriculture (36 percent), home economics (34 percent), and trade and industries (30 percent); African American students were most likely found in agriculture (55 percent) and home economics (29 percent) with only 16 percent in trade and industry programs. The lower participation by African American students in the trades most likely reflected the exclusion of African Americans from practicing in these occupations (Anderson, 1982). In addition, although distributive (sales) occupations had been funded in vocational education by the George-Deen Act of 1929, these programs were not offered in most Black schools (Ogbu, 1978).

During the 1930s, African American educators attempted to reduce educational and economic inequities in the North and the South through a Black vocational guidance movement that sought to improve the vocational counseling for African American students. They saw that African American students were either aspiring to very-low-level occupations or expecting to pursue an academic or professional education. These educators believed that more information on the wide range of middle-level skilled occupations would lead African American students to choose more of these occupations (Anderson, 1982). However, this movement had very little effect on the lower participation of Black students in the more lucrative job paths, due to the severity of the depression and the continuing exclusion of Blacks from these occupations. Instead, during the 1940s, the demand for civilian labor during World War II created more opportunities for African American men and women than any vocational guidance or training had been able to do. African American educational strategy finally moved away from vocational education and instead encouraged African American youth to aim for entrance into colleges and universities (Anderson, 1982). Thus, DuBois' vision that African American youth should strive for the highest level of education was finally fulfilled.

Black agricultural educators concerned about increasing the number of Black students in vocational agriculture note that most vocational agriculture teachers are white (Bowen, 1987). The historically and predominantly Black 1890 land-grant agricultural and mechanical colleges provide excellent training for many Black agricultural researchers and teachers (Taylor, Powers, and Johnson, 1990). However, the percentage of Black faculty at historically White 1862 land-grant colleges, which train the majority of vocational agriculture teachers, has remained very low (Bowen, 1987). In addition, while the percentage of Black students majoring in agriculture at the bachelor's level has not changed, the percentage of Black students obtaining master's degrees in agriculture has decreased. Consequently, the percentage of agricultural faculty who are Black is not likely to increase (Larke and Barr, 1987).

These studies offer various historical and structural reasons why African Americans might be found in lower-level vocational programs. According to Arnold and Levesque (1992):

A history of being limited to lower-level vocational education programs and occupations may explain any lingering overrepresentation in lower-level vocational education programs. However, it is also possible that Blacks may be underrepresented in the higher-level programs due to continuing racism and structural biases. (p. 20)

Hispanics

Although limited data availability often leads researchers to treat Hispanics as if they were a homogeneous group, the U.S. Hispanic population is diverse. The three largest Hispanic subgroups are Mexican Americans, Puerto Ricans, and Cubans. Recent immigrants from Central and South America constitute a fourth group (National Center for Educational Statistics, 1995). These subgroups are concentrated in different parts of the United States, their economic circumstances vary, and the timing of their immigration differs.

The issue of participation is central to vocational education. Consequently, researchers have extensively explored the factors that influence participation. However, little information exists about participation as it specifically relates to Hispanics. This situation has serious implications given the current Hispanic socioeconomic and demographic trends. According to Totti (1987), by the year 2005 Hispanics are predicted to be the largest ethnic minority in the United States.

The Hispanic population is growing even faster in the Pacific Northwest (Cook, 1986). While Hispanics are increasing in number, they have not benefited substantially from the economic growth of the 1980s and 1990s. Sotomayor (1988) reported that Hispanic workers are more likely to work in unskilled occupations. This situation held true especially for Hispanic women; wages remained low even though Hispanic females' participation in the workforce grew. Valdivieso (1985) noted that Hispanic children were more likely to live in poverty (70.5 percent) than Whites (47.6 percent), or African Americans (68.5 percent).

Furthermore, the educational outlook for Hispanics remains grim. As a group, Hispanics 20 to 24 years old have not graduated from high school (Valdivieso, 1985). In addition, dropout rates remain high. Sotomayor (1988) reported that, based on national survey data, 31 percent of 18-year-old Hispanics had not completed high school or obtained a general equivalency degree (GED). Oakes (1990) found that in elementary and secondary schools, students who were Hispanic, African American, low income, inner-city residents, or in "low-ability" classes had fewer opportunities than other students to participate in traditional academic mathematics and science programs for the following two reasons. First, Hispanic, African American, and low-income students were more likely than White and middle-income students to be assessed as low in academic ability and placed in lower-level tracks. Second, students in majority Black or disadvantaged schools were exposed to fewer demanding programs. Students in low tracks and in less advantaged schools were exposed to fewer math and science resources such as highly qualified teachers, equipment, and development of higher-level skills. Consequently, these lower opportunities perpetuated race and social class differences in math and science achievement.

In 1991, at the associate's degree level, Hispanic men were slightly less likely than White men to major in other technical/professional fields but were more likely to major in arts and sciences. Hispanic women were more likely than White women to earn associate's degrees in arts and sciences and in business, but were less likely to earn degrees in health-related fields. Between 1987 and 1991, differences in the fields studied by Hispanics and Whites at the associate's degree level narrowed for men and widened for women (NCES, 1995).

At the bachelor's degree level, in 1991, Hispanics were more likely than White to major in social and behavioral sciences and were less likely to major in technical/professional fields. Overall, Hispanic-White differences in the fields studied at the bachelor's degree level narrowed between 1977 and 1991, although almost all of the decrease occurred between 1977 and 1985 (NCES, 1995).

Wirsching and Stenberg (1992) suggested that length of residency, marital status, and educational attainment were predictive of participation of Hispanics in vocational education. Factors predictive of nonparticipation included age, barriers to participation (situational, institutional, and psychosocial), and degree of acculturation.

Native Americans

Vocational education for Native Americans needs to be understood in the context of all Native American education, which in turn operates within the context of Native American life. Originally, the federal government assumed full responsibility for the education of Native Americans, as their isolation on tax-exempt reservations provided states and localities with a rationale to withhold education (as well as other publicly supported) services. Hudson (1994) cites that in the 1800s, the federal government focused on two efforts to use education to attract Native Americans. First, the government supported missionary education through various religious groups; the goal was to Christianize Native Americans while providing them with basic literacy skills. Some of the mission schools that were established on reservations during this period still operate today, although it is part of a more diverse education system.

The federal government's second efforts focused on schools run by the Bureau of Indian Affairs (BIA). By 1900, the BIA had established twenty industrial training schools, providing instruction in basic literacy. The acknowledged goal of these schools was to "take the Indian out of the Indians." To help meet this goal, the training schools operated as off-reservation boarding schools, separating youth from the *negative* influences of their families and tribes. According to one historian, "the underlying intention of this policy of relocation was to assimilate Native Americans into the dominant culture." Children were placed in boarding schools in the early primary grades, and the schools were notorious in their attempts to eradicate any vestiges of traditional Indian cultures (Slater, 1992).

After the turn of the century, acceptance of Native American cultures was espoused by anthropologists and reformers, and, through their efforts by policymakers. This new view culminated in the 1928 Meriam report, which was harshly critical of the ethnocentric and indoctrination methods used by the boarding schools. Relatively rapid and major changes followed in the philosophy and practice of Native American education. Within five years, twelve boarding schools were closed or converted to day schools and curricula began to include information on Native American culture. Efforts to reform Native American education were assisted by a congressional study that revealed the deplorable living conditions on reservations. This study led to the passage of the 1934 Indian Reorganization Act (Hudson, 1994).

It was in the Indian Reorganization Act that the federal government first promulgated the notion of "self-determination" for Native Americans. The act increased tribal self-government and input into education, encouraged cultural and religious pluralism, and supported economic development for reservations. Native American teachers were trained, textbooks were published in Native American language, and "community" schools, designed to serve multiple tribal needs, became the new focus of the BIA's education efforts.

In the 1950s and 1960s, known as the Termination Era, the government reverted to the philosophy that Native Americans should be encouraged to integrate into the larger society. Financial support for 100 tribes was ended, a number of reservations were eliminated, and a federal relocation program was implemented to move Native Americans to urban centers. The effects of this policy were marked:

> *The majority of Native Americans who left the reservations became part of the undereducated, working poor—those engaged in part-time or lower paid manual labor. Many of these people . . . left the reservations but returned, unable to cope with urban life. The failure of so many Native Americans to adapt outside the reservation hastened the end of the termination policy. (Blood and Burnham, 1994, p. 25).*

The civil rights movement of the 1960s also helped end the Termination Era, as the rights of minorities, including Native Americans, were enforced with new legislation. In 1970, the Nixon administration returned federal policy to one of self-determination for Native Americans. Although the 1972 Indian

Education Act provided funds for adding Indian history and culture to educational programs, the larger focus of the new federal effort was to shift administrative responsibilities to tribes, rather than to increase funding. Thus, in 1975, the Indian Self-Determination and Education Assistance Act became the first of a series of laws that shifted federal administrative responsibilities to tribal leaders.

During the early 1990s, most Native Americans were enrolled in the public school system. About 85 percent of Native American K–12 students attend public schools, while 10 percent attend federally funded BIA schools and 5 percent attend private schools (Slater, 1992). At the postsecondary level, the federal government has attempted to increase educational opportunities for Native Americans on reservations by funding a number of postsecondary institutions on or near these sites. Hudson (1994) reported that in the early 1990s the BIA funded 24 tribally controlled postsecondary institutions, including 2 vocational institutes, 18 community colleges, and 4 four-year colleges. According to Hudson (1994), about 14 percent of all Native American postsecondary students attend these tribally controlled institutions. An additional five U.S. colleges and two Canadian colleges also serve Native Americans.

Values held by individuals with special needs are not always congruent with those of vocational educators. More importantly, they need not be congruent. The cultural values of one group do not need to be bent to fit the values of the dominant culture. Recognition and acceptance of the differences are usually what is needed. Marjorie Bear Don't Walk (1976) presents the position of the Native Americans:

> There developed a joke among Indians that if you sent any Indian to the moon, he/she would find a way to return to the reservation. Most of us do return to our reservations; most of us would prefer to be trained on or near our own homes. Most of us would like to find jobs on our own reservations. (p. 132)

Vocational educators who accept this expression of desire will find an initial basis for providing vocational education different from that of the past. However, the educational needs of Native Americans do not end merely with reservation-based and reservation-oriented programs. The important aspects must be addressed, as well. It must be determined whether training for a new social and economic role will cause a communication gap between Native American students and their parents and family. It is also important to determine how emotional support can be provided to help students and family members adapt to the new situations (Bear Don't Walk, 1976).

Limited-English Proficient Vocational Students

There are more than 40 million people in the United States who speak a native language other than English (Oxford, Lopez, Stupp, Peng, and Gendell,

1989). Although the majority of this population is Spanish speaking, it also includes persons who are Asian, European, Middle Eastern, African, and Native American. For example, between 1915 and 1985 more than 1 million refugees entered the United States: 730,000 from Southeast Asia, 100,000 from the former Soviet Union, 60,000 from other Eastern European countries, 30,000 from Latin America, 25,000 from the Near East, and 12,000 from Africa (Crandell, 1985). Several countries from the Caribbean are also included in this growing population.

Unlike some other special population groups, the number of nonnative speakers of English is expected to increase significantly. In fact, according to a study by Johnson and Packer (1987), immigrants will represent the largest share of the increase in the population and the workforce since the First World War. Johnson and Packer (1987) also reported that women, minorities, and immigrants will account for more than 80 percent of the net additions to the labor force by the year 2000.

Access to Vocational Education

Ensuring access to vocational education for special needs populations was one predominant theme of the Perkins Act. It was included because limited-English proficient (LEP) students are generally underrepresented in vocational-technical education programs at both secondary school and adult education levels. At the secondary level, LEP students' greater vocational coursetaking is mainly confined to occupational courses, and reflects to some extent the provision of work preparation courses specifically designed for these students. According to National Assessment of Vocational Education (NAVE) (1994), LEP students have less access to vocational schools than do other students.

Some school systems have had legal action sought against them for failing to provide access. In other words, they were discriminating against student entrance into vocational education programs based on their national origin. Historically, such suits are governed by the 1974 Lau decision made by the U.S. Supreme Court (*Lau v. Nichols*). The decision that a San Francisco school district was discriminating against 3,000 Chinese-speaking students was made based on Title VI of the Civil Rights Act of 1964, which prohibits exclusion from programs and denial of benefits to any person on the basis of race, color, or national origin (Bradley and Friedenberg, 1988). To more adequately meet the needs of LEP students, federal funds should be more closely targeted in institutions with a large concentration of immigrant populations.

Since 1976, the Office of Vocational and Adult Education of the U.S. Department of Education has funded a modest number of bilingual vocational training (BVT) programs. Probably the most important contribution made by these federal programs is development of the BVT model. The model is often considered to be the most effective instructional delivery for LEP vocational students (Friedenberg and Fields, 1993).

The BVT model consists of the following seven components:

1. Target recruitment specifically to LEP students.
2. Institute assessment procedures.
3. Use bilingual instructions and materials; simplify English.
4. Provide vocational English as a second language.
5. Offer counseling and support service.
6. Promote job development and placement.
7. Coordinate the previous six elements so that each supports the other (Friedenberg and Fields, 1993).

PARTICIPATION OF SPECIAL EDUCATION STUDENTS IN VOCATIONAL EDUCATION

Vocational education has a long history of serving special education students. Since the Americans with Disabilities Act (ADA) took effect in 1992, employers, professionals in vocational rehabilitation, and educators generally are turning more to vocational educators for answers to questions such as the following:

- How do you determine if an employee with a disability is ready to work?
- How do you decide if the functions of a job can be done by alternative means?
- How do you ensure that a student with a disability will get needed support once he or she is enrolled in a vocational education program (Morrissey, 1993)?

The ADA defines an *individual with a disability* as "one who has a physical or mental impairment that substantially limits one or more major life activities, one who has a record of such a disability, or is regarded as having such a disability" (Morrissey, 1993, p. 23). By law, educators must now provide programming and services to special populations, which include individuals with disabilities. According to data from the U.S. Department of Education (1989), there were 4.49 million young people who met the definition of handicapped being served in our public schools as of the 1987–1988 school year.

Of these young people with disabilities being served in the general school system, the number being served by vocational education doubled in a period of six years. The total number of students with disabilities in grades 7–12 taking part in vocational education grew from 20 percent to 40 percent from 1976–1983) (Conaway, 1987).

Education of the Handicapped Amendments of 1990 (PL 101-476)

This act, which began in 1975 as The Education of All Handicapped Children Act, was revised in 1983 and 1986 as Education Handicapped Act Amendments, and amended again in 1990 when its name was changed to the Individuals with Disabilities Education Act (IDEA). This act, as amended, was passed by Congress for educating disabled children and youth.

Rate of Participation

Until recently, reliable data has not been available to examine the actual rate of participation of handicapped students in vocational programs. That is, since 1983 when the U.S. Department of Education's Vocational Education Data System (VEDS) was discontinued, there has been no national data collected regarding the placement of students with disabilities in vocational education. (For a discussion of the problems associated with earlier vocational data collection efforts, see Benson, Hoachlander, and Johnson, 1980.) Thus, while it was possible from the extant research literature to describe exemplary programs and practices for disabled students, it was not possible to reliably measure the actual participation of handicapped students in vocational programs. However, with the completion of the High School Transcript Study of the Class of 1987 (more commonly known as the National Assessment of Education Progress [NAEP] Transcript Study), nationally representative data has now become available to describe the participation of handicapped students in vocational education (Kaufman, 1989).

Analyses presented by the National Assessment of Vocational Education (NAVE) (1989) have used this data to describe the characteristics of disabled students participating in vocational education. In their final report to Congress, NAVE reported that handicapped students had received essentially the same access to vocational education as other students. The report also indicated that the extent to which students were admitted to mainstream vocational courses varied somewhat by handicapping condition, as well as by severity of cognitive limitation; and the number of vocational credits they earned varied with demographic and other student characteristics.

Wagner (1991) observes that students with disabilities often need training in both work-related behaviors and specific job skills, if they are to function effectively in the competitive job market when they leave high school. A study by Wagner et al. (1993) explored the relationship of vocational education to school performance for students with disabilities. This analysis included a comparison of how students who took vocational education classes in high school fared in making the transition to adult roles and responsibilities, compared with other students. The data came from the National Longitudinal Transition Study of Special Education Students (NLTS). The NLTS is a nationally representative sample of more than eight thousand students in all eleven federal special education disability categories.

Wagner et al. (1993) used the NLTS data to examine whether disabled students who took vocational education in their most recent year in secondary school were more likely to have positive outcomes than nonvocational students, both during secondary school and in their early postschool years. The outcomes include (a) school performance as measured by students' school attendance, (b) grade performance as measured by whether students received one or more failing course grades, and (c) persistence in school, as measured by whether the student dropped out. The postschool outcomes included enrollment in postsecondary vocational or trade school, and incidence of paid employment.

Wagner et al. (1993) found a consistent pattern of relationships between enrollment in occupationally oriented vocational education and better school performance. Students who had occupational training were absent from school significantly fewer days than students who did not have such training, other factors being equal. Similarly, students taking occupationally oriented vocational education were significantly less likely to drop out of school when other confounding factors (such as disability and gender differences) were controlled. The NLTS estimates show that the likelihood of dropping out rather than persisting in school was three percentage points lower for vocational students than others. The analysis also indicates that vocational students were about three percentage points less likely than others to have failed a course.

Those youth who had been out of high school for up to two years, and had taken secondary vocational education classes, were 8 percent more likely to have attended a postsecondary vocational school in previous years than were nonvocational students. In addition, students who took vocational education in their last year in secondary school were 9 percent more likely to be competitively employed than youth who had not taken vocational education. Wagner (1993) also reports that if the secondary vocational education included work experience, the likelihood of employment increased an additional 14 percent beyond the increased probability associated with vocational enrollment alone.

The NLTS findings suggest that secondary vocational education does appear to have potential for improving both school performance and postschool outcomes of disabled students.

CHALLENGES FOR VOCATIONAL EDUCATORS

Minorities today face an uncertain future regarding their participation in vocational education. If planned and administered in ways that reflect quality, vocational education is not only an important tool for preparation for minority workers but also a way for America to overcome a growing social and economic crisis—the deterioration of living conditions for many of its citizens. Because of the economic and demographic development in America, there is now a window of opportunity for all minorities in vocational education. This opportunity will not be realized, however, if basic challenges are not met and resolved by the vocational education community.

Before describing these challenges, it is important to emphasize that the American vocational education community does have the potential and leadership capabilities to respond to these challenges that could strengthen America's social productivity. Jennings (1991) describes at least five major social and economic challenges facing all educators concerned with issues related to race, ethnicity, and the preparation of the workforce for the 1990s and beyond. These challenges are as follows:

1. **Demography**—Today's demographic scenario presents economic opportunities not just for minorities but the entire nation. However, vocational education will become increasingly important as a channel for providing minorities with career skills for the job market.
2. **Changing economy**—The deterioration of living conditions for poor and working-class Americans has led to what social scientists call a "permanent underclass" of young Blacks and Hispanics who have not been integrated into the American economy.
3. **Changes in the labor force**—According to the Workforce 2000 report, most labor force growth through the year 2000 will come from groups in the population that have been traditionally underutilized and suffer from labor market problems. Women, minorities, and immigrants could account for more than 70 percent of the net additions to the labor force between now and the year 2000. Vocational education is the arena where many of these new workers can be trained and channeled into higher paying jobs of the unfolding market in the next several years.
4. **How workers are trained**—This challenge is to find ways to impart vocational and advanced technologies skills to groups that have generally not been served effectively by American public schools.
5. **The politics of race**—Racial and ethnic tensions still have characterized social relations in American society. The vocational education community has a chance to turn potential confrontation into political and social opportunity.

Suggestions for Vocational Educators

Following is a list of suggestions to help vocational educators face the challenges concerning special needs populations:

- Expand the school's program, formal and informal, to include opportunities for minority students to authenticate their own intellectual growth and to share in their knowledge and experience.
- Improve the image of vocational education between minority youth and professionals.
- Fund a study to determine more accurate numbers of minorities participating in vocational education and the program types in which they participate.
- Vocational teacher education department heads should be sure that vocational special needs teacher educators and special needs courses include state-of-the-art information on serving LEP students.

- Devise methods of determining the readiness of minority students to cope with the challenge of college and graduate study. This involves going beyond traditional testing programs that have failed to discover potentially excellent minority students because they reveal more about one's past opportunity than about one's present potential.
- Encourage state directors to provide leadership regarding professional activities devoted to enhancing racially and ethnically diverse learning environments.
- Provide support for more ethnic minority doctorates in vocational education to ensure a future pool of talent for research on ethnic (as well as other) issues in vocational education, and to ensure future role models.
- Staff vocational education programs with people who are knowledgeable about minority cultures and are good role models and mentors for these groups.
- Relate the research and extension activities of the university to the needs of the total population of the state including urban Blacks, Hispanics, Native Americans, and poor Whites. Somehow the notion that this public benefaction known as a university must serve all of the people has to be reinforced.

SUMMARY

- In the 1960s and 1970s, much of the legislation passed by Congress dealt with providing equal education for all. As part of its efforts to help special population students, the Perkins Act requires states to provide assurances that these students have equal access to vocational education and that localities ensure their full participation in programs with Perkins money.

- Minorities who were incorporated into American society against their will are different from the White majority and from other minorities such as immigrants. Ethnic groups are unique according to several aspects of style: verbal and nonverbal communication, orientation modes, social value patterns, and intellectual modes. Stereotyping, discrimination, constraints imposed by self and family, low career aspirations, lack of confidence and initiative, and lack of sponsors are causes for low participation by these groups.

- Education is the real hope for American minorities; experience tends to confirm this. When minorities, including Blacks, Hispanics, and Native Americans, have received adequate and meaningful education, they have tended to be successful in such cultures, as that of the United States. While several types of education are crucial to this success, vocational education has demonstrated that it occupies a central position in minority affairs.

- In the past twenty-five years, vocational education has become more concerned with the role of serving persons with disabilities and has made progress in adapting and refining programs to prepare these "students at risk" vocationally. The Education of All Handicapped Children Act of 1975 launched an organized effort to provide a free and appropriated education for all handicapped children from ages 3 to 21. This act provided a number of grants to states and local school systems to improve vocational education and related services for handicapped individuals.

• Special needs groups and the individuals who make up special needs groups are a special challenge for vocational education. Defining, identifying, accepting, adapting, creating, and giving are terms that indicate separate challenges. In some cases, good solutions to these challenges are yet to be found.

DISCUSSION QUESTIONS AND ACTIVITIES

1. Describe some special programs in your state that provide support services for vocational students from special populations.

2. What are the patterns of access and participation for minorities in vocational education at the secondary level in your state?

3. What are the patterns of access and participation for minorities in vocational education at the postsecondary level in your state?

Library Research Questions

4. Determine the best strategies for increasing the participation of minority students from low socioeconomic backgrounds in vocational education.

5. According to research, minority students are less likely to participate in the following vocational courses at the postsecondary level: agriculture, home economics, and trade and industry. What are some of the possible reasons for this?

6. List some ways of providing more minority faculty as role models for minority students enrolled in vocational education.

7. Develop a historical review documenting how much impact vocational education had on helping the early-twentieth-century immigrants adjust to the working world of America.

8. Describe what is being done today through vocational education to help immigrants.

REFERENCES

Anderson, J.D. (1982). The historical development of Black vocational education. In H. Kantor and D.B. Tyack (Eds.), *Work, youth, and schooling* (pp. 180–222). Stanford, CA: Stanford University Press.

Arnold, C.L., and Levesque, K.A. (1992). *Black Americans and vocational education: Participation in the 1980s*. Macomb, IL: National Center for Research in Vocational Education.

Bear Don't Walk, M. (1976). Options for Native Americans in vocational education. In J.E. Wall (Ed.), *Vocational education for special groups* (pp. 125–135). *Sixth yearbook of the American Vocational Association*. Washington, DC: American Vocational Association.

Blood, P., and Burnham, L.H. (1994). *Meeting the vocational needs of the Native Americans* (pp. 21–25). Library of Congress, Federal Research Division.

Bowen, B.E. (1987). A minority perspective on minorities in agriculture. *Agricultural Education Magazine, 60*(6), 3–4.

Boykin, A.W. (1986). The triple quandary and the schooling of Afro-American children. In U. Neisser (Ed.), *The school achievement of minority children* (pp. 57–71). Hillsdale, NJ: Lawrence Erlbaum Associates.

Benson, C.S., Hoachlander, E.G., and Johnson, B.L. (1980). *An assessment of the reliability and consistency in reporting of vocational education data available from national information systems.* Washington, DC: National Institute of Education. (Contract No. 400-78-0039).

Bradley, C.H., and Friedenberg, J.E. (1988). *Teaching vocational education to limited-English proficient students.* Bloomington, IL: Meridian.

Cook, A.R. (1986). Diversity among Northwest Hispanics. *Social Science Journal, 23*(2), 205–216.

Commission on National Aid to Vocational Education (1914). *Vocational education,* Vol. 1. Washington, DC: United States Government Printing Office.

Conaway, C. (1987). Serving the handicapped: A progress report. *Vocational Education Journal, 62*(2), 25–26.

Crandell, J.A. (1985). *Directions in vocational education for limited-English proficient students and adults. Occasional paper No. 109.* Columbus: The Ohio State University, National Center for Research in Vocational Education. ERIC Document Reproduction Service No. ED. 264 436.

DuBois, W.E.B. (1903). *The souls of Black folk* (rev. ed.). New York, NY: Bantam.

Friedenberg, J.E., and Fields, E.L. (1993). Ethnic minority participation in vocational education. In C. Anderson and L.C. Rampp (Eds.), *Vocational education in the 1990s, II: A sourcebook for strategies, methods, and materials* (pp. 212–224). Ann Arbor, MI: Prakken Publishing Company.

Hudson, L. (1994). *National assessment of vocational education: Final report to Congress volume IV access to programs and services for special populations.* Washington, DC: Office of Educational Research and Improvement, U.S. Department of Education.

Ihle, E. (1986). *Black women's vocational education: History of Black women's vocational education in the South, 1865–present. Instructional modules for educators, Module II* (Module prepared for the Women's Educational Equity Act Program, U.S. Department of Education). Harrisonburg, VA: James Madison University.

Jennings, J. (1991). Minorities and vocational education: The challenges. *Vocational Education Journal, 66*(4), 20–21, 45.

Johnson, W., and Packer, A. (1987). *Workforce 2000: Work and workers for the 21st century.* Indianapolis, IN: D. Hudson Institute.

Kaufman, P. (1989). *Participation of special education students in high school vocational education: The influence of school characteristics.* Macomb, IL: National Center for Research in Vocational Education.

Larke, A., Jr., and Barr, T.P. (1987). Promoting minority involvement in agriculture. *Agricultural Education Magazine, 60*(6), 6–7.

Lazerson, M., and Grubb, W.N. (1974). *American education and vocationalism: A documentary history, 1870–1970.* New York, NY: Teachers College Press.

Longstreet, W.S. (1978). *Aspects of ethnicity.* New York: Teachers College Press.

Marshall, C. (1989). *More than black face and skirts: New leadership to confront the major dilemmas in education.* Charlottesville, VA: National Policy Board for Educational Administration. ERIC Document Reproduction Service No. ED 318 089.

Metzger, C. (1985). Helping women prepare for principalships. *Phi Delta Kappan, 67,* 292–296.

Morrissey, P. (1993). The ADA and vocational education. *Vocational Education Journal, 68*(8), 22–24.

National Assessment of Vocational Education (NAVE). (1989, August). *Handicapped and disadvantaged students: Access to quality vocational education.* Washington, DC: U.S. Department of Education.

National Assessment of Vocational Education (NAVE) (1994). *Final report to Congress volume II participation in and quality of vocational education.* Washington, DC: Office of Educational Research and Improvement, U.S. Department of Education.

National Center for Education Statistics (NCES) (1995). *The condition of education 1995: The educational progress of Hispanic students.* Washington, DC: Office of Educational Research and Improvement, U.S. Department of Education.

Oakes, J. (1990). *Multiplying inequalities: The effects of race, social class, and tracking on opportunities to learn mathematics and science* (National Science Foundation Report R-3928-NSF). Santa Monica, CA: RAND.

Ogbu, J.U. (1978). *Minority education and caste: The American system in cross-cultural perspective.* New York, NY: Academic Press.

Ogbu, J.U. (1986). The consequences of the American caste system. In U. Neisser (Ed.), *The school achievement of minority children* (pp. 19–56). Hillsdale, NJ: Lawrence Erlbaum Associates.

Oxford, R., Lopez, K., Stupp, P., Peng, S., and Gendell, M. (1989). *Projections of non-English language background and limited-English proficient persons in the United States to the year 2000.* Rosslyn, VA: InterAmerica Research Associates.

Slater, G. (1992). *Principal issues regarding Native Americans.* Papers presented at the Design Conference for the National Assessment of Vocational Education. Washington, DC: Office of Educational Research and Improvement, U.S. Department of Education.

Sotomayor, M. (1988). Educational issues and Hispanic populations in the U.S.A. *Journal of Vocational Special Needs, 10*(3), 7–9.

Taylor, W.N., Powers, L., and Johnson, D.M. (1990). The 1890 institutions at 100. *Agricultural Education Magazine, 63*(2), 8–9.

Totti, X. (1987, Fall). The making of a Latino ethnic identity. *Dissent,* Vol. 34, No. 4, 537–542.

U.S. Department of Education. (1989). *To assure the free appropriate public education of all handicapped children: Eleventh annual report to Congress on the implementation of the Education of the Handicapped Act.* Washington, DC: U.S. Department of Education, Office of Special Education and Rehabilitation Services, Division of Innovation and Development.

Valdivieso, R. (1985). *Hispanics and education data.* Washington, DC: National Center for Education Statistics.

Valverde, L.A. (1988). The missing element: Hispanics at the top in higher education. *Change, 20,* 11.

Wagner, M. (1991). *The benefits of secondary vocational education for young people with disabilities: Findings from the national longitudinal transition study of Special Education students.* Menlo Park, CA: SRI International. ERIC Document Reproduction Service No. ED 272 570.

Wagner, M., Blackorby, J., Cameto, R., and Newman, L. (1993). *What makes a difference?: Influences on postschool outcomes of youth with disabilities.* Menlo Park, CA: SRI International.

West, R.F., and Shearon, R.W. (1982). Differences between black and white students in curriculum program status. *Community/ Junior College Quarterly, 6*(3), 239–251.

Wirsching, T., and Stenberg, L. (1992). Determinants of Idaho Hispanic female participation in adult vocational education programs. *Journal of Vocational Education Research, 17*(3), 35–61.

8

VOCATIONAL INSTRUCTIONAL PROGRAMS AND TEACHER PREPARATION

This chapter examines many salient features of vocational programs. The major areas of focus are: vocational program areas of study, vocational enrollments by program area, teacher preparation, and selected entities influencing growth in vocational education programs.

AREAS OF STUDY

The hundreds of programs available for students fall into eight major areas of study:

1. **Agricultural education,** including horticulture, agricultural mechanics, and agribusiness.
2. **Business education,** including accounting office occupations and business management programs.
3. **Marketing education,** including general merchandising, apparel and accessories marketing, real estate, financial services and marketing, business and personal services marketing.
4. **Family and consumer sciences education,** which encompasses consumer and homemaking education as well as occupational fields such as food services.
5. **Trade and industrial education,** which includes a wide range of trades, including auto mechanics, carpentry, metalworking, graphic arts, and cosmetology.

6. **Health occupations,** such as practical nursing, registered nursing, medical and dental assistants, and radiologic technicians.
7. **Technology education,** which concerns materials, processes, and technologies that are used in manufacturing, construction, transportation, communication, and other components of industries.
8. **Technical education,** which involves a variety of technical occupation fields such as communications, engineering-related technologies, and computer sciences.

Agricultural Education

Vocational education in agriculture, in some form, has always been an integral part of American life. Hamlin (1956) points out that an agricultural school for orphans was established in Georgia in 1734 or shortly thereafter and a similar school, the Bethesda School in Savannah, Georgia was founded in 1740.

Teaching agriculture in public schools of less than college grade apparently began in certain elementary schools in Massachusetts in 1858. Teaching agriculture in a public secondary school seems to have begun in Elyria, Ohio, in 1902. The first agricultural teacher was employed by a public school in Carroll County, Georgia in 1903. Groups that later developed into 4-H clubs began in 1900. These groups received their initial impetus from county and local school superintendents in Illinois, Iowa, Mississippi and Ohio (Hamlin, 1956).

Agricultural education has consistently changed in its instructional programs to meet the needs of a dynamic, rapidly changing industry. Agriculture is becoming highly scientific and technical in such new frontiers as biotechnology, which deals with genetic engineering and tissue culture. Agricultural education is responding with more programs like agriscience, which consists of a series of laboratory courses that emphasize the basic biological and physical science principles and practices with agriculture (Scott and Sarkees-Wircenski, 1996).

Agricultural programs are increasingly being planned to prepare students for a wide range of career options when they complete the instructional sequence of courses. Like other areas of vocational education, more attention is being given to integrating academic subjects such as communications, mathematics, and science to the applications of technology. Agricultural education is being offered in grades 7 through 14 in more than 7,600 high schools and 570 postsecondary institutions in America. Many students begin career awareness and exploration programs in agriculture in the middle and junior high school years and continue this area of interest in the high school agriculture program. Some students continue their education for two or more years by enrolling in community colleges and four-year colleges or universities where they earn associates' degrees or baccalaureate degrees in agriculture or related areas (Lee, 1994).

Agricultural education ranges from traditional to high-tech courses that may include genetically modifying plants.

Agricultural occupation clusters are composed of groups of related courses or units of subject matter that are organized for carrying on learning experiences concerned with preparation for, or upgrading in, occupations requiring knowledge of and skills in agricultural subjects. The functions of agricultural production, supplies, mechanization, products, ornamental horticulture, forestry, agricultural resources, and the services related are emphasized in the instruction designed to provide opportunities for students to prepare for, or to improve their competencies in agricultural occupations (Mason and Husted, 1997).

The delivery system for vocational agriculture utilizes three major components: classroom and laboratory instruction, leadership development (FFA), and supervised agricultural experience programs. According to Lee (1994), classroom and laboratory instruction involves teaching students the underlying concepts and principles of agriculture, and providing them with opportunities to apply what they have learned in a "hands-on" environment. Supervised agricultural experiences (SAE) involve structured learning activities that build on what has been learned through the classroom and laboratory instruction. The FFA provides opportunities for students to become involved in a variety of career development events and professional development activities.

The profession in the mid-1980s began exploring innovative program approaches such as aquaculture, agrimarketing, infusing agricultural sciences into the curriculum, infusing international agricultural education into the instructional program, and so forth. All approaches were designed to maintain or increase student interest and enrollment in a program developed and delivered primarily to prepare people for employment in production agriculture, agribusiness, and natural resources occupations. However, in many instances, programs designed to emphasize vocational education were being threatened and, in many cases, phased out (Cox, McCormick, and Miller, 1989).

After the tremendous impact of the National Commission on Excellence in Education report, *A Nation at Risk* (1983), educational reform in this nation was launched. The intent of this reform was to improve the quality of education, especially in basic education. In 1985, then Secretary of Education, Terral Bell, and the Secretary of the U.S. Department of National Academy of Sciences' Board on Agriculture, John Block, undertook a companion comprehensive study of "Vocational Agriculture in Secondary Schools" (Cox, McCormick, and Miller, 1989).

Data from the National Longitudinal Study of the High School Class of 1972 revealed the following facts about agricultural education graduates:

- Agricultural education graduates participated less frequently in postsecondary programs when compared with nonagricultural education graduates.
- Participation in agricultural education had no substantive effect on postsecondary education attainment.
- Socioeconomic background variables (i.e., community, gender, ethnicity, father's education, mother's education, student's ability, and number of semesters completed of agricultural education) explained 29.77 percent of the variance in educational attainment (Gordon, 1985).

Results of this study suggest that more emphasis should be placed on counseling students to consider continuing their education beyond high school. In addition, secondary and postsecondary agricultural educators should clearly articulate their curricula programs. Also, more effort should be made to advise high school agricultural education students on the postsecondary opportunities available in their chosen career areas.

Vo (1997) cites that less than 2 percent of the jobs in America's agricultural industry relate to production. Most are nonproduction jobs, such as the following:

- Agronomist
- Livestock commission agent
- Winery supervisor
- Agricultural construction engineer
- Land surveyor
- Weed scientist
- Expert sales manager
- Log grader
- Mammalogist
- Rural sociologist

- College professor
- Geneticist
- Biochemist

- Environmental conservation officer
- Farm appraiser

Business Education

In colonial times, the apprentice usually had to discover the skills needed for business success and master them on his own. The demands of ambitious apprentices who urged employers to teach them bookkeeping after working hours resulted in organized business training. This was a major part of the beginning of vocational business education. Practical experience supplemented by study of "rules" became the foundation for advancement in business in the colonial period. According to Walker, Huffman, and Beaumont (1956), some rudimentary business courses were offered by individual teachers and by schools during the seventeenth and eighteenth centuries. Penmanship and an advanced arithmetic known as "casting accounts" were taught privately in Latin grammar schools.

Late in the eighteenth century, bookkeeping was taught by individuals, the forerunners of private business schools. Early in the nineteenth century, the business training became more specialized in "commercial" schools. Lack of leadership and status of business educators enabled traditionalists to retard the business education development in public schools for many years. As late as 1910, only one of seven high schools taught business-related subjects. The first organized course to prepare business teachers was given in Philadelphia in 1898 (Walker, Huffman, and Beaumont, 1956).

Business education has had to continuously change curriculum and instructional practices to keep pace with changes in business, equipment, organization, policy, and market demands. Instruction focuses on skill development with word processors, computers, high-speed copiers, laser printers, and fax machines. Business principles and concepts have also changed focus from secretarial office procedures to management systems and entrepreneurship, from a focus on the local economic community to an international one, and from computer application to information systems (Phillips, 1994). Business management was the most popular undergraduate major in 1994, making up 21 percent of all bachelor's degrees earned that year (National Center for Educational Statistics, 1997).

Marketing Education

The first comprehensive investigation of retail occupations was made in 1905 by the Women's Educational and Industrial Union in Boston, a society for the advancement of women in industrial work. Conditions revealed by this investigation motivated Mrs. Lucinda Wyman Prince to establish classes in retail selling as part of the society's activities. Within two years applicants for admission had to be turned away (Brown and Logan, 1956). The principles

Computer technology has become increasingly important in vocational and technical schools.

developed by Mrs. Prince have greatly influenced vocational practices. Mrs. Prince felt that the daily experiences of pupils must be the basis for the curriculum, that instruction should be largely individual, and training should prove itself in practice on the job.

Scattered and sporadic efforts to develop retail training continued through the first two decades of the century. The Committee of Nine of the National Education Association recommended in 1903 that advertising be included in the high school commerce curriculum. Retail sales training, patterned on the original Boston plan began in Providence, Rhode Island in 1910. Two years later Mrs. Prince organized the first retail training cooperative program in the Boston high schools. By 1915, the National Retail Dry Goods Association created the position of education director and appointed Mrs. Prince to this position (Brown and Logan, 1956).

The objectives of marketing education have changed since they were first introduced to secondary school programs in Boston in 1912. At that time, the objective was to provide cooperative training in retail store work for the purpose of improving the lot and quality of work sales personnel (Haas, 1972).

Marketing education is the instructional program designed to prepare individuals for the major occupational areas within marketing and management. Marketing, simply defined, is the selling of ideas, products, and services of all kinds to identified and qualified markets. Marketers manage the massive system of distribution that brings goods and services to industrial users and consumers worldwide. Marketing includes information gathering, recruiting, image building, promoting, training, campaigning, financing, lobbying, researching, and communicating. Marketing is a process that can be adapted to virtually every economic, social, or public activity, and is an essential ingredient in making our free enterprise system work Distributive Education Clubs of America (DECA Inc., 1992).

Nearly one-third of our nation's public schools offer marketing education programs. Recent data regarding the percentage of public high school graduates completing one or more courses in specific labor market programs of vocational education shows that 8.7 percent have been enrolled in marketing education programs (Scott and Sarkees-Wircenski, 1996). The Bureau of Labor Statistics (1992) estimated that nearly 80 percent of the nation's workforce will be engaged in service sector jobs by the year 2000 and to one degree or another, most of these workers will be involved in marketing. Marketing is a vital part of our economic system and students need expanded opportunities to enroll in marketing programs to prepare for the estimated 15,900,000 jobs projected by the year 2000 (DECA Inc., 1992).

Home Economics Education

The early developments in home economics education were scrutinized by educational leaders who attended the Lake Placid, New York, Conferences held annually from 1899 to 1908. These leaders were convinced that too little was being done in education to improve home and family living. Promoted by Mr. and Mrs. Melville Dewey and Ellen H. Richards, a sanitary engineer at Massachusetts Institute of Technology, these conferences attracted the participation of such leaders for chairperson of committees as Caroline Hunt, Abby Marlatt, Marion Talbot, Helen Kinne, Alice Norton, Ann Barrows and Isabel Bevier. Their deliberations covered school (elementary, secondary, vocational) and evening college and university programs, and the training of teachers. Home economics was defined by the Lake Placid Conference participants and later replaced the terms domestic science, domestic art, domestic economy, household science, and household arts. In their last conference in 1908, this group endorsed the David Bill, then in Congress, designed to give national financial assistance to the teaching of home economics (Lawson and Creighton, 1956).

Family and consumer sciences education is a new name and focus of home economics education, which is also called consumer and homemaking education and vocational home economics education. The new conceptual framework for home economics education was developed and accepted by those participating in the Scottsdale, Arizona, Conference of October, 23, 1993. The tripartite mission of family and consumer sciences is: empowering individuals, strengthening families, and enabling communities (American Home Economics Association, 1994).

The overriding mission of family and consumer sciences education is to prepare students for family life, work like, and careers in family and consumer

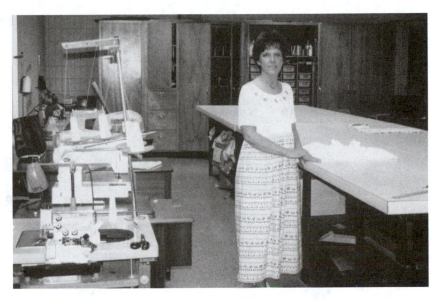

Many vocational programs such as Clothing and Textiles Management, Production, and Service are located in both the secondary schools and vocational technical centers.

sciences by providing opportunities to develop the knowledge, skills, attitudes, and behaviors needed for:

- Strengthening the well-being of individual and families.
- Becoming responsible citizens and leaders in family, community, and work settings.
- Promoting optimal nutrition and wellness.
- Managing resources to meet the needs of individuals and families.
- Balancing personal, home, family, and work life.
- Using critical- and creative-thinking skills to address problems in diverse family, community, and work environments.
- Facilitating successful life management, employment, and career development.
- Functioning effectively as providers and consumers of goods and services.
- Appreciating human worth and accepting responsibility for one's actions and success in family and work life (Stewart, 1994).

Most secondary students enroll in one or more vocational courses before they graduate with nearly half of those in vocational courses enrolled in consumer and homemaking courses. In 1987, 10.6 percent of high school graduates who completed one or more courses in specific labor market preparation programs were enrolled in occupational home economics (National Center for Educational Statistics, 1992).

Laboratory instruction provides students with opportunities to apply learned concepts and principles in the classroom through problem-solving and hands-on tasks. This student is working on an interior-decorating design project.

Trade and Industrial Education

The 1976 Centennial Exposition in Philadelphia showed America how far behind it lagged in the current theories. After seeing the Russians exhibit the typical exercises used as a basis for tool instruction, a number of industrial communities established evening classes to upgrade workers, notably in drawing. Because school authorities failed to consult and cooperate with factory employers or workers, these classes accomplished little, and all but disappeared in twenty-five years (Britton and Fick, 1956). To meet this crisis, the National Society for Promotion of Industrial Education was formed in 1906.

The major goal of trade and industrial education is for students to develop sufficient knowledge and skills to secure initial employment or advancements through experiences that (a) focus on performance skills required in an occupational field, (b) provide an understanding of and use of functional technology related to a chosen occupational area, (c) prepare individuals to deal effectively with personal and group relationship problems, (d) assist individuals in developing desirable work habits, ideals, and attitudes essential to job performance, and (e) provide relevant instruction to enable individuals to

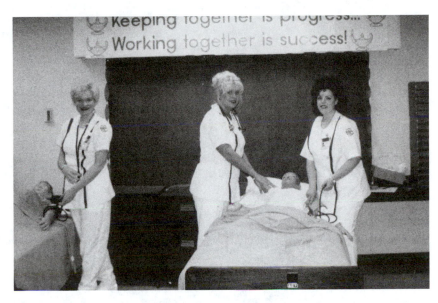

Some secondary vocational education students may choose to continue their health occupations experience by becoming Licensed Practical Nurses (LPN).

develop critical-thinking and problem-solving skills, manipulative skills, safety judgments, technical knowledge, and related occupational information preparing individuals for meaningful, productive employment in vocational industrial pursuits (National Association of Trade and Industrial Education, 1994).

Health Occupations Education

A limited number of programs in practical nursing were in operation after the Smith-Hughes Act of 1917, which broadly defined nursing as a trade and thus included under the trade and industrial provisions of the act (Calhoun and Finch, 1982). In 1956, practical nursing was included as part of the federal vocational education program. Venn (1964) points out that the program was usually conducted through a hospital or medical center, often with the cooperation of the local school district or a junior college.

The health occupations program is designed to acquaint individuals with the career options in the health services industry and to provide the knowledge, skills and attitudes necessary to succeed in the wide field of health occupation. Employment in the health services industry will continue to grow almost twice as fast as total nonfarm wage and salary employment. Demand for health care professionals is spurred by an aging population, new medical technologies that allow treatment of previously untreatable illnesses, and the

Specific occupational courses such as pharmacy technician may require both classroom instruction and clinical practice.

growth of outpatient and home care. Among the fastest growing areas are home health-care services and services provided in offices of physicians (U.S. Department of Labor, 1993).

There are four main issues in health care that have influenced the development of health-care occupations at the secondary level. They are the unequal valuableness of health care, questionable quality of health care, sky-rocketing costs, and responsibility for or control of health services (Sands, 1971). These four main issues are still relevant in the development of health care in today's society.

Technology Education

In October, 1904, Professor Charles R. Richards, Director of Manual Training at Columbia University, suggested the term "industrial arts" be substituted for manual training. The term was first used to designate work that developed as a reaction against the formalized courses inherited from Froebel (Foles,

Coover, and Mason, 1956). It was Froebel's recognition of the central importance of manual and industrial education that led to the major position manual training later occupied in kindergarten and elementary school.

Technology education (formerly industrial arts education) is the instructional program that acquaints people with their technological environment
and provides them with a broad knowledge of the applications of technology
in daily life. The Carl D. Perkins Vocational and Applied Technology Education Act of 1990 (PL 101-392) defined technology education as "an applied
discipline designed to promote technological literacy which provides knowledge and understanding of the impacts of technology including its organizations, techniques, tools, and skills to solve practical problems and extend
human capabilities in areas such as construction, manufacturing, communication, transportation, power, and energy" (American Vocational Association,
1990).

Technology education programs propose to help students:

- Develop an appreciation for the importance of technology.
- Make informed occupational and career choices.
- Apply tools, materials, processes, and technical concepts safely and effi-
ciently.
- Make wise consumer choices.
- Make appropriate adjustments to a rapidly changing environment.
- Recognize and deal with forces and trends that influence the future.
- Apply critical-thinking and problem-solving skills.
- Discover and develop individual talents.
- Apply creative abilities.
- Apply academic skills and the content of other school subjects (Interna-
tional Technology Education Association, 1993).

As an integral part of the school's curriculum, technology education
teaches students to understand, use, and control technology in an experimental laboratory environment. Students are taught the application of mathematics and science and how to use knowledge of technology to solve an
array of practical problems in the areas of communications, manufacturing,
construction, transportation, power, and energy.

Technical Education

The main thrust of technical education can be traced to the 1940s, when the
U.S. Office of Education recognized and proclaimed the need to train technicians who would work on jobs that required more limited competencies than
those of professional engineer but more than those needed by skilled
mechanics. As industry mushroomed after World War II, there were increasing demands for technical workers (Calhoun and Finch, 1982).

The technique of drafting and design technology has for many years constituted an important area of vocational education.

McMahon (1970) suggests that preparation for a technical occupation requires:

> *An understanding of, and ability to apply, those levels of mathematics and science appropriate to the occupation. And in those occupations that can be properly defined as technical, the mathematics and science required is more advanced than that required for a middle-type craft or skilled-trades occupations. (p. 23)*

The definition of technical is still somewhat unclear, with colleges, universities, vocational-technical schools, and technical institutes formulating their own definitions. However, Scott and Sarkees-Wircenski (1996) defined technical occupations as occupations that required workers to use higher levels of math, science, and technology to make decisions on the job than is normally required in skilled-trades occupations.

The majority of technical education programs are offered at the postsecondary level in public and private postsecondary institutions including community colleges, technical institutes, technical centers, engineering schools,

TABLE 8.1   Enrollment in Vocational Education Programs, 1960–1961 and 1978–1979.

| Program | Total Number Enrolled | | Percent Change |
	1960–61	1978–79	
Agriculture	805,322	971,726	21
Distribution	306,083	942,057	208
Health	62,160	798,520	1,185
Consumer and Homemaking	1,610,334	3,710,246	130
Technical	122,952	484,076	294
Trade and Industry	963,609	3,436,089	256
Occupational Home Economics	—	589,878	—
Industrial Arts	—	1,683,902	—
Office	—	3,469,134	—
Other	—	1,182,414	—
Total	**3,870,460**	**17,368,042**	**346**

Source: Warmbrod, J.R. (1981). Vocational education: Then and now. *VocEd, 56*(7), 30.

and four-year colleges offering technical programs of less than baccalaureate degree programs.

VOCATIONAL ENROLLMENTS BY PROGRAM AREA

The ensuing Vocational Act of 1963 declared that the major purposes of the federally-assisted program of vocational education include the maintenance, extension, and improvement of existing programs and the development of new programs so that persons of all ages in all communities will have access to high-quality vocational training or retraining. Subsequent federal legislation, principally the Vocational Education Amendments of 1968 and the Education Amendments of 1976, expanded the purposes of vocational education. With the passage of the Carl D. Perkins Vocational Education Acts (1984 and 1990) and the School-to-Work Opportunities Act of 1994, national attention has turned to the systems in place in this country for educating and training people for work.

From 1978–1979, total enrollment in secondary, postsecondary, and adult vocational education programs was more than four times greater than enrollment in 1960–1961 (Warmbrod, 1981). Table 8.1 displays enrollment in vocational education programs for 1960–1961 and 1978–1979.

From 1960–1961, 87 percent of all persons in vocational education were enrolled in home economics, trade and industry, and agricultural programs. For all programs in 1978–1979, consumer and homemaking, office occupations, and trade and industry accounted for one-fifth (20 to 22 percent) of the

TABLE 8.2 Distribution of Enrollment by Program Area, 1960–1961 and 1978–1979.

Program Area	Total Enrollment 1960–61 (%)	Enrollment in Six Programs 1978–79 (%)	Total Enrollment 1978–79 (%)
Agriculture	20.8	9.4	5.6
Distribution	7.9	9.1	5.4
Health	1.6	7.7	4.6
Consumer and Homemaking	41.6	35.9	21.5
Technical	3.2	4.7	2.8
Trade and Industry	24.9	33.2	20.0
Occupational Home Economics	—	—	3.4
Industrial Arts	—	—	9.8
Office	—	—	20.1
Other	—	—	6.8

Source: Warmbrod, J.R. (1981). Vocational education: Then and now. *VocEd, 56*(7), 31.

total enrollment as reported by Warmbrod (1981). Table 8.2 describes the distribution of enrollment by program area.

Secondary Level

Business was the most popular occupational program at the high school level, with more than half of all 1992 high school graduates completing at least one business course. Business was followed in popularity by trade and industry and then by technical and communications programs (NCES, 1995).

Although overall participation in occupationally specific curriculum declined somewhat over the decade from 1982 to 1992, trends varied by program area. The percentage of graduates completing at least one course in the technical and communications area, as well as the average number of credits earned in this program area, increased between 1982 and 1992. In contrast, both the percentage of graduates completing at least one trade and industry course and the average number of trade and industry credits earned declined over the decade (NCES, 1995).

Enrollments by Gender and Race

Males earn slightly more vocational credits than females, but females earn more of their vocational credits in consumer and homemaking education, while males earn notably more occupational credits. The pattern of vocational coursetaking also varies among racial/ethnic groups. Black and Native American students earn more vocational credits than other student groups;

Whites and Hispanics earn average amounts of vocational credits; and Asian American students earn fewer vocational credits than other students. Black students' higher level of coursetaking is confined mainly to the nonoccupational consumer and homemaking courses (NAVE, 1994).

Postsecondary Level

As was the case at the secondary level, the most popular 1992 postsecondary vocational program was business, with about 17 percent of all nonbaccalaureate students declaring a major in this area. Business was followed in popularity by health (11 percent) and then trade and industry programs. The combined technical fields (computers and data processing, engineering and science technologies, protective services, and communications technologies) accounted for 12 percent of all nonbaccalaureate majors (NCES, 1995).

In 1989, almost three-quarters of all postsecondary vocational students were enrolled in just three program areas: business (29 percent), health (22 percent), and technical (23 percent). An additional 15 percent were in the traditional trades, leaving only 11 percent of all postsecondary vocational enrollments in agriculture (10 percent), marketing (2 percent), family and consumer sciences (4 percent), and "undefined" areas (5 percent) (most likely students who are undecided) (Tuma, 1993).

Compared to secondary enrollments, these data show higher enrollments in health and technical fields and lower enrollments in the trades. According to Tuma (1993), postsecondary enrollment changes largely parallel employment projections. From 1986 to 1989, enrollments remained constant in most vocational fields, but deceased in business (39 percent to 28 percent) and increased in health (16 percent to 23 percent) and occupational home economics (2 percent to 5 percent). This matches U.S. Census Bureau data that show from 1990 to 2005, typists and word processors are among the fastest declining jobs, while nurses, medical assistants, home health aides, child-care workers, and food preparation workers are among the fastest growing or those with the largest job growth (U.S. Bureau of Census, 1992). A list of the fastest growing jobs for the twenty-first century is revealed in Appendix F.

Enrollments by Gender and Race

Although vocational program enrollments tend to be highly sex-typed, vocational students in general are 54 percent female and 46 percent male. Vocational students are more likely than other students in general to be Black or Hispanic; these students make up 18 percent of all postsecondary students but 24 percent of vocational students. Blacks are particularly likely to be overrepresented in vocational education, a fact that is not just due to their lower socioeconomic status (SES). Independently of SES, Blacks are more likely than individuals of other racial/ethnic groups to enroll in vocational programs rather than other types of postsecondary programs (NAVE, 1994). The reasons for this enrollment pattern are unclear.

TABLE 8.3 Distribution of Secondary Vocational Teachers
by Vocational Program Area

Program Area	Percent of Teachers in Area
Agricultural education	9
Business and office	33
Health occupations	3
Marketing and distributive education	4
Home economics	14
Trade and industrial education	20
Technical/communication	3
Other	12

Source: National Assessment of Vocational Education (NAVE) (1994).

Final report to Congress volume II: Participation in and quality of vocational education, p. 62. Washington, DC: Office of Educational Research and Improvement, U.S. Department of Education.

Note: Numbers do not add to 100 because of rounding.

Vocational education at the postsecondary level appears to offer the best hope for bringing the educationally, socially, and economically disadvantaged into the mainstream of American life.

TEACHERS IN VOCATIONAL EDUCATION

The Perkins Act calls for an assessment of "the preparation and qualifications of teachers of vocational and academic curricula." This section discusses the qualifications of teachers in secondary and postsecondary institutions, using measures of preparedness such as teaching experience, education credentials, nonteaching work experience, and occupational credentials.

Secondary Education

The percentage of occupational vocational education teachers in each of the main program areas is shown in Table 8.3. Business education is the largest field, followed by trade and industry. Together, these two fields comprise over half of all secondary vocational education teachers. Home economics teachers who prepare students for occupations make up 14 percent of the total; each of the other specific fields accounts for less than 10 percent.

Demographic Characteristics
From 1990 to 1991, vocational education teachers were a little older, on average, than nonvocational teachers (43.5 years as compared to 41.9 years). Gender differences between vocational education teachers and other teachers are

TABLE 8.4   Demographic Characteristics of Secondary Vocational and Nonvocational Teachers, 1990–1991

Demographic Characteristic	Vocational	Nonvocational
Average age (years)	43.5	41.9
Sex (percent)		
Male	52	51
Female	48	49
Race/Ethnicity (percent)		
Native American	1	1
Asian American	1	1
Black	9	6
White	88	90
Hispanic	2	3

Source: National Assessment of Vocational Education (NAVE) (1994).

Final report to Congress volume II: Participation in and quality of vocational education, p. 63. Washington, DC: Office of Educational Research and Improvement, U.S. Department of Education.

Note: Numbers may not add to 100 because of rounding.

not significant, but race/ethnic differences are. Vocational education teachers are more likely than others to be Black although most are White (Table 8.4).

There are few substantial differences in race or ethnicity by program area, although there are some differences by age. Agriculture teachers tend to be considerately younger (38.7 years) than average, while teachers in trade and industry tend to be older (45.6 years) (NAVE, 1994).

Education and Experience

Some formal postsecondary education is required for public school teaching in all states, and the credentials of teachers are considered to be measures of quality in educational institutions. Outside the regular education system, occupational credentials such as licenses reflect the acquisition of skills that can be essential for teaching vocational subjects. Work experience outside of teaching, if related to the subject taught in school, can be another valuable element in teacher preparation, especially for those teaching vocational subjects. Hamermesh and Rees (1984) suggest that work experience tends to improve performance, and pay scales usually recognize this improvement by rewarding experienced workers more than beginners.

Academic teachers in the school systems attempting to integrate academic and vocational subjects might also benefit from experience outside of school. Data on the teaching experience, nonteaching work experience, and educational and occupational credentials are provided in Table 8.5.

On the average, both academic and vocational teachers have about the same number of years of teaching experience—seventeen and eighteen years respectively, although teachers in vocational schools have less (fourteen

TABLE 8.5   Preparation of Secondary Academic and Vocational Education Teachers

Education and Experience	Academic Teachers	Vocational Teachers		
		All	Comprehensive Schools	Vocational Schools
Highest degree (percent)				
High school diploma or GED	0	2	1	4
Associate's degree or two-year certificate	*	6	2	22
Bachelor's degree	40	39	41	31
Degree above bachelor's	60	50	55	33
Nonteaching occupational certificate or license	0	4	2	10
Mean years of teaching experience	18	17	17	14
Related nonteaching work experience (percent)	19	66	63	78

Source: National Assessment of Vocational Education (NAVE) (1994).

Final report to Congress volume II: Participation in and quality of vocational education, p. 65. Washington, DC: Office of Educational Research and Improvement, U.S. Department of Education.

*Less than 1%.

years) than others. Secondary vocational teachers tend to have less formal education than academic teachers. Vocational teachers are much more likely than academic teachers to have related work experience. Only 23 percent of the secondary vocational teachers have nonteaching occupational licenses or certificates; that is one-third of the 66 percent who have occupational experience related to their teaching field.

Credentials and Work Experience

The tendency for vocational teachers to have less education and more work experience than academic teachers is heavily concentrated in trade and industrial education. According to Lynch (1993), this pattern of less education and more work experience goes back many years.

> *Beginning with the . . . 1917 Smith-Hughes Act and continuing to the present time, nearly all states substitute years of work experience [for] college preparation [in] certifying T&I teachers. In fact, only Hawaii and Wisconsin require the baccalaureate degree for initial certification. . . . Seven states require a baccalaureate degree and five states require an associate degree for full certification. Beginning teachers in 43 states may teach T&I programs without any college credits. (p. 11)*

Most states do require from sixteen to 200 hours of pedagogical preparation in the first year of teaching, typically obtained through workshops or college courses. Many states also require licensure in occupations such as cosmetology, health technologies, plumbing, and auto mechanics. In addition, twelve to eighteen states require individuals within the first year of teaching, or pre-service teachers lacking work experience, to pass National Occupational Competency Testing Institute (NOCTI) tests (Lynch, 1993).

Postsecondary Education

The characteristics of vocational teachers in public two-year postsecondary institutions differ somewhat from those of their secondary counterparts.

Demographic Characteristics

While secondary teachers are about equally distributed by gender, the faculty in two-year postsecondary institutions are more likely to be male (61 percent) than female (39 percent). This difference reflects a broader pattern in education. The more advanced the education level taught, and the higher the prestige and salaries, the more likely the faculty are to be male. Most elementary teachers are female; secondary teachers in grades 9 through 12 are about 50/50; two-year postsecondary faculty are about 60 percent male/40 percent female; and the proportions of male faculty in four-year institutions range from 71 percent in liberal arts colleges to 81 percent in private research universities. Although both academic and vocational faculty follow this postsecondary gender pattern, vocational faculty members are more likely than academic teachers to be male (Russel, Cox, Williamson, Bosmier, Javitis, Fairweather, and Zimbler, 1990).

The majority of vocational teachers at both levels are White (91 percent of postsecondary and 88 percent of secondary faculty). However, while secondary vocational teachers are more likely than others to be Black, there are few significant racial/ethnic differences between academic and vocational faculty at the postsecondary level (NAVE, 1994).

Education and Experience

As at the secondary level, two-year postsecondary vocational faculty have less formal education than their academic counterparts. This is especially the case for faculty in postsecondary trade and industry programs. Surprisingly, the distribution of highest degrees for two-year postsecondary vocational faculty is similar to that of secondary teachers. About 15 percent have less than a bachelor's degree, as compared to 12 percent of secondary teachers; 36 percent have B.A.'s, as compared to 39 percent of secondary teachers; and 50 percent of both groups have advanced degrees. Nonvocational faculty at the postsecondary level have considerably more education than at the seconary level (Hoachlander, Kaufman, Levesque, and Houser, 1992).

In their study, Hoachlander and others (1992) found that a substantial majority of postsecondary vocational faculty (71 percent) were trained in specific occupational fields, while a bare majority (53 percent) of nonvocational faculty were trained in specific academic fields, such as math, English, and social sciences. The proportion of vocational faculty with specific occupational training was fairly constant across subject matter fields, except for those in trade and industry. A smaller portion of trade and industry faculty have specific training than do other vocational teachers, and a larger portion were general education majors.

Research by Hoachlander and others (1992), also revealed that vocational faculty members in two-year postsecondary institutions had somewhat lower formal status than other faculty in public two-year postsecondary institutions. They were less likely to be professors and more likely to be assistant professors, instructors, or lecturers. Moreover, at each level of rank except one, the average salaries of vocational faculty were slightly lower than those of other faculty (the exception is at the professional level). The combination of lower status and lower pay within rank meant that the mean salaries of vocational faculty were lower than those of other faculty members ($30,953 versus $33,460).

Value of Occupational Experience and Formal Education

The fact that vocational education teachers in general, and trade and industry teachers in particular, have less formal education and more occupational experience than others has been at issue for some time. There is controversy about whether trade and industry teachers, or any teachers, should be able to teach in public schools without a college degree.

Historically, vocational educators have argued that work experience is indispensable for teaching students how to perform certain kinds of jobs. Indeed, it is hard to see how teachers who have never been auto mechanics, welders, or electricians could teach auto mechanics, welding or electrical wiring to students. According to NAVE (1994), the findings across many studies conducted over a period of forty years suggest that extensive occupational experience confers no particular benefits on vocational teaching, although a few years' experience has a positive impact. Formal postsecondary education is postively associated with desirable teacher and student outcomes. In essence, trade and industry teachers would be better off with more formal education and less occupational experience.

Implications for Teacher Preparation

Vocational education is changing as a result of reform activities at the federal, state, and local levels. States and localities are responding to the reforms called for in the Perkins Act and the federal School-to-Work initiative. Several states are undertaking fundamental reforms of secondary education to better prepare nonbaccalaureate students for the workforce. The reforms that teachers will need to be prepared for include

- an orientation toward workforce preparation for a majority of the secondary student body;
- emphasis on developing cognitive and technical skills in an integrated context;
- preparing nonbaccalaureate students for postsecondary education in community colleges and technical institutes through arrangements such as tech-prep programs; and
- student participation in work experience programs.

If such reforms are to be effected, there will have to be substantial changes in the way teachers are prepared in colleges and universities. Academic teachers will need more familiarity with the world of work, possibly through courses in business and technology, or through work experience outside of teaching. They will also need to learn how to apply features of their academic disciplines to work-related subjects. Vocational teachers will need more and more vigorous courses in the liberal arts. For many prospective vocational teachers, a greater emphasis on computers will be required. Beyond these changes in teacher education programs, states will need to tailor the preparation of their teachers to particular elements of reform in their system.

SELECTED ENTITIES INFLUENCING GROWTH IN VOCATIONAL EDUCATION PROGRAMS

American Vocational Education Research Association (AVERA)

The American Vocational Education Research Association was organized in 1966. It is a professional association for scholars and others with research interests in the relationship between education and work. AVERA information can be accessed via the Internet (http://www.lsu.edu/guests/avera). Followoing is a list of AVERA resolutions:

- To stimulate research and development activities related to vocational education.
- To stimulate the development of training programs designed to prepare persons for responsibilities in research in vocational education.
- To foster cooperative effort in research and development activities within the total program of vocational education.
- To facilitate the dissemination of research findings and the diffusion of knowledge.

Regular members are persons actively engaged in research and development activities related to vocational education. Members are entitled to the rights and privileges of the association without restriction. Student members of AVERA are persons actively pursuing graduate degrees as full-time resident students (as defined by the student's institution). Student members are entitled to the rights and privileges of AVERA members except they may not vote or hold elective office in the association. Emeritus members are members who have officially retired.

There is an annual business meeting of the association in conjunction with the American Vocational Association Convention. Between conventions, business of the association is conducted by the Executive Committee that is composed of the president, vice president (president elect), recording secretary, treasurer, membership secretary, historian, and past president.

AVERA organizes presentations of research reports, symposia, and other programs of interest to research scholars. AVERA members who are also members of the American Educational Research Association (AERA) form the Special Interest Group on Vocational Education within AERA. During AERA meetings, this Special Interest Group conducts special sessions on research in vocational education.

Publications originated by AVERA include: the *Journal of Vocational Education Research,* a refereed scholarly and quarterly publication, and the *Beacon,* a quarterly newsletter of the association. In addition, AVERA produces a directory of members and occasional monographs.

The Southern Regional Education Board (SREB)

The SREB High Schools That Work program is the nation's first large-scale effort to combine challenging academic courses and vocational studies to raise the achievement of career-bound high school students. The SREB-State Vocational Education Consortium is a partnership of states, school systems, and school sites. Superintendents, principals, teachers, and counselors in the multistate network are actively involved in making dramatic changes in the way they prepare students for work and further education in the twenty-first century. Launched in 1987 with 28 sites in 13 states, the consortium has rapidly expanded its High Schools That Work program to include more than 300 sites in 19 states. The Consortium includes—Alabama, Arkansas, Florida, Georgia, Kentucky, Louisiana, Maryland, Mississippi, North Carolina, Oklahoma, South Carolina, Tennessee, Texas, Virginia, and West Virginia—plus Delaware, Indiana, Kansas, and Pennsylvania (SREB, 1997). SREB information can be accessed via the Internet (http://www.peach.net/sreb).

National Center for Research in Vocational Education (NCRVE)

NCRVE's mission is to strengthen education to prepare all individuals for lasting and rewarding employment and lifelong learning. NCRVE is the nation's largest center for research, development, dissemination, and outreach in work-related education. Headquartered at the University of California at

This speaker is addressing vocational education participants at the 11th Annual High Schools That Work (HSTW) Staff Development Conference (July 9–12, 1997).

Berkeley (http://www.ncrve.berkeley.edu) since 1988, NCRVE is presently an eight-member consortium, with Berkeley assisted in its efforts by the University of Illinois, MPR Associates; University of Minnesota; RAND; Teachers College, Columbia University; the University of Wisconsin; and Virginia Polytechnic Institute and State University. The presence of NCRVE or one of its members in nearly every region of the country puts it in contact with the enormous diversity of educational institutions and labor markets in the United States. It also connects NCRVE with practitioners in each geographic region of the country (personal communication with Holly Holligan of NCRVE, October 16, 1997).

SUMMARY

- Among the vocational education students who concentrate their vocational course-taking, business and trade and industry ("the trades") are by far the two most popular program areas. Technical education courses are also relatively popular.

- Secondary vocational enrollments continue to be highly sex-typed. The lack of movement of females into male vocational areas is probably due to labor market growth in some traditionally female fields, such as health care, child care, food service, and other service industries. Males' movement into business may also result more from their interest in computer word processing skills than from interest in secretarial skills.

- Vocational education is a relatively large and stable part of postsecondary education system. Vocational programs serve a wider array of students, particularly special population students, than do other postsecondary programs, mainly by providing programs in more diverse and accessible institutions. Blacks and Hispanics are overrepresented in postsecondary vocational education, perhaps because of a greater interest in the shorter programs offered by these institutions, as well as greater concentration of nonpublic institutions in urban areas.

- Secondary vocational teachers tend to have less formal education than others, but they have more related occupational experience and credentials. This emphasis on occupational experience in lieu of formal education is concentrated in trade and industrial education, which has been guided by state policies in a tradition going back to the Smith-Hughes Act of 1917. The educational level of postsecondary vocational faculty is about the same as that of secondary vocational teachers. Those in trade and industry have even less formal education than their counterparts in secondary schools.

- Among the entities that had an impact on the growth of vocational education prior to the 1990s and beyond are the American Vocational Education Research Association (AVERA), Southern Regional Education Board (SREB), and the National Center for Research in Vocational Education (NCRVE).

DISCUSSION QUESTIONS AND ACTIVITIES

1. Describe the major program areas of vocational education.

2. What types of classes are available to postsecondary students and adults who desire to engage in the study of vocational education?

3. Describe the instructional delivery system for a typical postsecondary vocational area (**Library Research**).

4. Interview a technology education instructor and prepare a report for the class about the changes in the program resulting from federal funding.

5. Select a vocational field, preferably one other than your area of concentration, and prepare a report on its history and impact on your local community or state.

6. Describe the preparation of vocational education teachers for the eight major areas of vocational education.

7. How does today's vocational education compare with vocational education in the early 1960s? What changes have occurred during the past thirty-five years?

8. Develop a research paper on the demand and supply of secondary and postsecondary vocational teachers for the past ten years (**Library Research**).

REFERENCES

American Home Economics Association. (1994). *A conceptual framework for the 21st century.* Alexandria, VA: Author.

American Vocational Association. (1990). *The AVA guide to the Carl D. Perkins vocational and applied technology education act of 1990.* Alexandria, VA: Author.

Britton, R.K., and Fick, S.L. (1956). Fifty years of progress in trade and industrial education. *American Vocational Journal, 31*(9), 83–90, 104.

Brown, T.C., and Logan, W.B. (1956). Fifty years of progress in distributive education. *American Vocational Journal, 31*(9), 57–66, 111.

Calhoun, C.C., and Finch, A.V. (1982). *Vocational education: Concepts and operations.* Belmont, CA: Wadsworth Publishing Company.

Cox, D.E., McCormick, F.G., and Miller, G.M. (1989). Agricultural education model. *Agricultural Education Magazine, 61*(11), 9–12.

DECA Inc. (1992). *Marketing education and DECA: Essential factors in creating a quality work force.* Reston, VA: A report prepared by the Corporate National Advisory Board of DECA, an Association of Marketing Students.

Foles, R.G., Coover, S.L., and Mason, W.R. (1956). Fifty years of progress in industrial arts education. *American Vocational Journal, 31*(9), 75–82.

Gordon, H.R.D. (1985). Analysis of the postsecondary educational attainment of agricultural education graduates of the high school class of 1972. *Journal of Vocational Education Research, 10*(2), 11–18.

Haas, R.B. (1972). The origin and early development of distributive education—parts I, II, and III. In S.S. Schrumpf (Ed.), *The origin and development of distributive education* (p. 9). Hightston, NJ: McGraw-Hill Book Company.

Hamermesh, D.S., and Rees, A. (1984). *The economics of work and pay.* New York: Harper and Row.

Hamlin, H.M. (1956). Fifty years of progress in agricultural education. *American Vocational Journal, 31*(9), 39–46.

Hoachlander, E.G., Kaufman, P., Levesque, K., and Houser, J. (1992). *Vocational education in the United States, 1996–1990.* Washington, DC: U.S. Department of Education, National Center for Education Statistics.

International Technology Education Association. (1993). *Technology education: The new basics.* Reston, VA: Author.

Lawson, D.S., and Creighton, M. (1956). Fifty years of progress in home economics education. *American Vocational Journal, 31*(9), 67–74, 104.

Lee, J.S. (1994). *Program planning guide for agriscience and technology education.* Danville, IL: Interstate Publishers.

Lynch, R.L. (1993). *Vocational teacher education in U.S. colleges and universities and its responsiveness to the Carl D. Perkins Vocational and Applied Technology Education Act of 1990.* Draft report prepared for the National Assessment of Vocational Education. Athens, GA: University of Georgia, School of Leadership Lifelong Learning.

McMahon, G.G. (1970). Technical education: A problem of definition. *American Vocational Journal, 45*(3), 23.

Mason, R.E., and Husted, S.W. (1997). *Cooperative occupational education* (5th ed.). Danville, IL: Interstate Publishers, Inc.

National Assessment of Vocational Education (NAVE) (1994). *Final report to Congress volume II: Participation in and quality of vocational education.* Washington, DC: Office of Educational Research and Improvement, U.S. Department of Education.

National Association of Trade and Industrial Education (NATIE) (1994). *Workforce 2020: Action report school-to-work opportunities national voluntary skill standards.* Leesburg, VA: Author.

National Center for Educational Statistics (NCES) (1992). *Vocational education in the United States: 1969–1990.* Washington, DC: Office of Educational Research and Improvement, U.S. Department of Education.

National Center for Educational Statistics (NCES) (1995). *Vocational education in the United States: The early 1990s.* Washington, DC: Office of Educational Research and Improvement, U.S. Department of Education.

National Center for Educational Statistics (NCES) (1997, April). Quick facts. *Techniques, 7.*

National Commission on Excellence in Education. (1983). *A nation at risk: The imperative for educational reform.* U.S. Department of Education.

Phillips, J. (1994). All business is global. In A. McEntire (Ed.), *Expanding horizons in business education* (pp. 35–45). Reston, VA: National Business Association, National Business Education Yearbook, No. 32.

Russell, H., Cox, S., Williamson, C., Boismier, J., Javitis, H., Fairweather, J., and Zimbler, L. (1990). *Faculty in higher education institutions.* Washington, DC: U.S. Department of Education, National Center for Education Statistics.

Sands, W.F. (1971). The health care crisis: Can vocational education deliver? *American Vocational Journal, 46*(9), 24.

Scott, J.L., and Sarkees-Wircenski, M. (1996). *Overview of vocational and applied technology education.* Homewood, IL: American Technical Publishers.

Southern Regional Education Board (1997). *High schools that work: A dynamic program blends academic and vocational education to raise the achievement of career-bound students.* Atlanta, GA: Author.

Stewart, D. (1994). Home economics division considers name change. *Vocational Education Journal, 69*(6), 53–54.

Tuma, J. (1993). *Patterns of enrollment in postsecondary vocational and academic education.* Berkley, CA: MPR Associates.

U.S. Bureau of the Census. (1992). *Statistical Abstracts of the United States.* Washington, DC: U.S. Department of Commerce.

U.S. Department of Labor. (1993). The American work force: 1992–2005. *Occupational Outlook Quarterly, 37*(3), 2–44.

Venn, G. (1964). *Man, education, and work.* Washington, DC: American Council on Education.

Vo, C.D. (1997, April). This is agriculture? *Techniques,* Volume 72, Number 4, 30–33.

Walker, A.L., Huffman, H., and Beaumont, J.A. (1956). Fifty years of progress in business education. *American Vocational Journal, 31*(9), 47–54, 104.

Warmbrod, J.R. (1981). Vocational education: Then and now. *VocEd, 56*(7), 29–31.

9

DEVELOPMENT OF VOCATIONAL STUDENT ORGANIZATIONS

Vocational education's commitment to student organizations stems from the belief that the total development of individuals is essential to the preparation of competent workers. Research and experience have shown us that student organization activities are the most effective way to teach some of the critical skills that are necessary if students are to reach their fullest potential. The organizations are designed to allow students a vehicle for exploring their interest in an occupational field and to learn and refine leadership, social, and citizenship skills (Harris and Sweet, 1981).

Vocational student organizations (VSOs) bring together students interested in careers in specific vocational fields, providing them with a range of individual, cooperative, and competitive activities designed to expand their leadership and job-related skills. Some VSO activities are incorporated into the regular classroom curriculum, while others support curricular efforts outside the classroom. Student members take part in chapter meetings; serve on committees; run for elected positions; participate in local, state, or national workshops, conferences, and competitive events; help with chapter fundraising activities and community service projects; and serve as mentors for other vocational students. This chapter provides an overview of the following areas: Public Law 81-740, organizational structure and role of the vocational student organizations, federally recognized vocational student organizations, and vocational student organizations and the School-to-Work Opportunities Act of 1994.

PUBLIC LAW 81-740

Commonly referred to as Public Law 740, this act was passed in 1950 and was the only act to federally charter a vocational student organization. It clearly established the integral relationship of a vocational student organization to the instructional program and represented the first time that the U.S. Office of Education was recognized for being associated with vocational youth organizations. Public Law 740 allowed USOE officials to work with such organizations (Vaughn, Vaughn, and Vaughn, 1990).

Although the law chartered only one vocational student organization (the one for vocational agriculture), it established the pattern of treating existing and future vocational student organizations as integral parts of vocational instruction. It is because of this act that all vocational student organizations are now recognized as essential components of the education provided for students of vocational education (Vaughn, Vaughn, and Vaughn, 1990).

ORGANIZATIONAL STRUCTURE AND ROLE OF THE VSOS

VSOs are organized into local chapters that are typically formed by vocational students in a class or from several classes within a vocational program area. Each chapter is sponsored by an instructor who serves as the chapter faculty and advisor. State departments of education typically support VSO activities by designating state advisors for each vocational program area, and by providing administrative or financial assistance for local, state, and national meetings and conferences. Each VSO also has a national office, focusing on policies, guidelines, and curricula to assist instructors in implementing VSO programs.

Leadership skills are encouraged by having students participate in chapter planning and decision making, and by running for chapter offices. Fundraising and community service are also common activities that help build team spirit and individual initiative. In addition, local, regional, state, and national contests serve as "vocational skill Olympics."

While VSO contests can vary, the national contests follow a set format in which students complete industry developed written and performance tests of job-related skills. The written tests focus on relevant academic knowledge, while the performance tests assess vocational skills. For example, construction students may be required to build a cabinet, or the corner of a house; marketing students may develop an advertising campaign; business students may perform word processing or bookkeeping assignments; and livestock or crops raised by agriculture students may be judged on a variety of dimensions. Other performance tests assess leadership abilities through such activities as speeches and mock job interviews. While only a small percentage of students may make it to the national competition, many more participate in state competitions, with even more in regional and local competitions.

Because of such opportunities for student skill development, recognition, and leadership, VSO membership is widely regarded as a valuable adjunct to more formal education, particularly as a means to increase student motivation and professionalism.

Membership Status of VSOs

In the 1980s, membership growth that had continued in the 1960s and 1970s was stagnant or beginning to decrease for many VSOs (Hannah, 1993). Only FFA and the newer VSOs, such as Technology Student Association (TSA) and Health Occupations Students of America (HOSA), have had a continuing increase in membership size. This increase is probably attributed to the expanding opportunities in these fields. Table 9.1 shows membership size during 1997.

Hannah (1993) describes four reasons for the declining membership of vocational student organizations.

1. **Fewer students.** There's a smaller population of school-age children in the 1990s. Some call this the "baby bust" generation that began in 1965 and ended in 1976. According to census data from 1990, the number of 14- to 17-year-olds plunged 18 percent in the 1980s and the number of 18- to 24-year olds dropped 11 percent.
2. **Fewer electives.** With more students directed toward the college track, fewer students have the time or desire to take vocational programs. While most VSOs have been able to maintain their membership as a percentage of the vocational student population, overall membership dropped because of a decline in vocational course enrollment.
3. **Reduced state role.** Because of state budget cuts and the reduction in federal funds for VSO activities, many state supervisors have been told to limit their student organization time by 5 to 15 percent. Teachers say today they are held more accountable for students' success in meeting curriculum objectives, so they have less time for VSOs.
4. **Fewer teachers.** There has been a reduction in programs to prepare teachers in vocational education areas, which in turn affects VSOs. Many chapter advisors became associated with student organizations through their college experience. However, many vocational teachers today come from other disciplines or from industry and often don't recognize student organizations as a valuable learning opportunity.

TABLE 9.1   Nationally Recognized Vocational Student Organizations (VSOs)

Organization	Year Founded	Education Levels Served	Membership Size (1992–1993)	Membership Size[a] (1996–1997)
National FFA Organization (FFA)	1928	Secondary Postsecondary	400,000	452,885
Future Business Leaders of America-Phi Beta Lambda (FBLA-PBL)	1943	Middle Secondary (FBLA) Postsecondary (PBL)	275,000	250,000
Distributive Education Clubs of America (DECA)	1945	Secondary Postsecondary	180,000	136,511
Future Homemakers of America/Home Economics Related Occupations (FHA/HERO)	1945	Middle Secondary Postsecondary	285,000	242,000
Vocational Industrial Clubs of America (VICA)	1965	Secndary Postsecondary	300,000	245,000
Health Occupations Students of America (HOSA)	1976	Secndary Postsecondary	40,000	61,000
Technology Student Association (TSA)	1977	Elementary Middle Secondary	70,000	150,000
National Postsecondary Agricultural Student Organization (PAS)	1979	Postsecondary	Not available	1,122
Natonal Young Farmers Educational Association (NYFEA)	1982	Adult	25,000	14,403
Business Professionals of America (BPA)	1988	Secondary Postsecondary	58,000	45,314

Source: National Assessment of Vocational Education. (1994). *Final Report to Congress volume IV: Access to programs and services for special populations, p. 138.* Washington, DC: Office of Educational Research and Improvement, U.S. Department of Education.

[a]Information pertaining to membership size for 1996–1997 was obtained through personal communications with the VSOs during April 14–25, 1997.

FEDERALLY RECOGNIZED VSOS

The term federally recognized VSOs include student organizations for each vocational program area, at the middle school, secondary (high school), postsecondary, and in one case, the adult level. The following VSOs are associated with the vocational program areas:

Agriculture

- National FFA Organization (formerly Future Farmers of America)
- National Postsecondary Agricultural Student Organization (PAS)
- National Young Farmers Educational Association (NYFEA)

Business/Office

- Business Professionals of America (BPA)
- Future Business Leaders of America—Phi Beta Lambda (FBLA-PBL)

Consumer/Homemaking and Occupational Home Economics

- Future Homemakers of America/Home Economics Related Occupations (FHA/HERO)

Marketing

- Distributive Education Clubs of America (DECA)

Health Occupations

- Health Occupations Students of America (HOSA)

Trades and Technical Fields

- Vocational Industrial Clubs of America (VICA)

Technology Education (formerly Industrial Arts)

- Technology Student Association (TSA)

More information on the structure of each VSO is provided in Table 9.1. Although VSO participation is obviously dependent on student interest and enrollment in each vocational field, it also seems to be related to the length of time the VSO has been in existence.

Future Farmers of America (FFA)

The FFA is an intracurricular activity for vocational education agriculture. For many years previous to the FFA movement, vocational agriculture clubs existed in many parts of the United States. The movement received its first definite recognition as a state organization in Virginia. Professor Henry C. Groseclose of Virginia Tech, while confined to a hospital in 1926, wrote the constitution and bylaws of the FFA. This constitution and the bylaws with the accompanying ceremonies attracted national attention. Leaders of vocational education in agriculture in other states soon realized that such an organization was exceedingly worthwhile. Within two years after the FFA was founded, six

FIGURE 9.1   The Official FFA Emblem

states in the southern region had similar organizations. A national organization meeting was held in November 1928, at Kansas City, Missouri. At this
meeting national officers were elected and the National Constitution and
bylaws adopted (Phipps, 1972).

Prior to 1965, states that had separate schools for White and Black stu-
dents had two youth organizations for agriculture students—The Future
Farmers of America and The New Farmers of America (NFA) (Roberts, 1971).
The NFA was started as early as 1928, and the first convention was held at
Tuskegee Institute, in August 1935. Thirteen states were represented in the
organizational meeting (Hawkins, Prosser, and Wright, 1951). In 1965, the
NFA merged with the FFA (Vaughn, Vaughn, and Vaughn, 1990).

The FFA was expanded in 1963 to include students from off-farm agricultural programs, and girls were officially admitted into the organizations in
1969 (Vaughn, Vaughn, and Vaughn, 1990). The organization changed its
name in 1988 from Future Farmers of America to the National FFA Organization to reflect its evolution response to expanded agricultural opportunities
encompassing science, business, and technology in addition to production
farming (Mason and Husted, 1997).

Today, FFA members are preparing for agricultural careers through secondary high schools, technical schools, and four-year colleges and universities.

Address: Phone: (317)802-6060
National FFA Organization
6060 FFA Drive
P.O. Box 68960
Indianapolis, Indiana 46268

FIGURE 9.2 The Official FBLA-PBL Emblems

Future Business Leaders of America (FBLA) and Phi Beta Lambda (PBL)

The purpose of FBLA-PBL is to provide as an integral part of the instructional program additional opportunities for students in business and office education to develop vocational and career supportive competencies, and to promote civic and personal responsibilities.

The FBLA concept was developed in 1937 by Hamden L. Farkner of Teachers College, Columbia University, New York City (Vaughn, Vaughn, and Vaughn, 1990). Early in the 1940s, leading teachers in the South, saw an opportunity to help young people achieve success in their business careers through a national organization with state and local chapters. Sponsored by the National Council of Business Education, the Future Business Leaders of America established its first chapter, in Johnson City, Tennessee on February 3, 1942 (Santo, 1986). However, it did not become a national organization until 1946.

A separate postsecondary division of FBLA, Phi Beta Lambda (PBL) was established in 1958 and achieved independent status in 1969 (Binkley and Byers, 1982).

Address: Phone: (703)860-3334
FBLA PBL Inc.   Fax: (703)758-0749
1912 Association Drive
Reston, VA 20191

Distributive Education Clubs of America (DECA)

The mission of DECA is to enhance the education of students with interests in marketing, management, and entrepreneurship. Roberts (1971) points out that DECA had its origin in local clubs organized during the years 1938 to

FIGURE 9.3   The Official DECA Emblem

1942. These local clubs, known under various names such as Future Retailers, Future Merchants, Future Distributors, and Distributive Education Clubs were organized to meet the need for social and professional growth and the common interests of students in cooperative classes.

DECA began in 1947 as the Distributors Clubs of America. The first interstate conference was held that year in Memphis, Tennessee. In 1950, the name was changed to Distributive Education Clubs of America (Vaughn, Vaughn, and Vaughn, 1990). A postsecondary division of DECA-Delta Epsilon Chi (DEC) was established in 1961 to meet the needs of students enrolled in marketing and distributive education programs in junior colleges, community colleges, technical institutes, and area vocational technical schools. The first Junior Collegiate (postsecondary) National Conference was held in 1965 in Chicago (DECA Handbook, 1995).

Address: Phone: (703)860-5000
Distributive Education Clubs of America   Fax: (703)860-4013
1908 Association Drive
Reston, VA 20121

The Future Homemakers of America (FHA)

Once exclusively geared toward future housewives, FHA now has men as members. FHA focuses on consumer home economics and balancing work and family. FHA is the only in-school student organization with the family as the center focus.

As early as 1920, high school home economics students belonged to home economics clubs. The clubs had many different names (Junior Homemakers, Betty Lamp Clubs, and Future Homemakers) and structures. In Chicago, on June 11, 1945, a group of national officer candidates and a group of advisers drew up a temporary constitution. They also selected the name for the proposed national youth organization for students of home economics education: Future Homemakers of America (FHA/HERO Chapter Handbook, 1991).

In 1965, New Homemakers of America (a national organization for Black students enrolled in homemaking) merged with Future Homemakers of America (Vaughn, Vaughn, and Vaughn, 1990). The New Homemakers of America

FIGURE 9.4　The Official FHA/HERO Emblem

was founded on June 19, 1945 at Tennessee Agricultural and Industrial State College, Nashville (Hawkins, Prosser, and Wright, 1951). Prior to the New Homemakers of America, Blacks participated in developing homemaking clubs such as New Homemakers, Progressive Homemakers, and Young Homemakers. Future Homemakers of America Inc. (1996) cites Dr. Hazel Frost as the first national adviser for both FHA and NHA.

FHA expanded its organization in 1971 to include a division of Home Economics Related Occupations (HERO) for students studying occupational home economics (FFA/HERO Chapter Handbook, 1991). HERO was created to focus development on students who intended to be employed for gain in one of the many subfields of home economics (Adams, 1993).

Address:　　　　　　　　　　　　　Phone: (703)476-4900
Future Homemakers of America, Inc.　Fax: (703)860-2713
1910 Association Drive
Reston, VA 20191

Vocational Industrial Club of America (VICA)

The first national organization for students in trade and industrial (T&I) education, the Future Craftsmen of America, was formed by educators during the 1920s (VICA Leadership Handbook, 1989). The Future Craftsmen of America grew out of a recognition of the needs of students for industrial occupation. The organization failed in its second year of operation, but individual states kept the idea alive with organizations of their own (Binkley and Byers, 1982). Santo (1986) points out that the Future Craftsmen organization was destined for failure because its founders had not involved industry and labor.

In 1960, interest resurfaced for a national organization for T&I students among state supervisors and teacher trainers. At the American Vocational Association Convention, a committee was established to study the possibility of a national organization. By February 1965, existing vocational education groups agreed to finance the start-up effort including those from Alabama, Arkansas,

Presentation of VICA state winners to a local county board of education.

Georgia, Indiana, Ohio, Oklahoma, North Carolina, Missouri, South Carolina, Tennessee, Texas, Virginia, and West Virginia. The Future Farmers of America made the first financial contribution (VICA Leadership Handbook, 1989).

VICA was officially started at a Trade and Industrial Youth Conference in Nashville, Tennessee, in May 1965. The Postsecondary Division was officially formed in 1969. Today, VICA works directly with business and industry to maintain American productivity, quality, and competitiveness.

Address:
Vocational Industrial Club
  of America, Inc.
P.O. Box 3000
Leesburg, VA 20177

Phone: (703)777-8810
Fax: (703)777-8999

FIGURE 9.5   The Official VICA Logo

FIGURE 9.6   The Official Logo of Business Professionals of America (BPA)

Business Professionals of America (BPA)

Shortly after the passage of the Vocational Education Act of 1963, the need for a student organization to provide for students enrolled in vocational office programs was recognized. In 1964, at the AVA meeting, it was suggested that a study group be established to determine if state supervisors of office education wanted a youth group similar to those serving other curriculum areas of vocational education. Most did, and in July 1966, Iowa, Kansas, and Wisconsin formed the Vocational Office Education Clubs of America. The group was later incorporated as the Office Education Association (OEA). In 1988, the name of OEA was changed to Business Professionals of America with new logo, emblem, and colors (Business Professionals of America, 1988).

Unlike the FBLA, the BPA is intended for only those secondary and postsecondary students enrolled in vocational business and office education. Its aims are to develop the leadership abilities of its members, to promote interest in the nation's business system, and encourage competency in business office occupations (Mason and Husted, 1997).

Address: Phone: (614)895-7277
Business Professionals of America (BPA)   Fax: (614)895-1165
5454 Cleveland Avenue
Columbus, OH 43231

Health Occupations Students of America (HOSA)

The Health Occupations Students of America was formed in 1976 through the guidance of AVA's Health Occupations Division. The constitutional convention that formally established HOSA was held in Arlington, Texas, November 10–13, 1976 (Santo, 1986). HOSA serves secondary and postsecondary students enrolled in health occupations. HOSA's two-fold mission is to promote career development and opportunities in the health-care industry and to enhance the delivery of quality health services to all people. HOSA is the only

FIGURE 9.7   The Official HOE-HOSA Emblems

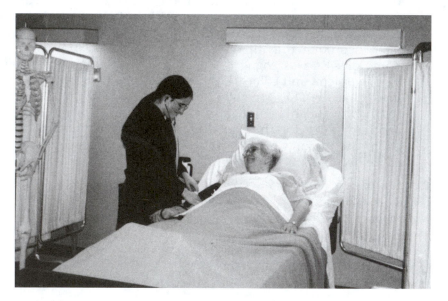

A HOSA student is shown taking the blood pressure of a patient during clinical practice.

student organization recognized by the Health Occupations Education (HOE) Division of the American Vocational Association.

Address: Phone: (972)874-0062
HOSA   Fax: (614)895-1165
6021 Morris Rd., Suite 10
Flowermound, TX 75028

Technology Student Association (TSA)

Industrial arts student groups have been in existence since the first industrial arts teachers decided to do something extra with their students after school (Santo, 1986). Desire on the part of students and advisors of Industrial Arts clubs triggered the establishment of AIASA (pronounced I-A-Sa). In 1957, an article written by Dr. Rex Miller regarding his high school club in Iowa generated interest in a national organization for students in industrial arts. Under Dr. Miller's leadership, the American Industrial Arts Student Association was officially organized at the 27th American Industrial Arts Association Convention in Tulsa, Oklahoma, in March 1965 (Vaughn, Vaughn, and Vaughn, 1990).

AIASA was organized as a sponsored program of the American Industrial Arts Association, and in 1978 was officially incorporated (Binkley and Byers, 1982). At the 1988 national conference, delegates voted to change the name to the Technology Student Association to reflect a commitment to the dynamic field of technology and the future (Scott and Sarkees-Wircenski, 1996). TSA is different from the other nine student organizations in vocational education in that the students may be in elementary school, middle school, or high school.

FIGURE 9.8   The Official TSA Emblem

FIGURE 9.9   The Official PAS Emblem

Address: Phone: (703)860-9000
Technology Student Association   Fax: (703)620-4483
1914 Association Drive
Reston, VA 20191

National Postsecondary Agricultural Student Organization (NPASO) or (PAS)

The formation of PAS began with a national seminar sponsored by the U.S. Office of Education at Cobleskill, New York, in 1966, to identify curriculum content, facilities, and requirements for postsecondary programs in agriculture (Vaughn, Vaughn, and Vaughn, 1990). According to Santo (1986), PAS was founded in 1979 and had its first Board of Directors meeting in Washington, D.C. the same year.

Today, PAS chapters are formed in postsecondary institutions that offer associate degrees or vocational diplomas and certificates in agricultural fields.

Address: Phone: (916)445-3898
National Postsecondary Agricultural
   Student Organization (PAS)
789 Sillman Way
Sacramento, CA 95831

National Young Farmers Educational Association (NYFEA)

NYFEA is a student organization for adults enrolled in agricultural education beyond high school. There was a Young Farmers Organization in existence prior to the development of the NYFEA. However, Vaughn, Vaughn, and Vaughn (1990) cite May 23, 1985 as the year when the Assistant Secretary for Vocational and Adult Education, Dr. Robert Worthington, officially recog-

FIGURE 9.10   **The Official Emblem of the National Young Farmers Educational Association**

nized the NYFEA as a vocational student organization. In April of 1988, the NYFEA was included in the U.S. Department of Education policy statement on vocational student organizations (Vaughn, Vaughn, and Vaughn, 1990).

This organization provides for the development and improvement of urban-rural network relationships especially appropriate for young farmer leaders when they leave the National FFA organization.

Address: Phone: (334)288-0097
National Young Farmers Educational
    Association, Inc.
P.O. Box 20326
Montgomery, AL 36120

VOCATIONAL STUDENT ORGANIZATIONS AND THE SCHOOL-TO-WORK OPPORTUNITIES ACT OF 1994

There are several opportunities for Vocational Student Organizations to perform a significant role in the various components of the School-to-Work Opportunities Act (STWOA). The act provides funds to states and local agencies that meet the requirements established by STWOA. Basic program requirements are categorized under three major components: (1) school-based learning, (2) work-based learning, and (3) connecting activities component.

School-Based Learning (Sec. 102, P.L. 103-239)

There are several elements under the school-based learning component that VSOs can become involved with. Significant attention is given to the importance of career guidance activities under STWOA. Every student that is part of a school-to-work program is required to participate in a career awareness or career exploration and counseling program no later than the seventh grade. Local VSO chapters can assist in this activity by exposing students to a wide variety of occupational clusters. In the initial stages, this may be in the form of business/industry representatives speaking and interacting with middle school students at the school site. The intermediate stage would involve industry tours and shadowing activities. Ultimately, students would choose a work-based learning experience in the form of an internship or mentor activity. All of these activities can be easily facilitated by VSOs because of their existing relationships with business/industry and labor.

Every student who participates in a school-to-work program is required to select a "career major" by at least the eleventh grade. One of the subcomponents of a career major is that the career major must prepare students for employment in a broad occupational cluster, therefore, making the VSOs a viable delivery vehicle for assisting students.

Work-Based Learning (Sec. 103. P.L. 103-239)

Clearly, the VSOs and their students have been tremendous ambassadors to the business/industry/labor environment for years. The local VSO advisor and his or her students can play an active role in contacting and recruiting potential employers to become involved with developing local partnerships.

Another element of the work-based learning component is that students receive instruction in workplace competencies. Employers today increasingly emphasize that academic and technical skills are not the only skills needed by students in order to enter the workplace. Today's high-performance workplace requires a diversity of general skills, such as teamwork, problem solving, positive work attitudes, employability, and participative skills, as well as critical thinking. These competencies make up the core of the educational programs on which VSOs are founded. VSO program administrators must work to infuse these competencies into school-to-work programs, both from the standpoint that they are required in order to meet the legislative provisions of the law and for the benefit of the students participating in the school-to-work program.

VSOs can play an integral role providing quality paid and nonpaid work experiences through school-based entrepreneurial and cooperative programs. Especially in rural areas, where even fewer opportunities exist for work-based learning, the VSOs can provide guidance and development strategies for initiating or expanding operating school-based enterprises.

The national VSO offices provide leadership at the national level in underscoring for Congress the important role that VSOs have provided for years in the delivery of vocational-technical education. Due to this effort, the legislation contains language stating that students participating in school-to-work programs must receive instruction in *all aspects of an industry*. The term "all aspects of an industry" has been defined as providing the students with all of the characteristics of the industry or industry sector that the student is

These two teachers are examining ways to advance student learning by improving curriculum and instructional planning between high schools and work sites.

preparing to enter—including planning, management, finances, technical and production skills, and the underlying principles of technology, labor and community issues related to that particular industry or industrial sector. This means that the instruction students receive related to their chosen career major should provide them with more than just the specific technical skills related to that industry.

Clearly, the various VSOs for years have provided extended learning competencies related to a variety of vocational areas. Their contribution has been even more valuable because the instruction the VSOs provided is comprehensive enough to ensure that the student understands and can competently navigate the area beyond the prerequisite academic and technical skills. It is this kind of well-rounded employee who can integrate a variety of skills and competencies that will be demanded by the high-performance workplace of tomorrow.

Connecting Activities (Sec. 104, P.L. 103-239)

Some of the connecting activities component of the School-to-Work Opportunities program include:

- matching students with work-based learning opportunities of employers;
- providing, with respect to each student, a school site mentor to act as a liaison among the student and employer, school, teacher, school administrator, and parent of the student, and community partners; and

- collecting and analyzing information regarding postprogram outcomes of participants in the School-to-Work Opportunities program, to the extent practicable, on the basis of socioeconomic status, race, gender, ethnicity, culture, and disability, and on the basis of whether the participants are students with limited-English proficiency, school dropouts, disadvantaged students, or academically talented students.

The VSOs' long standing relationship with business/industry representatives is an ideal conduit for these students to access work-based learning opportunities. Their previous interaction with each other through regional and state workshops, conferences, and contests should make the matching of students with the appropriate employer an instinctive process. The reader is urged to consult Appendix H to learn more about School-to-Work Opportunities and the Fair Labor Standards Act.

SUMMARY

- Public Law 740 is the only act to federally charter a vocational student organization. This act was passed in 1950. It clearly established the integral relationship of a vocational student organization to the instructional program and represented the first time that the U.S. Office of Education was recognized for being associated with vocational youth organizations.

- This interest in and support for VSOs derives from their role in working to foster the career, leadership, and personal development of vocational students. These basic goals are reflected in VSO operations and activities. Leadership skills are encouraged by having students participate in chapter planning and decision making, and by running for chapter offices. Fund-raising and community service are also common activities that help build team spirit and individual initiative. In addition, local, regional, state, and national contests serve as "vocational skill Olympics."

- The ten federally recognized VSOs include student organizations for each vocational program area, at the middle school, secondary (high school), postsecondary, and in one case, the adult level.

- The enactment of the School-to-Work Opportunities Act has generated an unprecedented amount of discussion and activity across the country among educators, business/industry and labor, and parents. Several references are made to Vocational Student Organizations within the text of the legislative provisions. It is clear that the VSOs can significantly strengthen any local school-to-work programs.

- The window of opportunity is here for significant systematic change to take place in the schools across this country. This piece of legislation has set a precedent for working collaboratively, recognizing the educational needs of all students, and providing a framework for complete restructuring of our traditional educational systems.

DISCUSSION QUESTIONS AND ACTIVITIES

1. How do FFA organization activities provide educational experiences for student-learners? How do they differ from other occupational areas?

2. Name the vocational student organizations associated with each vocational field. What contributions do these groups make toward realizing the goals of vocational education?

3. Select at least two vocational student organizations with which you are unfamiliar. Interview a student member and find out his or her impressions of the contributions of the organization to its individual members, the department, and the school.

4. How do the activities provided by a health occupations student organization provide educational experiences for student-learners?

5. How do the activities of the FHA-HERO student organization provide educational experiences for student-learners?

6. How do DECA activities provide educational experiences for student-learners?

7. Describe each vocational student organization.

For Exploration

8. Identify some of the barriers that students from special needs populations may experience in becoming involved in VSOs.

9. What are some of the major values students can acquire from membership in a VSO?

10. Describe the federal legislation that has guaranteed all students the right to participate in VSO activities.

11. Describe how you would establish a local vocational student organization.

12. Identify some of the benefits and advantages for students, teachers, schools, and communities that are provided by active VSOs.

13. Assume you are the advisor of a local chapter. Write a lesson plan in which you introduce the topic of the student organization to the related class.

14. Volunteer your services as a judge for VSO competitive events held statewide.

15. Research has shown that there is a decline in membership for VSOs. Describe at least five solutions for increasing the membership rate for individual vocational student organizations.

REFERENCES

Adams, D.A. (1993). The organization and operation of vocational education . In C. Anderson and L.C. Rampp (Eds.), *Vocational education in the 1990s, II: A sourcebook for strategies, methods, and materials* (pp. 35–59). Ann Arbor, MI: Prakken Publishing Company.

Binkley, H.R., and Byers, C.W. (1982). *Handbook on student organizations in vocational education.* Danville, IL: The Interstate Printers Publishers.

Business Professionals of America. (1988). History and organization: Office education association. *Chapter Management Reference,* 11–13. Columbus, OH: Author.

DECA Handbook (1995). Reston, VA: DECA, Inc.

FHA/HERO Chapter Handbook. (1991). Reston, VA: Future Homemakers of America.

Future Homemakers of America, Inc. (1996). History. *Traditions,* 104. Reston, VA: Author.

Hannah, G. (1993). Shift or drift. *Vocational Education, 68*(4), 21–25.

Harris, T., and Sweet, G. (1981). Why we believe in vocational student organizations. *Vocational Education, 56*(6), 33–35.

Hawkins, L.S., Prosser, C.A., and Wright, J.C. (1951). *Development of vocational education.* Chicago: Harper & Row.

Mason, R.E., and Husted, S.W. (1997). *Cooperative occupational education* (5th ed.). Danville, IL: Interstate Publishers.

Phipps, L.P. (1972). *Handbook on agricultural education in public schools.* Danville, IL: The Interstate Publishers.

Roberts, R.W. (1971). *Vocational and practical arts education* (3rd ed.). NY: Harper & Row.

Santo, G. (1986). Through the decades: A family album. *Vocational Education Journal, 61*(8), 39–57.

Scott, J.L., and Sarkees-Wircenski, M. (1996). *Overview of vocational and applied technology education.* Homewood, IL: American Technical Publishers.

Vaughn, P.R., Vaughn, R.C., and Vaughn, D.L. (1990). *Handbook for advisors of vocational student organizations.* Athens, GA: American Association for Vocational Instructional Materials.

VICA *Leadership Handbook* (1989). Leesburg, VA: National VICA.

APPENDIX A

ORDERING INFORMATION FOR VOCATIONAL EDUCATION VIDEOS

Quantity	No.	Title	Price Each	Amount
	1	Revisiting the Washington-DuBois Debate	$11.00	
	2	Revisiting the Dewey-Snedden Debate	$11.00	
	3	The Commission on National Aid to Vocational Education: A Reenactment of the 1914 Hearing	$11.00	
	4	Jobs: The Class of 2000	*	

Ways to order:

By Phone: (919)515–1756 or (304) 696–3079

By Fax: (919)515–9060 or (304)696–3077

By E-mail: gary_moore@ncsu.edu or gordon@marshall.edu

Mail Orders To:
  Dept. AEE
  Box 7607
  North Carolina State University
  Raleigh, NC 27695–7607
or
  Department of Adult and
    Technical Education
  Room 434, Harris Hall
  Marshall University
  Huntington, WV 25755–2460

*Mail Order To:
  WQED Video
  4802 5th Ave.
  Pittsburgh, PA 15213
  Phone: 1–800–274–1307

APPENDIX B

EUROPEAN-AMERICAN EVOLUTION OF VOCATIONAL EDUCATION

1802	Factory Act (England) required instruction for apprentices and limited children's hours of labor
1806	Lancastrian Schools, New York City
1820–1876	Mechanics Institutes (America)
1820	Common Schools (elementary)
1820	Boston Apprentices' Library
1821	First high school (Boston)
1827	Christian Brothers combine general and technical instruction
1827	Lyceum movement begins in United States
1832	School Workshops, France—Cesar Fichet
1836	Lowell Institute (Massachusetts)
1846	Associations formed to extend instruction in Sloyd, Sweden
1847	Sheffield Scientific School at Yale
1857	N.E.A. organized
1860	First U.S. Kindergarten, Froebel
1862–1890	Land-Grant College Act (Morrill Act)
1865	Imperial Technical School, Russia (Della Vos). Large group instruction to speed up training of apprentices
1868–1906	Rise of Trade Schools in: France, England, Germany, America
1871	Opening of "The Whittling School" in Boston
1873	First free manual training school—Salicis Manual Training School, France (Gustave Salicis)
1876	Manual training introduced to high schools, Philadelphia
1876	Introduction of Manual Arts and Arts and Crafts
1876	Boston School of Mechanical Arts (Runkle)

1880	First manual training school in St. Louis (Woodward—"put the whole boy in school")
1881	New York Trade School
1882	Sloyd School in Naas, Sweden, entirely for teacher training
1884	First public supported high school for manual training in Baltimore
1884	Industrial Education Association formed in New York City
1887	Hatch Act, providing federal funds for support of agricultural experiment stations
1888	Sloyd Association of Great Britain and Ireland formed. A system of manual training developed from a Swedish system included use of tools
1893	Manual training school, Boston—first public supported manual training school
1898	Technical high school established at Springfield, Massachusetts
1902	First Junior College in United States—Joliet, Illinois
1903	Term "Manual Arts" introduced at N.E.A. convention
1906	Massachusetts Commission on Industrial Education reports. State aid given for industrial education courses
1906	National Society for the Promotion of Industrial Education formed in New York City. (Beginning of Industrial Education)
1907	Wisconsin adopts vocational education
1908	New York adopts vocational education
1908	Beginning of cooperative education with formation of cooperative schools
1908	Beginning of formalized vocational guidance (Frank Parsons and Jim Brewer). Vocational Bureau and Breadwinners Institute opened in Boston
1909	First Junior High School, Berkeley, California
1912	N.S.P.I.E. promotes state and national legislation for vocational education (Prosser)
1913	Bonser proposes that industrial arts is both a subject and a method (School Arts Magazine)
1914	Smith-Lever Bill passed aid to agricultural education
1917	First Federal Publication of Policies for Vocational Education
1917	Russian Revolution
	World War I

APPENDIX C

QUOTATIONS OF BOOKER T. WASHINGTON

Any movement for elevation of the Southern Negro in order to be successful must have to a certain extent the cooperation of the Southern white.

We shall prosper in proportion as we learn to glorify and dignify labor and put brains and skill into the common occupations of life. It is at the bottom of life that we must begin and not at the top; nor should we permit our grievances to overshadow our opportunities.

An educated man on the street with his hands in his pockets is not one whit [sic] more benefit to society than an ignorant man on the streets with his hands in his pockets.

I have learned that it is important to carry education outside of the school building and take it into the fields, into homes, and into the daily life of the people surrounding the school.

The Negro should be taught book learning, yes, but along with it he should be taught that book education and industrial development must go hand in hand. No race which fails to do this can ever hope to succeed.

There is as much dignity in tilling a field as in writing a poem.

Learn all you can, but learn to do something, or your learning will be useless.

It seems to me that the temptation in education and missionary effort is to do for people that which was done a thousand years ago, or is being done for people a thousand miles away, without always making a careful study of the needs and conditions of the people we are trying to help. The temptation is to run all people through a certain educational mold, regardless of the condition of the subject or the end to be accomplished.

One of the weakest points in connect with the present development of the race is that so many get the idea that the mere filling of the head with a knowledge of mathematics, the sciences, and literature means success in life.

170

Is there not as much mental discipline in having a student think out and put on paper a plan for a modern dairy building as having him merely commit to memory poetry that somebody else thought out years ago?

The great thing for us as a race, is to conduct ourselves so as to become worthy of the privileges of an American citizen and these privileges will come. More important than receiving privileges is the matter of being worthy of them. Nobody likes to come in contact with a whining individual and nobody likes to be connected with a whining, despairing race.

When people, regardless of race or geographical location, have not been trained to habits of industry, have not been given skill of hand in youth and taught to love labor, a direct result is the breeding of a worthless, idle class, which spends a great deal of its time trying to live by its wits.

So long as the Negro is permitted to get education, acquire property, and secure employment, and is treated with respect in the business or commercial world, I shall have the greatest faith in his working out his own destiny in our Southern states.

The foundation of every race must be laid in the common everyday occupations that are right about our door.

A man's position in life is not measured by the heights which he has attained, but by the depths from which he has come.

We shall succeed not by abstract discussions, not by depending upon making empty demands, not by abuse of some other individual or race, but we will succeed by actually demonstrating to the world that we can perform the service which the world needs, as well or better than anyone else.

There are definite rewards coming to the individual or the race that overcomes obstacles and succeeds in spite of seemingly insurmountable difficulties. The palms of victory are not for the race that merely complains and frets and rails.

The colored boy has been taken from the farm and taught astronomy—how to locate Jupiter and Mars—learned to measure Venus, taught about everything except that which he depends upon for daily bread.

One of the saddest sights I ever saw in the South was a colored girl, recently returned from college, sitting in a rented one-room log cabin attempting day by day to extract some music from a second-hand piano, when all about her indicated want of thrift and cleanliness.

Source: Moore, G. E. (1993). *An informal conversation with Booker T. Washington and W.E.B. DuBois.* Raleigh, NC: North Carolina State University, University Council for Vocational Education.

PROSSER'S SIXTEEN THEOREMS

1. Vocational education should occur in the most realistic setting that replicates the work environment.
2. Vocational education should only be given where the training jobs are carried on in the same way, with the same tools, and the same machines as in the occupation itself.
3. Vocational education should provide students with thinking habits—technical knowledge and scientific problem-solving skills—and the manipulative skills required in the occupation itself.
4. Vocational education should be planned and delivered in a manner that capitalizes on the student's interest, aptitudes, and intrinsic intelligence to the highest degree.
5. Vocational education is not for everyone, but for those individuals who need it, want it, and are able to profit from it.
6. Vocational education should provide opportunities for students to repeat operations of thinking and manipulative skills until habits are formed characteristic of those required for gainful employment.
7. Vocational education should be taught by instructors who have successful experience in the application of skills and knowledge required of competent workers.
8. For every occupation there is a minimum of productive ability which an individual must possess in order to secure or retain employment in that occupation.
9. Vocational education should prepare individuals for the occupations as they currently exist in the work force and for future labor markets as a secondary concern.
10. Vocational education should provide opportunities for students to perform operations on actual jobs and not only simulated work tasks.
11. The only reliable source of content for specific training in an occupation is in the experiences of masters of the occupation.

12. For every occupation there is a body of content which is peculiar to that occupation and which practically has no functioning value in any other occupation.
13. Vocational education should meet the needs of individuals when it is needed and in such a way as they can benefit from it.
14. Vocational education is more effective when its methods of instruction are best suited to the particular characteristics of any particular group which it serves.
15. The administration of vocational education should be efficient in proportion as it is elastic and fluid rather than rigid and standardized.
16. While every reasonable effort should be made to reduce per capita cost, there is a minimum level which effective vocational education cannot be given, and if the course does not permit this minimum of per capita cost, vocational education should not be attempted.

Source: Prosser, C. A., and Allen, C. R. (1925). *Vocational education in a democracy.* NY: Century Company.

APPENDIX E

GROWTH OF VOCATIONAL EDUCATION PREPARATION AND RETRAINING

1917   **Smith-Hughes Act** (P.L.64-347). First vocational education act for high schools. Federal money for training in agriculture, home economics, trades, industry, and teacher training.

1918   The **Smith-Sears Act** (P.L. 178) provided federal funds for establishing retraining programs for World War I veterans.

1918   Commission on Reorganization of Secondary Education issues its famous **"Cardinal Principles of Secondary Education"**: health, command of fundamental processes, worthy home membership, development of a vocation, civic education, worthy use of leisure time, and ethical character.

1920   **Vocational Rehabilitation Act.** Training for handicapped persons.

1920   **Smith-Bankhead Act** (P.L. 236) authorized grants for vocational rehabilitation programs.

1923   **Gordon Bonser** advocated the inclusion of industrial arts into the elementary school with a study of manufacturing industries as the curriculum base with the goal being to develop an understanding of the functioning of our industrial society. Industrial arts was to be a general education subject desirable for all to take.

1925   Federal vocational education programs extended to territory of Hawaii (P.L. 68-35).

1926   The **American Vocational Association** was formed out of the merger of the national Society for Vocational Education (formerly NSPIE) and the Vocational Association of the Middle West.

1926   Vocational enrollment exceeded 850,000; states received $7.2 million for programs.

1929   The **George-Reed Act** expanded vocational education in agriculture and home economics.

1934   The **George-Ellzey Act** increased supplemental funding for agriculture, home economics, and trade and industrial education programs authorized by the Smith-Hughes Act of 1917.

1935   The **Bankhead-Jones Act** authorized grants to states for agriculture experiment stations.

1935   The **Social Security Act** provided vocational training for handicapped persons.

1935   The **National Youth Administration** provided vocational training and employment.

1935   The **Works Project Administration and Public Works Administration** provided vocational training, employment, and work relief.

1936   The **George-Deen Act** authorized an annual allotment of $12 million for agriculture, home economics, and trade and industrial education. Marketing occupations were recognized for the first time, and $1.2 million was authorized for them annually.

1938   The Civil Aeronautics Authority sponsored vocational training for pilots.

1940–1946   A series of ten **Vocational Education for National Defense Acts** were passed as war emergency majors to provide for vocational education programs to prepare war industry workers.

1944   The **Serviceman's Readjustment Act** ("GI Bill") provided vocational education opportunities for veterans

1946   The **George-Barden Act** authorized an appropriation of $28.5 million annually for the further development of vocational education. It is also known as the Vocational Education Act of 1946. It replaced the George-Deen Act of 1936.

1950   Federal vocational education program extended to the Virgin Islands (P.L. 81-462).

1956   The **Health Amendments Act** (P.L. 84-911) added practical nursing and health occupation programs to the list of vocational programs eligible to receive federal funds.

1956   Federal vocational education programs extended to Guam (P.L. 84-896).

1956   The **George-Barden Act Fishing Amendment** provided vocational education training in fishing trades, industry, and distributive occupations.

1958   The **National Defense Education Act** (NDEA) provided funds to support technical programs.

1961   The **Area Redevelopment Act** (P.L. 82-27) was an emergency measure born out of a recession, which authorized $4.5 million annually to be used for vocational education until 1965. It recognized the critical need for training due to unemployment and underemployment in economically distressed areas.

1962   The **Manpower Development and Training Act** (MDTA) authorized funds for training and retraining of unemployed and underemployed adults.

1963   The **Health Professions Educational Assistance Act** (P.L. 88-129) provided federal funds to expand teaching facilities for health programs and for loans to students preparing for the health professions.

1963   The **Vocational Education Act** for the first time mandated that vocational education meet the needs of individual students, not just the employment needs of industry. Its major purposes were to maintain, extend, and improve existing programs of vocational education and to provide part-time employment for young people who needed the earnings from such employment to continue their schooling on a full-time basis.

1963   The **Higher Education Facilities Act** (P.L. 88-204) authorized a five-year program of federal grants and loans to colleges and universities for the expansion and development of physical facilities.

1964   The **Civil Rights Act** (P.L. 88-352) established basic human rights and responsibilities in the workplace and prohibited discrimination on the basis of race, gender, national origin, or handicap. Other issues addressed equal employment opportunities, voting rights, equal education, fair housing, and public accommodation.

1964   The **Economic Opportunity Act** (P.L. 88-452) authorized grants for college work-study programs for students of low-income families; established a Job Corps program and authorized support for work-training programs to provide education and vocational training and work experience for unemployed youth; provided training and work experience opportunities in welfare programs; authorized support of education and training activities and of community action programs including Head Start, Follow Through, Upward Bound; authorized the establishment of the Volunteers in Service to America (VISTA).

1965   **Appalachian Regional Development Act** (P.L. 89-4). The purpose of this act was to provide public works, economic development programs, and the planning and coordination needed to assist in the development of the Appalachian region.

1965   **Higher Education Act of 1965** (P.L. 89-329) provided grants for university community service programs, college library assistance, library training and research, strengthening developing institutions, teacher training programs, and undergraduate instructional equipment. Authorized insured student loans, established a National Teacher Corps, and provided for graduate teacher training fellowships.

1967   The **Educational Professions Development Act** (P.L. 90-35) provided federal funds to address the training of teachers in critical shortage areas, and provided fellowships for teachers and other educational professionals. This act was instrumental in providing a vital source of college and university vocational teacher educators.

1968   The **Vocational Amendments** broadened the definition of vocational education to bring it closer to general education and provided vast sums of money to address the nation's social and economic problems. The act established a National Advisory Committee, expanded vocational education services to meet the needs of disadvantaged students, and established methods of collecting and disseminating information about vocational education. This act placed more emphasis on vocational programs at the postsecondary level. It also added cooperative education as one of the vocational education programs eligible to receive federal funds.

1971   The **Nurse Training Act** (P.L. 92-158) increased and expanded provisions for nurse training facilities.

1972   The **Education Amendments** established a National Institute of Education; general aid for institutions of high education; federal matching grants for state student incentive grants; a National Commission on Financing postsecondary Education; State Advisory Councils on Community Colleges; a Bureau of Occupational and Adult Education; state grants for the design, establishment, and conduct of postsecondary occupational education; and a bureau-level Office of Indian education.

1973   The **Comprehensive Employment and Training Act** (CETA) intended to continue the goals of the previous MDTA legislation, plus expand the previous services MDTA made available. It recognized the high unemployment level at that time, the increasing number of welfare recipients, the increasing number of economically disadvantaged rural and urban communities with hard core unemployed, the significantly large number of youth unable to find part-time or full-time employment, and the increasing number of people in minority groups who were unskilled and unemployed.

1974   The **Education Amendments** (P.L. 93-380) encouraged the development of individualized education plans (IEPs) for children with special needs participating in Title I of the 1965 Elementary and Secondary Education Act (ESEA). These amendments also included the Women's Educational Equality Act of 1974 which was designed to assist states in bringing about educational equity for women Other important provision of these amendments included support for career education, establishment of the National Center for Educational Statistics, and research into the problems of providing bilingual education.

1975   The **Education of All Handicapped Children Act of 1975** (P.L. 94-142) launched an organized effort to provide a free and appropriate education for all handicapped children ages 3–21. This act spelled out the assurances for handicapped youngsters including due process, written individualized education plans, bias free testing and assessment, and measures to protect the confidentiality of records. In addition, a number of terms related to handicapped individuals were clearly defined. This act provided a number of grants to states and local school systems to improve vocational education and related services for handicapped individuals.

1976   The **Educational Amendments** continued the trend of omnibus legislation to extend and revise previous legislation and to redirect American education in an attempt to correct some of the nation's problems including changing the public's attitude toward the roles of men and women in society. This act required the development of programs to eliminate sex discrimination and sex stereotyping. It also required the development of a national vocational education data reporting and accounting system and required states to develop an evaluation system.

1978   The **Career Education Act** (P.L. 95-205) established the comprehensive career development concept, which viewed the individual as progressing through various planned experiences, a series of dimensions that total a complete cycle. These dimensions begin with career awareness at an early age, add employability skills, and end with educational awareness.

1978   The **Comprehensive Employment and Training Amendments of 1978** provided for continuation of the Comprehensive Employment and Training Act of 1973 and the manpower Development and Training Act of 1962. Ensured coordination and cooperation among all federal, state, and local private and public agencies involved in the vocational education and training of workers.

1982   The **Job Training Partnership Act** (JTPA) replaced CETA and enlarged the role of state governments and private industry in federal job training programs, imposed performance standards, limited support services, and created a new program of retraining for displaced workers.

1984   The **Carl D. Perkins Vocational Education Act** amended the Vocational Education Act of 1963 and replaced the amendments of 1968 and 1976. It changed the emphasis of federal funding in vocational education from primarily expansion to program improvement and at-risk populations.

1990   The **Carl D. Perkins Vocational and Applied Technology Education Act** amended and extended the previous 1984 Perkins Act. The intent of this act was to assist states and local school systems in teaching the skills and competencies necessary to work in a technologically advanced society for all students. A major goal of this legislation was to provide greater vocational opportunities to disadvantaged individuals. The act provided funds for the integration of academic and vocational education and the Tech Prep programs, and articulated programs between high schools and postsecondary institutions. The act eliminated set-asides for support services for special populations giving states and local agencies greater flexibility in how funds are best used to serve special populations.

1992   The **Job Training Reform Amendments** (P.L. 101-367) revised the JTPA of 1982 to change the focus of manpower programs toward improving services to those facing serious barriers to employment, enhancing the quality of services provided, improving a accountability of funds and the programs they serve, linking services provided to real labor market needs, and facilitating the development of a comprehensive and coherent system of human resource services. One of the new provisions of special interest to vocational educators was the requirement for on-the-job training contracts and the development of individual service strategies (ISSs) which is an individualized employability development plan for each JPTA participant. This act is devoted to serving special populations who face the greatest employment barriers.

1993   The Family and Consumer Science became the new name for home economics education.

1994   The **Goals 2000: Educate America Act** (P.L. 103-227) was a blueprint for improving America's schools through the establishment of eight national goals and the development of voluntary academic and skill standards to assist state and local agencies in helping every child meet criteria that will ensure that youngsters are learning what they need to learn in order to function as a family member, involved community member, and competent worker. The act identified ten elements which constitute a suggested framework for developing a local Goals 2000 Plan.

1994   The **Improving America's School Act** (P.L. 103-382) was a reauthorization of the Elementary and Secondary Education Act (ESEA) of 1965 which placed primary emphasis on serving disadvantaged students. The major goal of Title I has been revised to improve the teaching and learning of children in high-poverty schools to enable them to meet the challenging academic and performance standards being established by the Goals 2000 Act. This act increased opportunities for vocational and applied technology education to provide input into state and local educational plans and strengthened vocational and applied technology education in fourteen different areas.

1994   The **Improving America's School Act** (P.L. 103-382) was a reauthorization of the Elementary and Secondary Education Act (ESEA) of 1965 which placed primary emphasis on serving disadvantaged students. The major goal of Title I has been revised to improve the teaching and learning of children in high-poverty schools to enable them to meet the challenging academic and performance standards being established by the Goals 2000 Act. This act increased opportunities for vocational and applied technology education to provide input into state and local educational plans and strengthened vocational and applied technology education in fourteen different areas.

1994   The **School-to-Work Opportunities Act** (STWOA) provided a framework to build a high quality skilled workforce for our nation's economy through partnerships between educators and employers. This act emphasized preparing students with the knowledge, skills, abilities, and information about occupations and the labor market that facilitated the transition from school to continuing education and work. Key elements of this act included collaborative partnerships, integrated curriculum, technological advances, adaptable workers, comprehensive career guidance, work-based learning and a step-by-step approach.

FASTEST GROWING JOBS FOR THE TWENTY-FIRST CENTURY

Occupation	% Increase	Total by 2005
Home health aides	138	827,000
Human services workers	136	445,000
Personal and home care aides	130	293,000
Computer engineers and scientists	112	447,000
Systems analysis	110	956,000
Physical therapy assistants	93	118,000
Physical therapists	88	170,000
Paralegals	86	176,000
Special education teachers	74	625,000
Medical assistants	71	308,000
Detectives	70	100,000
Correction officers	70	479,000
Child-care workers	66	1,135,000
Travel agents	66	191,000
Radiological technicians and technologists	63	264,000
Nursery workers	62	116,000
Medical records technicians	61	123,000
Operations research analysts	61	72,000
Occupational therapists	60	64,000
Legal secretaries	57	439,000
Preschool and kindergarten teachers	54	669,000
Manicurists	54	55,000
Producers, directors, actors, and entertainers	54	198,000
Speech-language pathologists and audiologists	51	110,000
Flight attendants	51	140,000
Guards	51	1,211,000
Insurance adjusters	49	220,000
Respiratory therapists	48	109,000
Psychologists	48	212,000
Paving equipment operators	48	107,000

Source: Leftwich, K. (1994). Outlook to 2005. *Vocational Education Journal, 69* (7), 29.

APPROPRIATIONS FOR VOCATIONAL EDUCATION FOR FISCAL YEARS 1952 TO 1966

Year	Amount (in $ millions)
1952	26,273,383
1953	25,811,591
1954	25,811,591
1955	30,811,591
1956	33,638,330
1957	38,008,534
1958	40,888,411
1959	44,638,411
1960	47,683,393
1961	49,842,068
1962	53,619,101
1963	90,169,303
1964	135,586,109
1965	292,091,671
1966	416,902,278

APPENDIX H

SCHOOL-TO-WORK OPPORTUNITIES AND THE FAIR LABOR STANDARDS ACT

EXHIBIT 1a
STANDARDS FOR 16- AND 17-YEAR OLDS

The following standards apply to 16- and 17-year-old youths employed in nonfarm jobs.

Hours Limitations

- None Under FLSA: Federal law does not limit either the number of hours nor the time of day that the youth 16 years of age and older may work.
- Some state laws do restrict the hours that 16- and 17-year-olds may work.

Occupation Limitations

Minors may perform all work except in 17 occupations considered too hazardous for all youth under the age of 18. The Hazardous Occupations Orders (HOs) are:

HO1	Manufacturing and storing explosives;
HO2	Motor-vehicle driving and outside helper, including driving motor vehicles or working as outside helpers on motor vehicles or driving as part of any occupation;
HO3	Coal mining;
HO4	Logging and sawmilling;
HO5*	Work using power-driven woodworking machines, including the use of saws on construction sites;
HO6	Work where exposed to radioactive substances;
HO7	Work involving the operation of power-driven hoisting devices, including the use of fork lifts, cranes and nonautomatic elevators;
HO8*	Work using power-driven metal forming, punching, and shearing machines (but HO8 permits the use of a large group of machine tools used on metal, including lathes, turning machines, milling machines, grinding, boring machines and planing machines);
HO9	All mining other than coal mining, including work at gravel pits;
HO10*	Work involving slaughtering or meatpacking, processing, or rendering, including the operation of power-driven meat slicers in retail stores;
HO11	Work involving the operation of power-driven bakery machines;

HO12*   Work using power-driven paper-products machines, including the operation and loading of paper balers in grocery stores;

HO13   Work in manufacturing of brick, tile and kindred products;

HO14*   Work involving the use of circular saws, band saws, and guillotine shears;

HO15   All work in involving wrecking, demolition and ship-breaking;

HO16*   All work in roofing operations; and

HO17*   All work in excavating, including work in a trench as a plumber.

EXHIBIT 1b

STANDARDS FOR 16- AND 17-YEAR-OLDS

The following standards apply to 16- and 17-year-old youths employed in nonfarm jobs.

Exceptions to Occupation Limitations

Special Provisions for Student-Learners and Apprentices—The seven HOs identified with an asterisk permit the employment of apprentices and student-learners in vocational education programs under certain conditions. Student-learners in STW programs will meet the student-learner exemption if the student is employed under a written agreement which provides that:

(1) all hazardous work will be performed under the direct and close supervision of a qualified and experienced person;

(2) safety instructions will be given by the school and reinforced by the employer with on-the-job training;

(3) the job training follows a schedule which reflects organized and progressive skill developments; and

(4) the work in the hazardous occupation is *intermittent* and for *short periods of time* and is under the direct and close supervision of a journeyman as a necessary part of such apprenticeship training.

The written agreement must be signed by the employer and placement coordinator (or school principal). Copies of the agreement must be kept on file by both the school and the employer.

Note: To qualify as an apprentice, one must obtain the appropriate certificate from the local U.S. Department of Labor Bureau of Apprenticeship and Training (BAT) office, or a state office approved by BAT.

EXHIBIT 2
STANDARDS FOR 14- AND 15-YEAR-OLDS

The following standards apply to 14- and 15-year-old youths employed in nonfarm jobs.

Hours Limitations

The hours 14- and 15-year-olds may work are limited to:

- outside school hours,
- no more than 3 hours on a school day,
- no more than 18 hours in a school week,
- no more that 8 hours on a nonschool day,
- no more than 40 hours in nonschool weeks,
- between 7 A.M. and 7 P.M. (between June 1 and Labor Day they may work as late as 9 P.M.).

Occupation Limitations

In addition to the Hazardous Occupations listed in Exhibit 1a that are prohibited for minors under the age of 18, 14- and 15-year-olds may not work in the following occupations:

- cooking, other than at lunch counters and snack bars, and within the view of the customer;
- manufacturing, mining, processing;
- most transportation jobs;
- most in warehouses and workrooms;
- on construction jobs except in the office;
- in any job involving hoists, conveyor belts, power-driven lawn mowers and other power-driven machinery.

No Exceptions to Occupation Limitations

Occupation limitations are strictly enforced for 14- and 15-year-old youth, with no exceptions. The student-learner provisions applicable to some Hazardous Occupations for youth 16 and 17 years of age (as listed in Exhibit 1b) do not apply to minors under the age of 16.

EXHIBIT 3
SPECIAL PROVISIONS FOR 14- AND 15-YEAR-OLDS UNDER WECEP

The Work Experience and Career Exploration Program (WECEP) includes special provisions that permit 14- and 15-year-old STW enrollees to be employed during school hours and in occupations otherwise prohibited by regulation.

WECEP is designed to provide a carefully planned work experience and career exploration program for 14- and 15-year-old youths, including youths in STW programs, who can benefit from a career-oriented educational program. WECEP is designed to meet the participants' needs, interests, and abilities. Among other things, the program helps dropout-prone youths to become reoriented and motivated toward education and helps to prepare them for the world of work.

A state education agency with a school-to-work program may obtain approval from the Department of Labor for STW enrollees participating in WECEP to be employed:

- up to 3 hours on a school day,
- up to 23 hours during a school week,
- any time during school hours,
- under variances granted by the Wage and Hour Administrator that permit employment of WECEP participants in otherwise prohibited activities and occupations.*

Any representative of the Governor who is interested in establishing a WECEP may forward a letter of application to the Administrator of the Wage and Hour Division, U.S. Department of Labor, Room S3502, 200 Constitution Avenue, N.W., Washington, DC 20210. The provisions for WECEP are set by Regulations 29 CFR Part 570.35a. Approval to operate a WECEP is granted by the Administrator of the Wage and Hour Division for a two-year period.

*Note: The Regulations do not permit issuance of WECEP variances in manufacturing, mining, or in any of the 17 hazardous occupations orders listed in Exhibit 1a.

EXHIBIT 4
STANDARDS FOR FARM JOBS

The following standards apply to minor employed in farm jobs.

Hours Limitations

- Minors 16 years old may be employed in any farm job at any time.
- Fourteen- and fifteen-year-old farm workers may be employed outside school hours in any occupation not declared hazardous. Children who move from a school district where schools have closed for the summer vacation and live in another district where the schools are still in session, may work during the hours that the school is in session in the new district. After May 15, it is assumed that school is closed for the summer.
- With written parental consent, 12- and 13-year-olds may be employed outside school hours in any nonhazardous job on the same farm where their parents are employed.
- Minors under 12 years of age may be employed outside school hours in any nonhazardous job with written parental consent but only on farms not subject to the minimum wage provisions of FLSA.
- Minors of any age may perform work at any time on a farm owned or operated by the minor's parents or persons standing in place of the parents.

Occupation Limitations

- Once teenagers reach age 14, they may perform the same agricultural work as an adult except occupations that involve the agricultural hazardous occupations orders.
- Agricultural hazardous occupations orders apply to minors under age 16. These orders are listed in Child Labor Bulletin 102—*The Child Labor Requirements in Agriculture under the Fair Labor Standards Act.*

Exemptions

Exemptions from the agricultural hazardous occupations orders applicable to tractors and certain other farm machinery apply to 14- and 15-year-old student-learners enrolled in vocational education programs and holders of certificates of completion of training under 4-H programs.

Source: U.S. Departments of Education and Labor. (1995). *School-to-work opportunities: Work-based learning and the fair labor standards act* (1st ed.). Washington, DC: Authors.

APPENDIX I

EXCERPT FROM THE ATLANTA EXPOSITION ADDRESS

The following excerpt reflects Booker T. Washington's belief that the future of his race lay in pursuing manual occupations in the South and in receiving an education that would inculcate the values of hard work.

Ignorant and inexperienced, it is not strange that in the first years of our new life we began at the top instead of at the bottom; that a seat in Congress or the state legislature was more sought than real estate or industrial skill; that the political convention of stump speaking had more attractions than starting a dairy farm or truck garden.

"Cast down your bucket where you are"—cast it down in making friends in every manly way of the people of all races by whom we are surrounded. Cast it down in agriculture, mechanics, in commerce, in domestic science, and in the professions.

Gentlemen of the Exposition, as we present to you our humble effort at an exhibition of our progress, must not expect overmuch. Starting thirty years ago with ownership here and there in a few quilts and pumpkins and chickens, remember the path that has led from these inventions and production of agricultural implements, buggies, steam engines, newspapers, books, statuary, carvings, paintings, the management of drug-stores and banks, has not been trodden without contact with thorns and thistles.

The wisest among my race understand that the agitation of questions of social equality is the extremist folly, and that progress in the employment of all the privileges that will come to us must be the result of severe and constant struggle rather than of artificial forcing. In all things that are purely social we can be as separate as the fingers, yet one as the hand in all things essential to mutual progress.

In conclusion, may I repeat that nothing in thirty years has given us more hope and encouragement, and drawn us so near to you of the white race, as this opportunity offered by the Exposition.

Source: Washington, B. (1901). *Up from Slavery*. Garden City, NY: Doubleday & Company, Inc.

GLOSSARY

Adult Education College, vocational, or occupational programs, continuing education or noncredit courses, correspondence courses and tutoring, as well as courses and other educational activities provided by employers, community groups, and other providers.

Advisory Committee A group serving strictly in an advisory capacity, with the educational policy remaining under the control of the superintendent of schools. It usually consists of seven to twelve persons—teachers, businesspersons, labor leaders, parents, and students. If a steering committee is used, some members may be asked to serve on it.

Apprentice A person who learns a trade by working under the guidance of a skilled master.

Appropriations (Federal Funds) Budget authority provided through congressional appropriation process that permits federal agencies to incur obligations and to make payments.

Area Vocational School/Center A high school, a department of a high school, a technical institute or vocational school, a department or a division of a junior-community college, or a university used exclusively or principally to provide vocational education to students who are entering the labor market.

At-risk Populations Certain segments of society, all who have disabilities and/or disadvantages, such as members of minority groups, women, persons who are economically and/or academically disadvantaged, and those who are physically and/or mentally disabled.

AVA (American Vocational Association) An organization composed of vocational educators whose members receive the *Vocational Education Journal*. Other services include insurance, annual conventions, and professional relationship services with other associations.

Bilingual Education   Formal learning and training for individuals with limited-English proficiency to prepare them for occupational entry and to provide them with instruction in the English language so that they will be equipped to pursue such occupations in an English language environment.

BPA (Business Professionals of America)   The vocational organization for those secondary and postsecondary students enrolled in vocational business education programs.

Calling   Used to denote a ministerial position. It may also be used to denote any vocation in which an individual is employed who regards their vocation as an end in itself and one from which they receive a high degree of personal satisfaction.

Career Guidance and Counseling   The term *career guidance and counseling* means programs that (a) pertain to the body of subject matter and related techniques and methods organized for the development in individuals of career awareness, career planning, career decision-making, placement skills, and knowledge and understanding of local, state, and national occupational, educational, and labor market needs, trends, and opportunities; (b) assist individuals in making and implementing informed educational and occupational choices; and (c) aid students to develop career options with attention to surmounting gender, race, ethnicity, disability, language, or socioeconomic impediments to career options and encouraging careers in nontraditional employment.

Commission on National Aid to Vocational Education (1914)   The purpose of this Commission was to determine (1) the need for vocational education, (2) the need for federal grants, (3) the kinds of vocational education for which grants should be made, (4) the extent and conditions under which aid should be granted, and (5) proposed legislation.

DECA (Distributive Education Clubs of America)   The national vocational organization for secondary and postsecondary students who are enrolled in marketing education programs.

DECA Chapter   A local student organization consisting of marketing education students.

Disabled   Referring to those students, ages 3 to 21, who are disabled mentally, educationally, and/or physically. They may be in public elementary and secondary schools or they may have been placed in private schools by public agencies.

Disadvantaged   Characterizing individuals who are economically and/or academically disadvantaged to the extent that they cannot actively participate in vocational programs.

Douglas Commission (1905)   This commission was responsible for investigating the status of vocational education and making recommendations for any required modifications. The growing interest in vocational education during the first decade of the twentieth century led to the appointment of this commission by Governor William Douglas of Massachusetts.

Early Leaders in School-To-Work   Florida, Oregon, Tennessee, and Wisconsin were among the first states to enact statutory provisions for school-to-work initiatives. Washington state was recognized nationally as the first to pass legislation to specifically invest state funds in the development of school-to-work transition programs.

E-mail   Electronic mail. A basic Internet service that allows user to exchange messages electronically.

English Poor Law (enacted in 1601)   Its basic intent was to equip the children of poor families in England with a salable skill. This approach was considered very successful and greatly influenced vocational education in America.

FBLA (Future Business Leaders of America)   A national vocational organization for students enrolled in secondary business courses. Students do not have to be in a vocational program to belong.

Federal Board for Vocational Education   The functions of the Federal Board had been determined to fall within three classifications: (1) efficient administration of the federal funds; (2) research and studies to promote and improve vocational education; and (3) assistance to the states in their promotion and development activities. The Federal Board operated from July 1917 to October 10, 1933.

FFA Organization (Future Farmers of America)   The national vocational organization of secondary students in vocational agriculture programs.

FHA (Future Homemakers of America, Inc.)   The national vocational organization for junior and senior high school students enrolled in home economics occupations education. The organization's goal is to help youth assume active roles in society as wage earners, community leaders, and family members.

High Technology   State-of-the-art computer, microelectronic, hydraulic, pneumatic, laser, nuclear, chemical, telecommunication, and other technologies being used to enhance productivity in manufacturing, communication, transportation, agriculture, mining, energy, commercial, and similar economic activity, and to improve the provision of health care.

Higher Education   Study beyond secondary school at an institution that offers programs terminating in an associate's, baccalaureate, or higher degree.

HOSA (Health Occupations Students of America)   The national vocational organization for secondary and postsecondary students who are enrolled in health occupations education.

Industrial Revolution   A rapid major change in an economy (as in England in the late eighteenth century) marked by the general introduction of power-driven machinery or by an important change in the prevailing types and methods of use of such machines.

Internet   The Internet is a network of tens of thousands of computer networks. The networks consist of over a million computer systems. These computers and networks communicate with each other by exchanging data according to the same rules, even though the individual networks and computer systems use different technologies.

Journeyperson   A skilled worker who has completed an apprenticeship program.

Labor Force   Persons employed as civilians, unemployed, or in the armed services during the survey week. The "civilian labor force" comprises all civilians classified as employed or unemployed.

Land-Grant System   State agricultural and mechanical college or university that has three functions—resident instruction (college/university), research, and extension.

Lyceum Movement   The American lyceum movement served as a means of building up useful knowledge in natural sciences among people of the smaller towns of America. It lasted until the middle of the nineteenth century.

Manual Training   A course of training to develop skill in using hands to teach practical arts (as woodworking and metalworking).

Maintenance Act   Also known as the Second Morrill Act. It authorized additional funds from the sale or lease of public lands to more fully support and maintain the agricultural and mechanical arts programs established in the original Morrill Act.

Marketing Education   The process of understanding and using various combinations of subject matter and learning experience related to the performance of activities that direct the flow of goods and services, including their appropriate utilization, from the producer to the consumer or user.

Morrill Act of 1862   Federal legislation that appropriated public lands for the establishment of a college of vocational education in each state. It is also known as the Land-Grant College Act.

NAM (National Association of Manufacturers)   NAM was organized in 1895 in response to a period of economic depression. NAM was interested in securing an adequate supply of trained workers and in reducing the power of the growing labor movement.

Nation at Risk   A 1983 report of the National Commission on Excellence in Education. This influential report observed that the United States was losing ground in international economic competition and attributed the decline in large part to the relatively low standards and poor performance of the American educational system.

NEA (National Education Association)   A professional organization for teachers, supervisors, administrators, and others interested in education.

NSPIE (National Society for the Promotion of Industrial Education)   The purpose of the society was to bring to public attention the importance of industrial education (the term used then for vocational education) and to promote the establishment of institutions for vocational training.

Nontraditional Student   Program enrollees, both male and female, who enroll in areas of study traditionally considered appropriate only for the opposite sex.

NPASO or PAS (The National Postsecondary Agricultural Student Association)   The vocational organization for those students enrolled in agriculture/

agribusiness and national resources programs in postsecondary institutions.

NYFEA (The National Young Farmers Educational Association) The vocational student organization for adults enrolled in agriculture classes, usually through the local vocational program.

Occupational Specific Instructional Program Instructional programs whose expressed intent is to impart work-related knowledge and skills at the secondary and postsecondary levels. The term has been historically applied to vocational programs offered in grades 11 and 12 at the secondary level, and to postsecondary vocational and technical education programs at the sub-baccalaureate level. The concept, however, applies to any program designed to prepare individuals for work at any level and thus encompasses baccalaureate and postbaccalaureate programs related to professional education.

Postsecondary Education The provision of a formal instructional program whose curriculum is designed primarily for students who have completed the requirements for a high school diploma or its equivalent. This includes programs whose purpose is academic, vocational, and continuing professional education, and excludes avocational and adult basic education programs.

Russian System This was essentially a laboratory method of teaching. This method consisted of a set of exercises that were arranged in what was considered to be a logical order for teaching purposes.

SCANS (Secretary's Commission on Achieving Necessary Skills) This 1991 report emphasized the importance of developing a range of work-related skills that spanned both academic and vocational programs. As a rule, this report focused little, if any, emphasis on specific "difficult" skills, such as knowing how to operate a drill press or build a brick wall, and considerable emphasis on the development of thinking skills and interpersonal skills of the workplace.

School-to-Work Opportunities Act (STWOA) Legislation designed to address the nation's serious skills shortage through partnerships between educators and employers was signed into law by President Bill Clinton on May 4, 1994, as Public Law 103-239. This act is a giant step toward the development of an educational system that matches students' educational attainment and corresponding skills more closely to job opportunities. It also reinforces the need to prepare students with high levels of technical skills and related academic competencies.

Secondary School The term *secondary school* means a nonprofit day or residential school that provides secondary education, as determined under state law, except that it does not include any education provided beyond grade 12.

Sex Bias Behavior, attitude, or prejudice resulting from the assumption that one sex is superior to another.

Sex Discrimination   The denial of opportunity, privilege, role, or reward on the basis of sex.

Sex Equity   The elimination of sex bias and sex stereotyping.

Sex Stereotyping   Attributing behaviors, abilities, interest, values, and roles to an individual or group on the basis of sex.

School-to-Work Transition Programs   Includes the following programs:

Apprentice Training   Programs registered with the Department of Labor or a state apprenticeship agency in accordance with the act of August 16, 1937, commonly known as the National Apprenticeship Act, which are conducted or sponsored by an employer, a group of employers, or a joint apprenticeship committee representing both employers and a union, and that contain all terms and conditions for the qualification, recruitment, selection, employment, and training of apprentices.

Cooperative Education   Allows students to earn school credit in conjunction with paid or unpaid employment that is in their vocational field of study. These programs usually involve employers in developing a training plan and evaluating students.

School-Based Enterprise   A class-related activity that engages students in producing goods or services for sale or use to people other than the participating students themselves.

Tech Prep   Programs consisting of the 2 or 4 years of secondary school preceding graduation and 2 years of higher education, or an apprenticeship program of at least 2 years following secondary instruction, with a common core of required proficiency in mathematics, science, communications, and technologies, designed to lead to an associate's degree or certificate in a specific career field. Also referred to as 2 + 2 programs.

Work Experience   Allows students to earn school credit in conjunction with paid or unpaid employment. In contrast with cooperative education programs, these programs may or may not involve employment that is in the student's vocational field of study or involve employers in developing a training plan and evaluating students.

Sloyd System (Sweden)   The Sloyd System advocated that manual labor in a prevocational sense should be taught as part of general education.

Smith-Hughes Act of 1917   Federal legislation that provided an annual grant of approximately $7.2 million in perpetuity to the states for the promotion of vocational education in agricultural, trade and industrial, and home economics education.

Socioeconomic Status   Constructed from data on father's occupation, father's education, mother's education, family income, and material possessions in the household.

Special Education   Curriculum provided to secondary students who have a disability and have developed an Individualized Education Plan (IEP).

Special Populations   The federal regulations pertaining to the Carl D. Perkins Vocational and Applied Technology Education Act of 1990 define special populations as individuals with disabilities, educationally and economically disadvantaged individuals, individuals of limited-English proficiency, individuals who participate in programs designed to eliminate sex bias, and individuals in correctional institutions.

State Councils   Advisory groups, each of which advises its state's board of vocational education on policies that would strengthen that state's vocational education program. Their policy objectives are (1) to achieve considerable public involvement in shaping vocational education policy, (2) to provide independent assessments of vocational programs and activities, and (3) to establish mechanisms that will improve vocational education policies and the policy-making process.

State Plan   A written plan submitted to the U.S. secretary of education for a two-year period that shows how that state proposes to use funds provided through a particular vocational education act.

Statute of Artificers (passed in 1562)   Transformed apprenticeship from a local to a national system in England.

Technical/Professional Fields   A group of occupationally oriented fields of study, other than engineering and computer science, that includes agriculture and agricultural sciences, architecture, business and management, communications, education, health sciences, home economics, law, library and archival sciences, military sciences, parks and recreation, protective services, and public affairs.

Technology Education   An applied discipline designed to promote technological literacy that provides knowledge and understanding of the impacts of technology including its organizations, techniques, tools and skills to solve practical problems and extend human capabilities in areas such as construction, manufacturing, communication, transportation, power, and energy.

Tribally Controlled Community College   An institution that receives assistance under the Tribally Controlled Community College Assistance Act of 1976 or the Navajo Community College Act.

TSA (Technology Student Association)   The national organization for elementary, middle, and senior high school students who are enrolled in or have completed technology education courses.

Vocational Education   Organized educational programs offering a sequence of courses that are directly related to the preparation of individuals in paid or unpaid employment and in current or emerging occupations requiring other than a baccalaureate or advanced degree. Such programs should include competency-based applied learning, which contributes to an individual's academic knowledge, higher-order reasoning, problem-solving skills, work attitudes, general employability skills, and the occupational specific skills necessary for economic independence as a productive and contributing member of society. This term also includes applied technology education.

Vocational Student Organizations (VSOs)   Those organizations for individuals enrolled in vocational education programs that engage in activities as an integral part of the instructional program. Such organizations may have state and national units that aggregate the work and purposes of instruction in vocational education at the local level.

VICA (Vocational Industrial Clubs of America)   A nonprofit national vocational organization for secondary and postsecondary students enrolled in trade and industrial occupations programs.

Workplace Mentor   An employee or individual approved by the employer at a workplace who possesses the skills and knowledge to be mastered by a student, and who instructs the student, critiques the performance of the student, challenges the student to perform well, and works in consultation with classroom teachers and the student's employer.

WWW (World Wide Web)   The collection of different services and resources available on the Internet and accessible through a Web browser.

INDEX

Page references in *italics* indicate figures. Page references followed by "t" indicate tables.